PLACE IN RETURN BOX to remove this checkout from your record.
TO AVOID FINES return on or before date due.

DATE DUE	DATE DUE	DATE DUE
NOV 8 0 1996		
DEC 1 1 1994		
	SEP 0 0 2010	

MSU Is An Affirmative Action/Equal Opportunity Institution

Politics Against Democracy

Richard Stöss

Since the mid-1980s there has been a resurgence of organised right-wing extremism in West Germany. This is the third wave since 1945 (after the successes of the Socialistische Reichspartei in 1950–52and the NPD in 1966–69), and according to the criteria of size of membership and election success, it is likely to be the strongest. Athough the organised core of right-wing extremism in West Germany is small (fluctuating between 20,000 and 30,000 members) and the election success of right-wing extremist parties, such as the Republikaner, is limited, surveys have shown that up to 40 per cent of the population show themselves to be susceptible to anti-democratic slogans. Given the magnitude of the immigration in the 1980s and early 1990s from eastern Germany and East European countries an the resurgence of extremist nationalism and racism, right-wing movements should be watched closely. Based on a wealth of empirical data, this study offers a timely overview of the causes and manifestations of right-wing extremism in West Germany and discusses possible counter-measures.

Richard Stöss is a lecturer at the Zentralinstitut für sozialwissenschaftliche Forschung, Free University of Berlin.

GERMAN STUDIES SERIES
General Editor: Eva Kolinsky

Volker Berghahn and Detlev Karsten, *Industrial Relations in West Germany* (cloth *and* paper editions available)

Eva Kolinsky (ed.), *The Greens in West Germany: Organisation and Policy Making*

Eva Kolinsky, *Women in West Germany: Life, Work and Politics*

Peter J. Humphreys, *Media and Media Policy in West Germany: The Press and Broadcasting since 1945*

Eckhard Jesse, *Elections: The Federal Republic of Germany in Comparison*

Alan Kramer, *The West German Economy, 1945–1955*

GERMAN STUDIES SERIES

Politics Against Democracy
Right-wing Extremism in West Germany

Richard Stöss

Translated from the German by
Lindsay Batson

BERG
New York/ Oxford
Distributed exclusively in the US and Canada by
St. Martin's Press, New York

First published in 1991 by
Berg Publishers Limited
Editorial offices:
165 Taber Avenue, Providence, RI 02906, USA
150 Cowley Road, Oxford, OX4 1JJ, UK

© Richard Stöss 1991

All rights reserved.
No part of this publication may be reproduced in any form
or by any means without the written permission of
Berg Publishers Limited.

British Library Cataloguing in Publication Data

Stoess, Richard
Politics against democracy: the extreme right in
West Germany (Extreme Rechte in der
Bundesrepublik). – (German studies)
I. Title II. Series
320.943

ISBN 0–85496–190–9

Library of Congress Cataloging-in-Publication Data

Stoess, Richard.
[Extreme Rechte in der Bundesrepublik. English]
Politics against democracy: right-wing extremism in West Germany
Richard Stoess: translated by Lindsay Batson.
p. cm. — (German studies series)
Translation of: Extreme Rechte in der Bundesrepublik.
Includes bibliographical references.
ISBN 0–85496–190–9
1. Germany (West)—Politics and government. 2. Fascism—Germany
(West) 3. Conservatism—Germany (West) 4. Right and left
(Political science) I. Title II. Series.
DD260.4.S7413   1991
320.943—dc20   91–3811
CIP

ISBN 0 85496 190 9

Printed and bound in Great Britain by
Billing and Sons Ltd, Worcester

Contents

Tables, Figures, Maps and Appendix Documents	v
List of Abbreviations	xi
Introduction	1

1. **Everyday Scenes of Right-wing Extremism** — 4

2. **What is Right-wing Extremism? Definitions – Aims – Policies** — 14
   - Antipathy towards Democracy — 15
   - The 'National Question' and 'National Opposition' — 17
   - Conceptions of the 'National Question' — 22
   - Old and New Nationalism — 26
   - 'Historical Revisionism' — 28
   - Right-wing Extremism as a Research Topic — 36

3. **Repressing and Glossing Over the Past. Right-wing Extremism as an Integral Part of West German Political Culture** — 38
   - Anti-democratic Attitudes in West Germany — 38
   - The Silent, Inexorable Return of the Past — 53
   - The Political Integration of Right-wing Extremism after 1945 — 82

4. **The Development of Organised Right-wing Extremism** — 100
   - Overview of Development — 101
   - Post-war Right-wing Extremism (1945–65) — 106
   - New Right-wing Extremism (1966–88) — 142
   - Outlook: Further Electoral Success? — 192

5. **Causes and Countermeasures** — 206
   - The Causes of Right-wing Extremism in West

Contents

Germany	207
Anti-Fascism – Problems and Perspectives	221
6. Summary of the Theories Outlined in this Analysis	230
Appendix: Selected Documents	237
Bibliography	257
Index	262

Tables, Figures, Maps and Appendix Documents

Tables

2.1.	The territorial development of Germany, 1871–1957	22
2.2.	Right-wing extremist solutions to the national question	25
3.1.	Hitler: Would he have been one of the greatest German statesmen had it not been for the war? (1955–78)	43
3.2.	Evaluation of the 'Third Reich' (1975–78)	43
3.3.	Sympathies for a man like Hitler (1954–83)	44
3.4.	Socio-structural characteristics of those with right-wing extremist attitudes in comparison with the population as a whole	47
3.5.	Xenophobia in the Federal Republic of Germany (1982)	49
3.6.	Attitudes to foreign workers living in ghettoes	50
3.7.	Feelings of national pride in major European countries (1983)	52
3.8.	Automatic arrest in the three Western zones	62
3.9.	Review of de-Nazification in the Western zones (FRG), 1949/50	69
3.10.	German views on de-Nazification (1952)	70
3.11.	Results of the Nuremberg trials	74
3.12.	Review of the prosecution of Nazi war criminals by (West) German courts, 1945–85	78
3.13.	The prosecution of Nazi criminals in the eyes of the population (1974–79)	79
3.14.	The potential for right-wing extremist opposition in the 1949 Bundestag elections	88

vii

Tables, Figures, Maps and Appendix Documents

3.15.	Bürgerblock votes in the Bundestag elections, 1949–61	93
4.1.	Phases of development of organised right-wing extremism, 1945–88	103
4.2.	Election results in Lower Saxony, 1947–53	111
4.3.	DRP election results, 1950–63	114
4.4.	DG election results, 1950–64	128
4.5.	NPD election results, 1965–88	146
4.6.	NPD members by occupation and social class, 1966–70	150
4.7.	Election results of the Bundestag parties, 1969–87	154
4.8.	Development of membership of the Junge Nationaldemokraten, 1970–87	157
4.9.	AUD election results, 1965–78	159
4.10.	FAP election results, 1980–89	190
4.11.	Republikaner election results, 1986–89	205
5.1.	The prosecution of war criminals in the eyes of the population (1988)	218
5.2.	The criminal prosecution of neo-Nazis in the eyes of the population (1980–85)	219

Figures

2.1.	Anti-democratic potential	18
2.2.	Components of right-wing extremism	27
2.3.	'Germany Must Perish'	32
3.1.	'And then in 1933, lots of brown beings from outer space came and murdered and ravaged everywhere and disappeared from the earth again in 1945'	39
4.1.	Development of the membership of organised right-wing extremism, 1954–87	104
4.2.	Development of the membership of organised right-wing extremism in comparison with the NPD, 1965–87	105
4.3.	Development of right-wing extremist parties, 1945–88	107
4.4.	Development of extreme right-wing	

Tables, Figures, Maps and Appendix Documents

	journalism, 1961–87	108
4.5.	Development of NPD membership, 1964–87	148
4.6.	Recorded crimes committed by German right-wing extremists, 1974–87	167
4.7.	Development of the membership of extreme right-wing youth organisations, 1959–87	170
4.8.	Development of the membership of organised neo-Nazis, 1975–87	172
4.9.	Leaflet issued by Erwin Schönborn in 1977	179
4.10.	An example of the propaganda material issued by Gary Rex Lauck	184
4.11.	Development of DVU membership, 1971–87 (including subsidiary organisations and Liste D)	195
4.12.	A comparison of the development of membership in the NPD and the DVU	197
5.1.	The interrelation between individual causes of right-wing extremism and causes relating to society as a whole	221

Maps

2.1.	Territorial losses after the First World War	20
2.2.	Occupied Germany, 1945–49	23

Appendix: Selected Documents   237

Unless otherwise stated, all documents are from the archives on parties at the Zentralinstitut für sozialwissenschaftliche Forschung at the Freie Universität Berlin.

1. Wahlprogramm der Deutschen Reichspartei zur Bundestagswahl 1953
   Source: Dudek and Jaschke, *Rechtsextremismus*, vol. 2, p. 38f.
2. Außenpolitisches Zehn-Punkte-Programm der Deutschen Gemeinschaft (1954)
3. Nationaldemokratisches Manifest (1978)
4. 24 Thesen zum Nationalismus (1977) [Junge Nationaldemokraten]
   Source: Meyer and Rabe, *Unsere Stunde die wird kommen*, pp. 232ff.
5. Ausländische Arbeiter in Deutschland (1979) [NPD leaflet]

ix

Tables, Figures, Maps and Appendix Documents

6. Aktion Neue Rechte, Grundsatzerklärung (1972)
7. Aktionsfront Nationaler Sozialisten, Kampfprogramm für die Hamburger Bürgerschaftswahl, 1978
   Source: Broder, *Deutschland erwacht*, Cologne, 1978, p. 104

List of Abbreviations

AAR	Aktion Ausländerrückführung – Volksbewegung gegen Überfremdung und Umweltzerstörung *Action 'Send Foreigners Home' – People's Movement to Prevent Overpopulation by Foreigners and Ecological Destruction*
ANJÖ	Arbeitsgemeinschaft nationaler Jugendbünde Österreichs *Working Association of Austrian Nationalist Youth Leagues*
ANR	Aktion Neue Rechte *Action for a New Right*
ANS/NA	Aktionsfront Nationaler Sozialisten/Nationale Aktivisten *Action Front of National Socialists/National Activists*
APO	Außerparlamentarische Opposition *Extra-parliamentary opposition*
AUD	Aktionsgemeinschaft Unabhängiger Deutscher *Action Community of Independent Germans*
AVP	Aktionsgemeinschaft Vierte Partei *Action Community for a Fourth Party*
AVS	Arbeitsgemeinschaft (ehemals politisch) verfolgter Sozialdemokraten *Working Association of (Formerly Politically) Persecuted Social Democrats*
BBI	Bürger- und Bauerninitiative *Citizen and Farmer Initiative*
BDS	Bund Deutscher Solidaristen *League of German Solidarists*
BFD	Bund Freies Deutschland *League for a Free Germany*
BHE	Block der Heimatvertriebenen und Entrechteten *Bloc of Expellees and Victims of Injustice*

List of Abbreviations

BHE-DG	Deutscher Gemeinschaftsblock der Heimatvertriebenen und Entrechteten *German Fellowship Bloc of Expellees and Victims of Injustice*
BHJ	Bund Heimattreuer Jugend *League of Patriotic Youth*
BNS	Bund Nationaler Studenten *League of National Students*
BP	Bayernpartei *Bavarian Party*
BVN	Bund der Verfolgten des Naziregimes *League of Victims of the Nazi Regime*
BvW	Bund versorgungsberechtigter ehemaliger Wehrmachtsangehöriger und deren Hinterbliebener *League of Former Members of the Armed Forces Entitled to Pensions, and their Dependants*
CDU	Christlich Demokratische Union *Christian Democratic Union*
CSU	Christlich-Soziale Union *Christian-Social Union*
DA	Deutsche Aktionsgruppen *German Action Groups*
DA	Deutscher Anzeiger *(a weekly newspaper)*
DAF	Deutsche Arbeitsfront *German Labour Front*
DAJ	Deutsche Arbeiter-Jugend *German Workers Youth*
DAP	Deutsche Arbeiterpartei *German Workers Party*
DAP	Deutsche Aufbau-Partei *German Reconstruction Party*
DB	Deutscher Block *German Bloc*
DBI	Deutsche Bürgerinitiative *German Citizen Initiative*
DFP	Deutsche Freiheits-Partei *German Freedom Party*
DG	Deutsche Gemeinschaft

List of Abbreviations

	German Community
DKP	Deutsche Kommunistische Partei
	German Communist Party
DKP	Deutsche Konservative Partei
	German Conservative Party
DNS	Dachverband der Nationalen Sammlung
	Peak Association of the Nationalist Rally
DNVP	Deutschnationale Volkspartei
	German National People's Party
DNZ	Deutsche National-Zeitung
	(weekly newspaper)
DP	Deutsche Partei
	German Party
DRP	Deutsche Rechtspartei
	German Rightist Party
DRP	Deutsche Reichspartei
	German Reich Party
DSB	Deutsche Soziale Bewegung
	German Social Movement
DSU	Deutsch-Soziale Union
	German Social Union
DU	Demokratische Union
	Democratic Union
DU	Deutsche Union
	German Union
DVU	Deutsche Volksunion
	German People's Union
DWZ	Deutsche Wochen-Zeitung
	(*a weekly newspaper*)
DZP	Deutsche Zentrums-Partei
	German Centre Party
EBF	Europäische Befreiungsfront
	European Liberation Front
EVD	Europäische Volksbewegung Deutschlands
	European People's Movement of Germany
FAP	Freiheitliche Deutsche Arbeiterpartei
	Free German Workers Party
FDP	Freie Demokratische Partei
	Free Democratic Party
FSD	Freie Sozialisten Deutschlands

List of Abbreviations

FSVP	Free Socialists of Germany Freie Sozialistische Volkspartei Free Socialist People's Party
FVP	Freie Volkspartei Free People's Party
GB/BHE	Gesamtdeutscher Block/Block der Heimatvertriebenen und Entrechteten All-German Bloc/Bloc of Expellees and Victims of Injustice
GDP	Gesamtdeutsche Partei All-German Party
GLU	Grüne Liste Umweltschutz Green List for Environmental Protection
HIAG	Hilfsgemeinschaft auf Gegenseitigkeit der ehemaligen Angehörigen der Waffen-SS Mutual Aid Association of Former Combat SS Members
HJ	Hitler-Jugend Hitler Youth
HLA	Hamburger Liste für Ausländerstopp Hamburg List to Stop Foreign Immigration
HNG	Hilfsorganisation für nationale politische Gefangene und deren Angehörige Organisation for the Support of National Political Prisoners and their Dependants
JBA	Jugendbund Adler Youth League Eagles
JDB	Jungdeutschlandbund Young Germany League
JDG	Junge Deutsche Gemeinschaft Young German Community
JF	Junge Front Young Front
JN	Junge Nationaldemokraten Young National Democrats
KNJ	Kameradschaftsring nationaler Jugendverbände Comradeship Circle of Nationalist Youth Associations
KPD	Kommunistische Partei Deutschlands Communist Party of Germany

List of Abbreviations

NDBB	Nationale Deutsche Befreiungsbewegung
	National German Liberation Movement
NDP	Nationaldemokratische Partei
	National Democratic Party
NF	Nationalistische Front
	Nationalist Front
NG	Notgemeinschaft
	Emergency Association
NLA	Nationalliberale Aktion
	National Liberal Action
NPD	Nationaldemokratische Partei Deutschlands
	National Democratic Party of Germany
NR	Nationalrevolutionäre
	National Revolutionaries
NRAO	Nationalrevolutionäre Aufbauorganisation
	National Revolutionary Preparatory Organisation
NRB	Nationalrevolutionärer Bund
	League of National Revolutionaries
NRKA	Nationalrevolutionärer Koordinationsausschuß
	National Revolutionary Coordinating Committee
NSDAP	Nationalsozialistische Deutsche Arbeiterpartei
	National Socialist German Workers Party
PdA	Partei der Arbeit
	Labour Party
PO	Politische Offensive
	Political Offensive
RdS	Ring deutscher Soldatenverbände
	Ring of German Soldiers Associations
REP	Republikaner
	Republicans
SA	Sturm-Abteilung
	Storm Detachment
SDS	Sozialistischer Deutscher Studentenbund
	Socialist German Students League
SdV	Sache des Volkes
	The People's Cause
SED	Sozialistische Einheitspartei Deutschlands
	Socialist Unity Party of Germany
SPD	Sozialdemokratische Partei Deutschlands
	Social Democratic Party of Germany

List of Abbreviations

SRP	Sozialistische Reichspartei *Socialist Reich Party*
SS	Schutz-Staffel *Security Squad*
SVB	Solidaristische Volksbewegung *Solidaristic People's Movement*
SzT	Sammlung zur Tat *Action Rally*
TfD	Tatgemeinschaft freier Deutscher *Action Fellowship of Free Germans*
UDG	Unabhängige Deutsche Gemeinschaft *Independent German Community*
VAPO	Volkstreue Außerparlamentarische Opposition *Extra-Parliamentary Opposition Loyal to the People*
VDNV	Vereinigung Deutsche Nationalversammlung *Association for a German National Assembly*
VdS	Verband deutscher Soldaten *Association of German Soldiers*
VSBD	Volkssozialistische Bewegung Deutschlands *Movement for People's Socialism in Germany*
VVN/BdA	Vereinigungen der Verfolgten des Naziregimes/Bund der Antifaschisten *Associations of Victims of the Nazi Regime/League of Anti-Fascists*
WAV	Wirtschaftliche Aufbau-Vereinigung *Economic Reconstruction Association*
WJ	Wiking Jugend *Viking Youth*
WSG	Wehrsportgruppe *Martial Sports Group*
Z	Zentrum *Centre Party*

Introduction

Since the mid-1980s there has been a resurgence of organised right-wing extremism in West Germany. This is the third wave of organised right-wing extremism to have occurred since 1945 (following the successes of the Sozialistische Reichspartei in 1950–2 and the NPD in 1966–9), and in terms of membership and electoral success, it seems likely to supersede the preceding waves. In relation to the political situation in other Western countries, this development is frequently described as 'normalisation' of the party spectrum, a term that I would regard as unfortunate.

In 1967, Scheuch and Klingemann proposed the following theory: 'The potential for radical right-wing political movements exists in all Western industrial societies. . . . Viewed from this perspective, right-wing radicalism is a "normal" symptom of liberal industrial societies.'[1]

Despite the fact that there are few, if any, comparable studies on this subject, there is nevertheless no doubt at all that right-wing extremism has existed and still exists in all Western European states.[2] However, the situation in Germany is unique.

When one considers the historical facts, national socialism represents the most radical form of Fascism that existed between the two world wars, and the consequences of its inhuman, aggressive policies, which were experienced by Germany, Europe and the whole world, have neither been overcome nor forgotten. Even today, the legacy of national socialism still has a

---

1. Erwin K. Scheuch in collaboration with Hans D. Klingemann, 'Theorie des Rechtsradikalismus in westlichen Industriegesellschaften', in *Hamburger Jahrbuch für Wirtschafts- und Gesellschaftspolitik*, vol. 12, Tübingen, 1967, pp. 11–29, quotation pp. 12ff.

2. European Commission committee to investigate 'The Resurgence of Fascism and Racism in Europe', report on their findings, December 1985; Klaus von Beyme (ed.), *Right-wing Extremism in Western Europe*, London, 1988 (first published in *West European Politics*, vol. 11, no. 2, April 1988); Hans-Ulrich Thamer and Wolfgang Wipperman, *Faschistische und neofaschistische Bewegungen*, Darmstadt, 1977.

lasting influence on West Germany's political culture, since there has never been any serious thorough, critical examination of the Nazi past. Characteristically, both historical and contemporary right-wing extremism are dealt with by repressing them and minimising their significance. For example, the responsible authorities are still trying to establish whether the Republikaner, founded in 1983, is a *radical* or an *extremist* right-wing organisation. Moreover, strategists within both the ruling parties and the opposition are seriously considering the new party as a possible coalition partner, as a means either to retain or to gain power, as the case may be.

We are constantly reminded that the past is part of everyday modern life – forty-five years after the end of the Nazi regime. The so-called 'historians' dispute' is a good example. In April 1989, for example, the former Auschwitz warder, Gottfried Weise (nicknamed 'Tell of Auschwitz'), who had been sentenced to life imprisonment for mass murder, was able to escape abroad from under the judiciary's nose. And in June, a Berlin judge had a plaque removed and destroyed, which had been mounted on the wall of the Berlin Supreme Court by the Deputy President of the Berlin Parliament, Hilde Schramm, and the Charlottenburg Bürgermeisterin, Monika Wissel, as a memorial to the 500 victims of the War Court, which once sat in that building. Although 'Roses for the Public Prosecutor'[3] was more typical of the 1950s and 1960s, apparently the 1970s and 1980s have seen no radical change in the unwillingness of the judiciary to draw conclusions in a self-critical light from its own past.

This is by no means 'normal', and it would be wrong to attempt to offset German Fascism/right-wing extremism against comparable manifestations in other countries, or even to try to trivialise it or excuse it in this way. On the contrary, it means that West Germany and its people have a special duty actively and committedly to support human rights, tolerance, democracy, peace and international understanding, at both the national and international

---

3. In this brilliant 1959 film by Wolfgang Staudte, the Public Prosecutor Dr Wilhelm Schramm, who until 1945 had been an ardent supporter of the Nazi regime in his capacity as an adviser to the court-martial, helps a like-minded comrade to flee abroad by holding back the order for his arrest. The Public Prosecutor subsequently receives a bunch of roses as a sign that the venture has been successful.

Introduction

levels. This requires a genuine distancing from national socialism and a subsequent rejection of right-wing extremism.

Occasionally, right-wing extremism in West Germany makes the headlines in the international press. There is no need for this. On the other hand, there are certain forces – generally from the conservative camp – who endeavour to trivialise right-wing extremism and to portray left-wing radicalism as the real threat to democracy. This likewise does not do justice either to the historical guilt burden, which is a legacy of German Fascism, or to the current challenge presented by right-wing extremism.

The organised core of right-wing extremism in West Germany is small. Over the past thirty years, membership figures have fluctuated between 20,000 and 40,000. The electoral success of right-wing extremist parties is also limited. Admittedly, they have occasionally been successful in gaining seats in individual *Land* parliaments, but they have not been represented at the national parliamentary level since 1953, although the NPD only just failed the 'five per cent hurdle'[4] in 1969, and today it is predicted that the Republikaner have a good chance of gaining seats in the next Bundestag. (It is already known that they will have two MPs from Berlin.) On the other hand, extreme right-wing attitudes are alarmingly widespread: in polls, up to 40 per cent of the population have been shown to be susceptible to anti-democratic slogans. Hence a considerable degree of latent right-wing extremism exists, which could, or rather will, manifest itself when the country is faced with particular economic and political conditions.

The recent successes of right-wing extremism prompted me to write this book. It is based on empirical evidence and is intended to give a concise, analytical and yet committed overview of the causes and manifestations of right-wing extremism in West Germany, and discuss countermeasures to it.

The manuscript was completed in November 1988 and amended in the summer of 1989 to include information regarding the Republikaner.

Richard Stöss
Berlin

---

4. Five per cent clause: the clause of the electoral law that debars parties with less than 5 per cent of the vote from entering parliament.

1
Everyday Scenes of Right-wing Extremism

Reports of right-wing extremism appear almost daily in the West German media. Here is a brief survey of events which occurred in the first three months of 1988.[1]

January 1988

Fulda: Some 200 members of the right-wing extremist group Wiking Jugend (WJ),[2] which has existed since 1952, together with Nazis from the Netherlands, Switzerland and Austria, crossed over into the neighbouring *Land* of Bavaria after their New Year's Eve demonstration at the GDR border was banned by the Hessian authorities. Several hundred Hessian police officers on the other side of the state boundary were unable to intervene, while only twenty police officers were on hand in Bavaria to deal with the situation.

Ahrensburg: Various youth organisations have spoken out against the sale of right-wing extremist newspapers. In a joint leaflet, they demanded the banning of right-wing extremist organisations and of the weekly newspapers *Deutsche National-Zeitung* and *Deutsche Wochen-Zeitung*, both of which are published by Dr Gerhard Frey, whose right-wing extremist newspapers have a total weekly circulation of 110,000 copies.

Berlin: Following a proposal by the SPD, the Berlin Parliament (House of Representatives) decided to commission a committee

---

1. Compiled from the press service, *Blick nach rechts* [Look Right], published by the SPD.
2. The organisations named in this overview are examined in more detail in the following chapters.

to investigate the involvement of the former Senator of the Interior, Heinrich Lummer (CDU), with right-wing extremist organisations, particularly the NPD. Lummer had been accused of having paid DM 2,000 to right-wing extremist organisations during his time as Senator of the Interior.

Berlin: A 16-year-old schoolgirl was sentence to four days' arrest on probation by a juvenile court. She was charged with incitement and grievous bodily harm. She had set her dog on a Turkish woman, who had been bitten several times on the leg by the animal. In doing so, the young girl shouted, 'When Hitler was still alive, the jews were burnt to death. The same thing ought to happen to the Turks.'

Düsseldorf: The North Rhine-Westphalian Minister for the Interior, Herbert Schnoor, commented on the increasing brutality of right-wing extremist activities. The SPD described the neo-Nazi FAP as a particularly militant group. Schnoor, supported by the North Rhine-Westphalian *Land* parliament, had called upon the Federal Minister of the Interior Zimmermann to ban the FAP. However, Zimmermann opposed the demand on the grounds that the party was far too insignificant to merit being banned.

Munich: The DVU, the largest right-wing extremist group in the Federal Republic of Germany, has permission to use a town hall for its rallies, following a ruling by the Bavarian Administrative Court, which overturned a ruling by the *Bürgermeister* of Passau.[3] (The DVU is led by the right-wing extremist publisher, Dr Gerhard Frey.)

Hannover: Skinheads affiliated to right-wing extremist circles raided a youth centre in the centre of town. Visitors were critical of the fact that police officers on duty in the vicinity of the youth centre did not take any measures to stop the attackers, who were throwing tear gas and smoke bombs into the youth centre.

---

3. After further lengthy legal battles, the event eventually took place on 18 September 1988.

February 1988

Düsseldorf: The Minister for the Interior of North Rhine-Westphalia, Schnoor, again warned that neo-Nazis are becoming increasingly militant. The FAP were at the forefront of this, he said. Recently, for example, members of the FAP in Essen vandalised one of the offices of the German Communist Party (DKP).[4] In Bielefeld a passerby was shot and injured outside the headquarters of the right-wing extremist organisation, the Nationalist Front (NF). In several towns, radical slogans have been daubed on the walls of houses.

Augsburg: The Catholic peace movement, Pax Christi, in the diocese of Augsburg, has announced that it would like to rename the 'General Dietl Barracks'[5] 'Lieutenant Kitzelmann Barracks'. Pax Christi justified its suggestion by pointing out that General Dietl is said to have been a committed supporter of Hitler who, even in November 1943, was appealing for blind faith in the Führer. Lieutenant Michael Kitzelmann from Allgäu, on the other hand, had trusted in the power of the Catholic Church and had made no secret of his disgust at the despicable, unchristian ideology professed by Hitler. Kitzelmann had been condemned to death and executed in 1942 for subverting the army.

Frankfurt: Green Party representatives on the Town Council proposed that Adolf Hitler lose his status as Freeman of the City. Despite the fact that a ruling to that effect had been made by the Hessian Minister of the Interior several years after the end of the war, Hitler has never formally been stripped of his honorary status.

Munich: The DVU intends to stand in all constituencies for the 1989 European elections. According to the DVU executive, it is supported in this by the NPD, the second largest right-wing extremist organisation (after the DVU itself) in West Germany.

---

4. Three FAP members were later convicted as a result of this, and charged with disseminating national socialist paraphernalia, coercion and grievous bodily harm (they had beaten up the two elderly employees in the DKP office).

5. German army barracks in the town of Füssen in the Allgäu.

Everyday Scenes of Right-wing Extremism

The DVU, for its part, is supporting the NPD in its Landtag election campaigns in Baden-Württemberg in March and in Schleswig-Holstein in May.

Heidelberg: Detonators for dynamite, a live mine detonator, a grenade, a live, loaded bazooka, a rifle-grenade and live US infantry ammunition, together with a large number of tear gas guns, were seized by police during a raid on a house as part of their investigations regarding an attack on a hostel for people seeking political asylum. Posters of swastikas were also found.

Stuttgart: A proposal by the SPD Landtag representatives in Baden-Württemberg to redraft the school history and social studies syllabuses so that the background to anti-Semitism and neo-Nazism could be explained more thoroughly, and that positive steps were taken to discourage an undemocratic, friend – foe way of thinking, was rejected by the CDU, who hold the majority of seats.

Uelzen: Supporters of the FAP met at a motorway service station in Allertal. They were immediately escorted back to their cars by the police to prevent arguments breaking out with anti-Fascists. In the afternoon, members and supporters of the party met in Uelzen to hold a party conference.

Travemünde: The regional division of the NPD in Schleswig-Holstein held a press conference in the Strandhotel on the occasion of its regional party conference, which took place in the neighbouring town of Plön. Approximately sixty NPD members conducted their party conference, which met with counter-demonstrations, under heavy police guard.

March 1988

Berlin: How to combat radical right-wing, militarist and neo-Nazi tendencies was the subject of a parliamentary question tabled by the SPD in the House of Representatives. The SPD expressed its opposition to right-wing extremist incidents in Berlin schools and to the way in which national socialism has

7

been marginalised in the current discussions regarding German history. At the same time, the party renewed its proposal from last November to promote school visits to former concentration camps.

Hannover: A juvenile court in Hannover sentenced two neo-Nazis to one and a half years' suspended imprisonment for arson. Their attacks on a police station and on a house where a number of immigrant families were living had been planned in the flat of the Hannover FAP leader, Sigfried Müller.

Sindelfingen: Several bars in the town centre were raided by skinheads. They inflicted serious injuries on one citizen, and destroyed the furnishings in two bars.

Stuttgart: Huge anti-Israeli and anti-Jewish slogans have been sprayed in pedestrian subways and on street walls in and around Stuttgart.

Weinheim: The Weinheim councillor, Günter Deckert (formerly a member of the NPD, now a member of the 'Deutsche Liste'), is planning the 'sixth Kurpfälzer meeting' for next month, which right-wing extremists from all over Germany are expected to attend.

Boppard: The CDU local government politician, Willi Brühl, is to be made head of the *Kant Gymnasium* [grammar school]. Brühl has been an honorary member of the traditional association of the '6th mountain division' of the Waffen SS since March 1982.

Meldorf: The NPD has held its main election campaign rally in preparation for the Baden-Württemberg *Land* parliament elections. The NPD is backed in this election by Dr Gerhard Frey's DVU. Apart from Frey, the other main speakers at the rally were the national chairman of the NPD, Martin Mußgnug, and the regional chairman, Jürgen Schützinger.

This brief catalogue of incidents with right-wing extremist connections indicates the extent and complexity of the phenomenon that is the subject of this book. It is not merely a question

Everyday Scenes of Right-wing Extremism

of right-wing extremism in the narrow sense of parties and other organisations, of press and literature, demands and manifestos, meetings and election campaigns, bribery and provocations, demonstrations and counter-demonstrations, increasing militancy, violence and brutality. It is also a question of right-wing extremism as an everyday, integral part of political culture as a whole, such as 'clandestine delight' at xenophobic incidents, latent anti-Semitism, the 'brown zone' between bourgeois-democratic and right-wing extremist parties, and last but not least, the omnipresence of the Nazi past: Hitler is still a Freeman of some cities, the army preserves many of its old traditions, school curricula are in many cases in need of revision, SS sympathisers are appointed to important positions in the Civil Service, etc.

The continuous presence of the Nazi past is likewise reflected in the following report from the *Frankfurter Rundschau* (15 February 1988), and is worthy of comment:

Explosive Nazi Files Stolen
Report of Blackmail Using Secret Documents Confirmed

BERLIN, 14 February (*Deutsche Presse Agentur*). The spokesman for the US military mission in Berlin, Thomas A. Homan, has indirectly confirmed the theft of 80,000 Nazi files from the Berlin Document Centre (BDC). When questioned on Sunday, Homan said that investigations as to the whereabouts of the missing files have been underway for years. In the course of their investigations, the US authorities have been working closely with the Berlin authorities, he said.

Homan was not prepared to discuss details of the disappearance of the files, which were published on Sunday in the *Berliner Morgenpost*. The investigations had proved difficult, he said, because some 30 million files are stored in the archives. When questioned, the Berlin judiciary refused to comment on the incident. The files of all members of the NSDAP are kept in the BDC.

The *Berliner Morgenpost* had reported that, over the years, 'some highly explosive and to this day top secret files' regarding leading figures in the Third Reich had been stolen. Until now, only a few leading German and US politicians had been informed about the so-called 'document affair', which has only recently come to light, despite the fact that it has been smouldering since the beginning of the eighties.

According to the newspaper, 'enormous sums of money' – over

20 million marks – had been 'cashed in by a close-knit, organised gang who had blackmailed prominent figures' with the BDC documents. These people had paid to keep their own Nazi past a secret.

The newspaper later states that the Public Prosecutor's Office in Berlin is 'keeping an eye' on the deputy director of the BDC as the suspected culprit.

It is not possible to describe here all the finer points of the scandal, which first became public in February 1988. It turns out that the authorities had been aware of the thefts since 1980, and apparently they have been thoroughly investigated, but without success. Nothing could be proved about any of the approximately forty (German) employees at the BDC. It is claimed that the Document Centre is carefully guarded, and is practically inaccessible to German academics, although it is the German authorities who grant access to the files. The public is denied access to the 'explosive' collection of files, on the grounds of maintaining data protection and the protection of the individual's right to privacy.

> Even today, West German modern historians are repeatedly turned away from the doors of the BDC, and the West Berlin administration continues brusquely to reject enquiries from German academics. The reason: protecting the civil liberties of Nazi criminals and so-called fellow travellers. Access for the purposes of research is only granted when the former Nazi member himself – or, in the case of his death, his family – has given permission.[6]

Thus the state protects Nazis from academics who wish to research the past. One can only speculate as to its motives: it is highly likely that the files on 10.7 million NSDAP members, 600,000 SS members and 200,000 SA members contain the papers of many prominent politicians, lawyers, captains of industry, journalists, etc. This could also be the reason why for some twenty years, the German government has refused to allow the Americans to pass the BDC over to German hands. In 1978 the SPD MP, Karl-Heinz Hansen, claimed that the government (at the time an SPD–FDP coalition) wished to conceal the identity of

---

6. *Frankfurter Rundschau*, 16 February 1988.

former Nazis, and in doing so caused considerable anger within his own party.

In the light of outrage among the mass media regarding the theft of the files, the German government is apparently now giving way, and is conducting meaningful negotiations regarding taking over responsibility for the archive. The number of Nazis still alive is, after all, declining rapidly, and any interests of descendants that may be classified as politically relevant can easily be satisfied by means of the Protection of Information Act.

This case clearly shows the extent to which we Germans make heavy weather of our past. Whether the story about the gang of blackmailers and the 20 million marks extortion money is true is of secondary importance, although it is noteworthy that reporting centred on this aspect.

Finally, with regard to this examination of press reports on right-wing extremism in West Germany in the first three months of 1988, I shall examine the results of the Baden Württemberg *Land* elections of 20 March, or more precisely, their political evaluation.

First, the election result itself: right-wing – or rather, right-wing extremist – splinter parties won a total of 4.6 per cent of the vote, which they obtained mainly from the CDU camp. The latter, however, was just able to hang on to its absolute majority.[7] The largest part of the 4.6 per cent went to the NPD (2.1 per cent), and the Republikaner (REP), led by the former Waffen-SS member Franz Schönhuber, received 1 per cent. None of the minor right-wing parties was able to win a seat in parliament.

What is really interesting about the otherwise undramatic election results was the question of whether co-operation between the two largest right-wing extremist organisations, the NPD and the DVU (possibly together with the Republikaner), to form a 'united right' following the example of the *Front National* under Jean-Marie Le Pen in France, would bring about a new trend in voting behaviour among right-wing voters.

Since the end of the 1970s, right-wing extremist parties have consistently polled less that 1 per cent of the vote in both

---

7. The other results were as follows: SPD 32 per cent, FDP 5.9 per cent, **Green Party** 7.9 per cent.

national and regional elections. The Republikaner were the first to break out of this in Bavaria in 1986, where they received 3 per cent of the vote. In 1987, Frey's DVU, backed by the NPD, stood in the *Land* elections as 'Liste D' (D standing for Deutschland). Owing to an enormous financial outlay, the alliance managed to enter parliament in Bremen, albeit with only one MP. Nevertheless, it was the first right-wing extremist parliamentary seat at regional level for twenty years. Consequently, the 'nationalist opposition' celebrated the Baden-Württemberg elections as a major victory and considered themselves well on the way to gaining seats in the Bundestag. The DM 700,000 received from the state as reimbursement of their election campaign costs contributed towards financial consolidation within the NPD.

The results achieved by the right-wing parties dominated discussions about the Baden-Württemberg election results. The CDU tried to allay people's fears, saying that the growth of the right-wing parties was no cause for alarm and that democracy was not threatened. Moreover, claimed the CDU, people who voted for the right-wing parties should not simply be branded as extremists. For the most part, they were disaffected protest voters from farmers and the middle class, who had to be won back by the democratic parties. Radical splinter parties had no chance of success in the medium term, they claimed. The SPD, the unions and the Green Party responded rather differently. They warned of the dangers of trivialising the success of the right, which had occurred in a *Land* with no serious economic or social problems. The chairman of the Central Council of Jews in Germany, Heinz Galinski, declared himself profoundly depressed about the success of the right-wing extremists. The democratic parties, he said, should not be content simply to carry on as usual.[8]

Amid all this squabbling, most of which was motivated by party politics, only a handful of points raised offered anything constructive. One example was the deputy president of the Landtag in Baden-Württemberg, Dr Alfred Geisel, who said in an interview:[9]

8. *Frankfurter Rundschau*, 22 March 1988.
9. *Blick nach rechts*, July 1988, p. 3.

Everyday Scenes of Right-wing Extremism

All democratic parties, even the SPD, must take these types of development on the right-wing extremist spectrum, which have been manifested in the regional elections, more seriously. We must stop playing down right-wing extremist groups and activities. The modern history and social studies curricula in our schools must at long last concentrate on reappraising the roots of anti-Semitism, xenophobia and national socialism. What the public is told regarding right-wing extremist activities must be markedly improved. Parliaments must discuss such events in greater depth. It would be fatal if democratic parties were to accommodate these extremist trends in their political activity in an attempt to win back lost votes.

But it is not easy to translate even these level-headed proposals into practice. Just as we Germans make heavy weather of our Nazi past, so are we ineffective[10] in dealing with contemporary right-wing extremism. Why do we gloss over right-wing extremism and national socialism? Why is Hitler still a Freeman of some cities? Why doesn't the public have access to Nazi files? Why don't schools devote more attention to explaining the roots of national socialism, neo-Fascism and anti-Semitism? Why do we dismiss the election results of right-wing extremist parties?

In the next chapter, before describing right-wing extremism in West Germany, I would like to define a number of terms and set out the basic political aims of right-wing extremism.

---

10. Wolfgang Fritz Haug, *Der hilflose Antifaschismus*, Cologne, 1977.

2
What is Right-wing Extremism?
Definition – Aims – Policies

There are very many different descriptions of the object of this analysis to be found in the literature and in everyday language: for example, neo-Fascism, Fascism, national socialism, nationalism, right-wing extremism, right-wing radicalism, totalitarianism. As all these terms are so confusing, I think it would be useful to attempt to delineate the parameters of this analysis, and to define – or at least to describe – the terms used in this book.

First, it must be pointed out that the terms Fascism, right-wing extremism, etc. are frequently used in everyday politics as war cries. 'Fascist' is a political word of abuse. It is usually Conservatives who find themselves denounced as right-extremist, Fascistic or Fascist, but from time to time the accusation of Fascism is also levelled at members of the left. In each case, the aim is to discredit the political opponent – with the result that Fascism is diluted. People think that as there is no difference between Conservatism and Fascism, Fascism cannot be so bad after all.

The equation of right-wing extremism with left-wing radicalism and of Fascism with communism in the expression totalitarianism,[1] is likewise politically motivated, and in my opinion is not appropriate to a differentiated analysis because all either supposed or actually non-democratic systems are measured by the same yardstick, and the relation to totalitarianism depends on the definition of democracy. Hence it is quite often the case that democratic socialism is treated as a totalitarian ideology and hence excluded from the democratic consensus.

---

1. The concept of totalitarianism cannot be dealt with here. See Hannah Arendt. *The Origins of Totalitarianism*, New York, 1951; Uwe Backes and Eckhard Jesse, *Totalitarismus – Extremismus – Terrorismus. Ein Literaturführer und Wegweiser zur Extremismusforschung in der Bundesrepublik Deutschland* (2nd edition) Opladen, 1985.

This book examines right-wing extremism. Right-wing extremism is used here as a collective term to include all manifestations in public life that are directed against the democracy of Western industrial societies.

In conjunction with this it is often pointed out that left-wing extremism, such as exists in those states with 'real existing socialism', can be anti-democratically structured. I do not wish to contradict this, and nothing could be further from my mind than to try to minimise Stalinism. However, one important difference must be taken into account: right-wing extremism seeks to eradicate democracy, while socialism aims to abolish capitalism. While right-wing extremism only concentrates on one specific form of civil rule, without questioning its economic bases,[2] socialism is principally concerned with changing the relations of production. For, according to communist ideology, social equality – and hence social justice – can only be achieved by abolishing private ownership of the means of production and by eliminating the unequal distribution of economic power. Without social justice, however, so the theory goes, there cannot be any true democracy. Right-wing extremism is fundamentally anti-democratic in terms of its ideology and aims, whereas socialism is only anti-democratic when it is abused by bureaucracy, or becomes perverted. Hence equating socialism with Stalinism is just as unjustified and meaningless as equating Conservatism with Fascism.

Antipathy towards Democracy

This book examines antipathy towards democracy in the West German political system. By this I mean efforts aimed at the

2. Sometimes right-wing extremist organisations claim to pursue anti-capitalist goals by criticising big business or the 'servitude of interest' (Zinsknechtschaft). The combination of nationalist and socialist aims is shown, for example, in the expression 'national socialism'. In actual fact, it is pure propaganda intended to appeal to and gain the support of the working class. The 'left-wing Fascist' rhetoric is not directed against an economic principle but against supposed or real *political* consequences of an unequal distribution of economic power (discrimination of the middle class or rather, the petty bourgeoisie as against big business). This results in the traditional right-wing extremist demand for the 'dominance of politics over the economy'.

elimination or permanent restriction of democratic structures and processes. Three important characteristics should be emphasised:

1. As a rule, anti-democratic thinking combines extreme nationalism with an imperialist striving towards power supremacy, or at least hostile attitudes towards other states. Conjuring up an external threat not only serves expansionist or 'revisionist' goals, it also provides justification for *Gleichschaltung*, or a forced closing of the ranks at home and suppression of opposition or deviant opinion.

2. Anti-democratic concepts are directed against parliamentarian-pluralist systems of government. The banning of political parties, pressure groups and unions converges with the establishment of a one-party state claiming to integrate all sectors of society and which represents the most important pillar of state control, together with the military and big business (and, if applicable, the Church). Any form of opposition is ruthlessly suppressed. Fascist systems of government must be distinguished from authoritarian systems of government (although the boundaries are fluid). Authoritarian systems do tolerate political parties, pressure groups and parliaments, but without granting them any real rights of control and participation, in the face of a ruling executive whose power is almost unlimited.

3. The societal model of anti-democratic thought is that of a community in harmony with the natural order of things. Nation and state merge to form an empire whose unity is usually personified by a leader. This model epitomises the realisation of 'true' people's power in contrast to the hated liberalism, which purportedly divides and weakens the nation.

Antipathy towards democracy is manifested in everyday life in two ways: as an integral part of political thought, and as concrete political practice. The difference between anti-democratic *attitudes* and anti-democratic *behaviour* is more significant than it appears to be at first sight. Before a person becomes politically committed to the extreme right (that is, openly confesses his or her affiliation to right-wing extremism), he or she usually develops a corresponding consciousness and appropriate political sympathies. Theoretically speaking, anti-democratic attitudes are the prerequisite for anti-democratic behaviour. And, since such attitudes are not necessarily expressed in political behaviour, and in any case, only a small proportion of the population is politically active, the extent of anti-democratic attitudes is many times greater than the extent of actual anti-democratic practice.

This does not mean, however, that only politically active right-wing extremism is relevant to our analysis. The inactive right-wing extremists of today could become the active ones of tomorrow. With good reason, organised right-wing extremism views those people with a potential for right-wing opinions as supporters (e.g. as voters) and as a reserve from which the new generation can be recruited. More important still is the fact that passive right-wing extremists encourage active right-wing extremism by tolerating it. The national socialist dictatorship, for example, was not based on the fact that all Germans were active Nazis. They were in the minority. The Nazi regime was sustained primarily by 'fellow travellers', and it profited from an underdeveloped anti-Fascist consciousness in Germany.

The difference between right-wing extremist views and right-wing extremist behaviour can also be expressed verbally in terms of latent and manifest right-wing extremism.

Antipathy towards democracy does not follow any standard ideology. It is, rather, a heterogeneous mixture of the most diverse combinations of reasons and viewpoints, which in Germany is reflected in fragmentation of its organisations. It expresses a large number of competing concepts and aims, which on the one hand are concerned with the re-establishment of national unity (of the German Reich) and on the other, its internal structure.

The 'National Question' and 'National Opposition'

The fact that it is precisely the 'national question' that forms the core of right-wing extremist thought and behaviour in West Germany and that nationalism here is practically a synonym for right-wing extremism, is not always readily comprehensible to

Figure 2.1 Anti-democratic potential

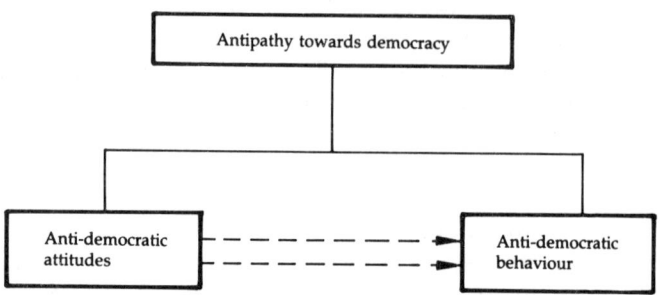

foreign observers. In contrast to most Western European countries, experience has shown that democratic nationalism has not found any broad response in Germany in the long term,[3] because, traditionally, the Germans have enormous problems regarding 'their' nation. For example, there has always been a considerable discrepancy between ethnic and political boundaries: the Germans have, for the most part, lived in separate states. Until the mid-nineteenth century the area of the German empire was a patchwork of small states covered with a dense network of customs boundaries. The national unity propagated at the time by democratic and liberal forces, however, did not occur in the course of a democratic process from below, but came mainly as a result of economic and military pressure from Protestant Prussia in the north of Germany, which then also formed the hegemonial power of the German Empire, founded in 1871. This was thus a 'Little Germany' solution: Catholic Austria, which had previously been conquered by the army, and being Prussia's most serious contender in the fight for the supremacy in Germany, was excluded. The Prussian king, as German Emperor, reigned over a kingdom that was largely Protestant, but that had strong Catholic influences in the west and the south. (Since then, an unusual feature of the structure of conflict in Germany and in the Federal Republic of Germany has emerged – namely, class conflict is eclipsed by religious conflict.)

3. The exception proves the rule, and in this case the main exceptions are democratic liberalism and social democracy. After 1945, the SPD, particularly under the chairmanship of Kurt Schumacher, represented a policy of all-German socialism.

What is Right-wing Extremism?

The Little German Empire, created in the spirit of an authoritarian state under the dominating influence of military, imperialistic and unquestioningly anti-democratic forces, strove for a 'place in the sun' in the club of the colonial powers at the beginning of this century – and failed. After the First World War, Germany lost the following territories as a result of the Peace Treaty of Versailles (1919):

- Northern Schleswig to Denmark.
- Eupen and Malmedy to Belgium.
- Alsace-Lorraine to France.
- Western Prussia, Posen, parts of Outer Pomerania and Upper Silesia to Poland.
- The Memel region, first to the Allies, then to Lithuania.
- The Saar territory became a mandate of the League of Nations, and Danzig was declared a 'free city'.

German unification with Austria[4] was forbidden. Austria, for its part, had to hand over southern Tyrol and south Styria to Italy and the Sudetenland to Czechoslovakia.

1919 was also the year the first German democratic republic, the 'Weimar Republic',[5] was born, which right-wing extremist forces fought particularly vehemently. They could not come to terms with military defeat, the collapse of the Empire, the 'shameful dictate' of Versailles and the hated republic. They considered it the 'decline of the Western world'. Their struggle was aimed at revoking the Treaty of Versailles and the abolition of parliamentary democracy. Two schools of thought can be distinguished. The German Nationalists[6] continued the tradition of authoritarian Prussian conservatism. They demanded a 'powerful state' and the restoration of the monarchy on a constitutional basis. Political parties, trade unions and associations

---

4. In the First World War Austria fought on Germany's side.
5. The first democratically elected German parliament with full democratic rights, the National Assembly, was forced to assemble in Weimar to elect the *Reichspräsident* and a cabinet and to pass the constitution, since revolutionary battles were still raging in the capital, Berlin.
6. The German National People's Party (DNVP) existed from 1918 until 1933.

Map 2.1 Territorial losses after the First World War

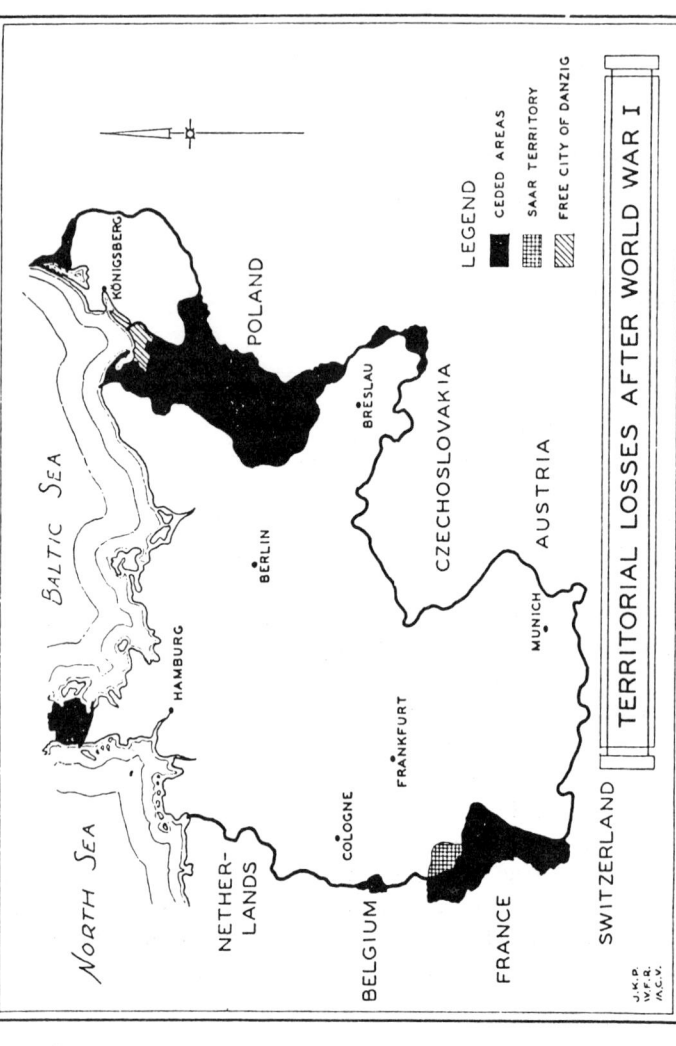

Source: James K. Pollock and Homer Thomas (1952), *Germany in Power and Eclipse*, New York/Toronto/London, p. 26.

were not to be abolished completely, in view of their political influence, but their scope was to be considerably restricted. The national socialist viewpoint was different:[7] in their view, the Wilhelminian[8] order had failed and so was no model for solving post-war problems. Hence the Nazis presented themselves as a revolutionary movement, directed against both the workers' organisations and big business and large landowners, a movement that despised traditional conservatism just as much as middle-class liberalism and proletarian (internationalist) socialism. Their propaganda heralded a 'Third Reich'[9] beyond all known world-views as a supposed synthesis of nationalism and socialism,[10] and a completely new order in the form of a *Führer*-state based on a people's community (*Volksgemeinschaft*) with the slogan: 'One nation, one empire, one Führer'.

Following the Second World War, Germany was again forced to accept considerable territorial losses. All areas to the east of the Oder-Neisse Line were lost: East Pomerania, East Brandenburg, Lower and Upper Silesia and the southern part of East Prussia went to Poland. The northern part of East Prussia was annexed to the Soviet Union. The Saar region received political autonomy but was under the economic control of France. The remainder was occupied by the three Western allies (Great Britain, France and the United States) and the Soviet Union. In 1949 the three Western zones became the Federal Republic of Germany (FRG) while the Soviet zone became the German Democratic Republic (GDR).

Politics, under the banner of nationalism, has only served to harm the German nation-state in the long term, and with its two world wars has brought immeasurable misery upon both the German and the other European peoples. Nevertheless,

---

7. The NSDAP existed from 1919 until 1945, initially under the name DAP in 1919/20.
8. Wilhelm II, the last German emperor, 1888–1918.
9. The title of a right-wing extremist polemical work against the Weimar Republic, written by Arthur Moeller van den Bruck. The first empire lasted from 911 to 1806, the second empire from 1871 to 1918, and the third empire, according to Moeller, was to rise from the ruins of the Weimar Republic. The characterisation 'Third' Reich also indicated his political position.
10. In their 1920 party manifesto they demanded the voluntary expropriation of land and the abolition of 'unearned income'. In 1928, however, Hitler declared definitively that the NSDAP firmly supported the principle of private property.

Table 2.1 The territorial development of Germany, 1871–1957

Year	Area km²		Losses km²	%
1871–1918	540,860			
1919–1933	470,550		70,310	13
Since 1945: FRG[11]	248,330			
GDR	107,570			
Total		355,900	114,650	24
Total losses since 1871			184,960	34

German nationalism has not died out. Rather, the enormous territorial losses and the division of Germany was and still is perceived by certain strata of the population as national disgrace and humiliation, as a loss of historical and national identity. This develops into a need to regain national unity and strength, and hence also to restore the status quo. After both the First and Second World Wars, revisionist aims were pursued by the very political forces that had been responsible, or partly responsible, for the dismantling of the nation.

Conceptions of the 'National Question'

The fact that, after 1945, all attempts to form a unified right-wing extremist party failed, despite repeated attempts, is due to the fact that the various groups and factions have widely disparate opinions regarding the best path to German unity and the internal structure (particularly in economic and social terms) of the German Empire, which they claim still exists from a legal point of view,[12] but which must be recreated in a political sense. Traditionally, the right-wing extremist camp in Germany is

11. Including the Western sectors of Berlin and the Saarland, which were only incorporated into the Federal Republic in 1957.
12. According to the official interpretation of the law in West Germany, the German Reich (in its boundaries of 1937) continues to exist in a legal sense, for although the victorious powers declared a peace treaty settlement for the whole of Germany, it has never been ratified. Hence the rights and responsibilities of the four powers towards Germany as a whole, it is claimed, still exist. The argument is that the German nation was divided against its will and therefore is

What is Right-wing Extremism?

Map 2.2 Occupied Germany 1945–49

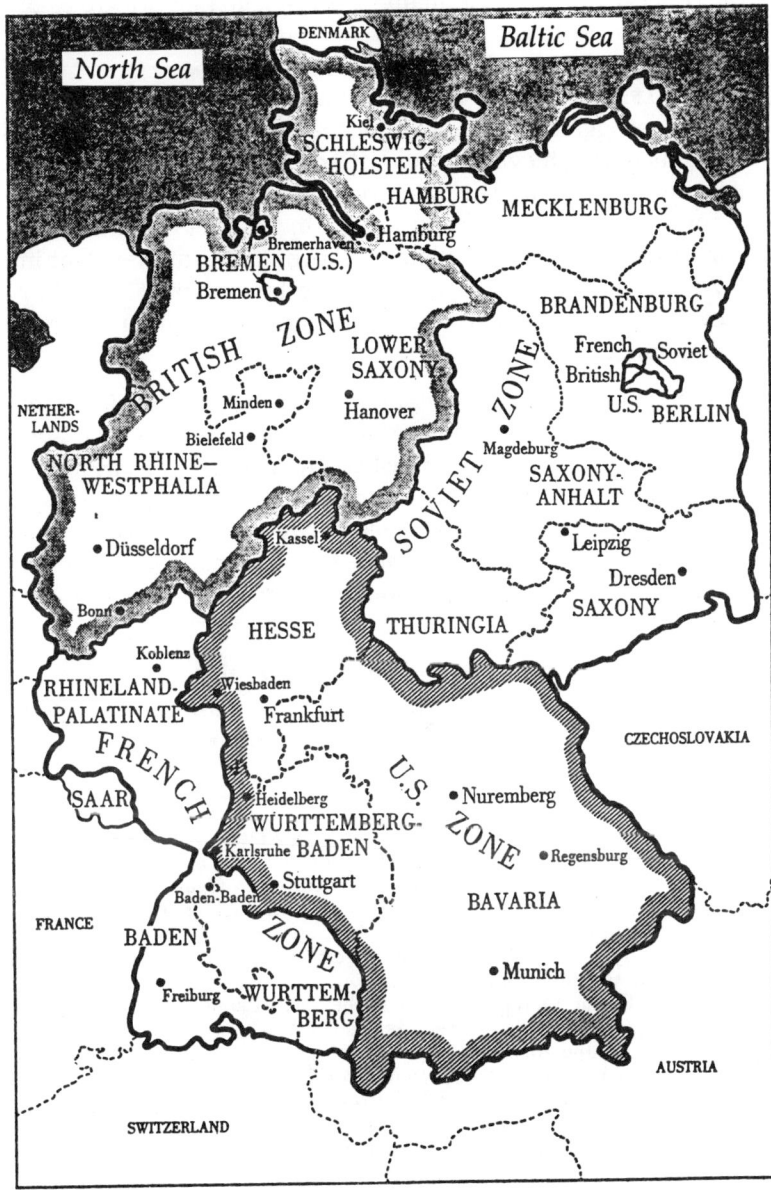

Source: John Gimbel (1986), *The American Occupation of Germany*, Stanford, p. XVI.

divided. With regard to the 'national question', four opposing concepts exist in West Germany, the fundamental principles of which can be outlined as follows:

1. A *pro-Eastern, national-Bolshevist conception*, which is based on the Tauroggen Convention[13] or the Treaty of Rapallo,[14] and is aimed at achieving reunification by means of a German-Soviet agreement. This concept has comparatively few supporters, which is hardly surprising in the light of the escalating Cold War and the militant anti-communism prevalent in West Germany, but is distinguished by emphatic 'social' or even (petit-bourgeois) 'socialist' visions of the social order in a reunified Germany.

2. A *pro-Western, anti-Bolshevist conception*, usually consisting of statist middle-class property-owners, who believe that German unity can be accomplished by a 'policy of strength', alongside the Western allied powers. While the so-called 'Atlanticists' favour an alliance between the European and North American states, the anti-American nationalists advocate a concept of Europe modelled on de Gaulle's 'Europe of the Mother Countries'.

3. A *European-neutralist conception* considers that unification of Germany will only be possible on the basis of a united Europe as a 'Third Power' or 'Third Front' between America

---

entitled to the right of self-determination with regard to its national unity. The treaties with Eastern bloc states in the 1970s (with the Soviet Union, Poland, East Germany and Czechoslovakia) were only intended to regulate the peaceful coexistence of the existing states and to prevent the existing boundaries from being redrawn by military means, until such time as a peace treaty of this kind is made. Officially, under international law, West Germany has never recognised East Germany as a result of the treaties.

13. In a mill near Tauroggen (today in the Soviet Republic of Lithuania) in December 1812, the Prussian General Prince von Yorck personally concluded a convention with the Russian General Diebitsch under which the Prussian auxilliary corps in Napoleon's Russian campaign was declared neutral. This convention caused the uprising of Prussia against the French occupation.

14. Treaty concluded near Genoa in April 1922 between Germany and the Soviet Union by which both states renounced all financial claims resulting from the First World War (the Western powers, in contrast, demanded vast reparations from Germany). The beginning of a period of good relations between the two countries.

What is Right-wing Extremism?

Table 2.2 Right-wing extremist solutions to the national question

	Foreign policy orientation	Economic and social policy
National-Bolshevist conception	Alliance with the Soviet Union (anti-Western)	Emphatically social/petit bourgeois 'socialist'
Pro-Western conception	Alliance between Western Europe and North America (Atlanticists)	
	Alliance of European nations (Gaullist) (Western/ anti-Bolshevist)	Middle-class property-owners/ capitalist
European-neutralist conception	Alliance of European states as a 'Third Power' between America (USA) Asia (USSR)	'Third Path' between capitalism and communism
National neutralist conception	Bloc-free nation-state	'Third Path'

and Asia (or, respectively, between the United States and the Soviet Union). Supporters of this school of thought usually promulgate theories of national revolution or nationalist liberation, and also propagate a 'Third Path' between East and West domestically, between capitalism and communism, between freedom and order.

4. *A national-neutralist conception*, which is related to European neutralism and is essentially consistent with the concepts of European neutralism in its domestic policies, rejects both East and West integration and proceeds from the assumption that the major powers will only agree to reunification if the future Germany accepts the status of a neutral and bloc-free nation-state.

All neutralists have differing opinions on the 'arms question': one group describes itself as pseudo-pacifist and supports 'unarmed neutrality', while another propagates 'armed neutrality' in an effort to promote what it feels to be the 'desire for defence' in the German people.

Due to the insignificance of the various national-Bolshevist positions, disputes among West German right-wing extremists were mostly between the supporters of pro-Western and of neutralist conceptions.

Old and New Nationalism

The heterogeneity of West German right-wing extremism is not only a consequence of the existence of these four parallel and competing aims, but also of the competition between differing ideological traditions. We distinguish between groups that are oriented towards authoritarian or Fascist methods of rule from the Weimar Republic, or towards German nationalism or national socialism,[15] on the one hand, and those who are concerned with finding up-to-date solutions suited to the new national and global political circumstances resulting from the Second World War, on the other. I describe the former as *'Old Nationalism'* (or 'Old Right'), and the latter as *'New Nationalism'* (or 'New Right').

Old Nationalism identifies itself broadly with the ideas of the German Nationalists or Nazis, but does not, as a rule, aim to restore historical national socialism. On the contrary – and despite highly resentful attempts to justify the past – a certain amount of criticism is levelled at the 'Third Reich': there is a desire to avoid the mistakes and failings of the Nazi dictatorship and, in a certain sense, to make a fresh start. Favoured links are the left wing of the Nazi movement, or the 'Harzburg Front',[16] the symbol of a 'national opposition' combining all right-wing extremist groups. In fact, the influential right-wing extremist

---

15. National socialism is the German variation of Fascism which (as we know) was an international phenomenon.

16. The 'Harzburger Front' resulted from the merging of the nationalist opposition (Deutschnationale, Nazis, Stahlhelm and other 'fatherland' associations and influential people) in the final phase of the Weimar Republic. However, this right-wing extremist battlefront collapsed in 1932 because not all members of the alliance wanted to commit themselves to supporting Adolf Hitler in the presidential elections.

Figure 2.2 Components of right-wing extremism

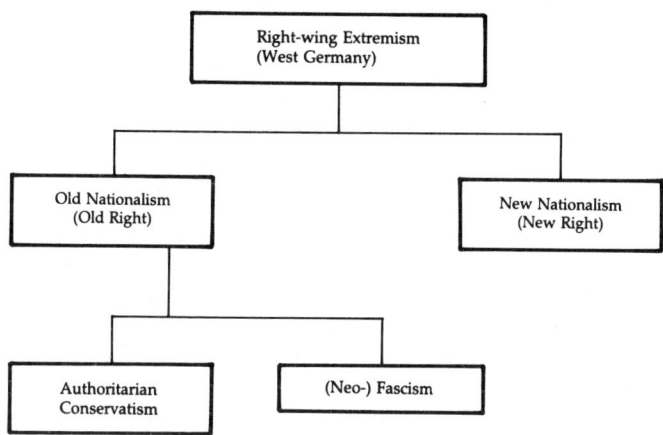

parties of Old Nationalism in West Germany are, for the most part, 'Harzburg Front' organisations; in other words, organisations that have both a Nazi and a national-conservative (German nationalist) wing competing for power and influence within their own parties. Old Nationalism is characterised by pronounced statist and military thinking and a foreign policy preference for pro-Western or European-neutralist concepts; above all, their ideas are anti-Bolshevist. Therefore, it is in a certain sense close to the democratic bourgeois parties, with which it is forced into permanent rivalry for electoral support.

New Nationalism emerged toward the end of the 1940s. Politically, it distances itself from Old Nationalism, which it criticises as 'Fascist' and 'reactionary' and considers to be historically outmoded. It seeks new political thinking in a world that has been transformed by the Second World War. It considers the common philosophies (national socialism, German nationalism, liberalism, socialism) to be old-fashioned, outdated positions, which are incapable of solving the 'national question'. It sees the re-emergence of the classic party spectrum from the Weimar period as a revival of veterans whose anachronistic status had long been proved by the failure of the Weimar Republic. New Nationalism denounces the Western-zone state as 'authoritarian', 'undemocratic', 'imperialistic', 'materialistic', 'consumerist' and 'big capitalist'. It dismisses the claim that the

German Reich legally still continues to exist and argues for its recreation from the grass-roots upwards. In a populist vein, it confronts the authoritarian statism of the bourgeois-democratic parties and the Old Right with the self-realisation of the people by national revolution. The theoreticians of the New Right seek a 'Third Path' between capitalism and communism, between idealism and materialism, between East and West. The sympathies of New Nationalism have always been with the national liberation struggles of the peoples of Asia, Africa and Latin American, whom it identifies as fellow sufferers of the German people who are occupied and divided by colonial masters (the allied victors). It seeks a 'Third Power', a 'Third Front', comprised of the states of Europe and the Third World united against the 'imperialist superpowers', the United States and the Soviet Union. It also develops concepts of a neutral, bloc-free and largely demilitarised united Germany with a powerful state, a plebiscitary (or even Soviet) democracy, extensive local self-government and co-operative organisation of production. Market-dominant companies are to be taken into public ownership and the structurally weak middle classes should be given special assistance by the state.

'Historical Revisionism'

According to West German right-wing extremism, the 'national question' involves more than merely recreating the Empire as a territorial unit and European power. It is equally a question of fighting its 'suppression' in an ideological and propagandist sense, in order to re-expose the German national identity, which they claim was deliberately annihilated by the victors. The struggle for 'historical truth' and the revision of official historiography, which they maintain was decreed by the allies and implemented by their German accomplices, therefore forms a central plank of right-wing extremist policy.

According to the revisionists, the 'historical truth' goes something like this:

> The four victorious allies deliberately smashed the German Empire in 1945 in order to destroy it permanently as a power factor. Both the

What is Right-wing Extremism?

liberal democracy in the West and the communist peoples' democracy in the East imposed systems of rule, values and philosophies on the defeated German people, which are alien to the German way of thinking and German tradition. The aim of this dictate by the victorious powers was solely to cement the dependence of parts of Germany on the individual superpowers and to prevent a German self-awareness or national consciousness ever developing again. These 'un-German' ways of life were drummed into the Germans in the course of their re-education, with the main aim of engendering on the population a permanent guilt complex. This guilt complex consists of two main elements: Germany's sole guilt for the Second World War, and the extermination of the Jews (known as 'the war guilt lie' and 'the Auschwitz lie' respectively).

That, then, is a brief outline of the revisionist view of history, which they hold up against the established record of history and attempt to substantiate with their own 'research'. This 'research' serves two main purposes: first, to deny that Germany was solely responsible for the Second World War, to emphasise the fact that the victors had their share of guilt and war crimes, and to expose the war trials and Nazi trials (see p. 72 below) as 'political justice' and, therefore, illegal. Second, it strives to cast doubt on the holocaust as an historical fact, to relativise it, or even to claim that the Jews themselves were responsible for their fate.

The net result of revisionism, then, is the suppression of historical truth, glossing over and relativising the past, the deflection of Germany's own guilt and failings by diverting attention to the supposed or actual injustices of others, and last but not least, the vindication of right-wing extremist power ambition.

To illustrate this, and perhaps help the reader to gain some insight and understanding of it, here is a poem that trivialises Hitler ('who only wanted peace') and national socialism, and claims that 'foreign hordes' were responsible for the destruction of 'Great Germany'.[17]

---

17. Renate Schütte, *Der Wind schlägt um. Gedichte, Kritik*, 43/1978, p. 16.

Remains of Germany

Oh beautiful Germany,
how small you have become! –
Divided up and in enemy hands,
occupied by foreign hordes.

You wanted to flourish and prosper,
and support a free nation.
The world could not forgive you for that.
It had to devastate you

and pushed the blame onto the man,
who had only wanted peace,
and his people, blinded then,
only offered him contemptuous ingratitude.

But the values he once created,
will never be completely lost.
Great Germany, hear our cry:
'One day you will rise again!'
                               Renate Schütte

The origins of historical revisionism go back to the era of national socialism. Even then, attempts were made to justify the persecution of Jews and the war policy. For example, in 1944 the deputy government press officer and later right-wing extremist publisher, Helmut Sündermann,[18] published a series of articles under the title 'The War Forced on Us'.[19] After 1945, with the war trials and de-Nazification, right-wing extremists felt obliged to develop strategies to justify themselves in the interest of exonerating the accused, and right-wing extremist organisations were likewise forced to legitimise their political goals.

In the 1950s, this prompted a growing flood of revisionist literature claiming that the Treaty of Versailles had been the real cause of the war and emphasising the fact that guilt was shared

---

18. Sündermann, who died in 1972, founded the Druffel publishing company in 1952, which published many revisionist writings including the book by Rassinier, *Was ist Wahrheit?* Today the company is run by his stepson, Dr Gert Sudholt.

19. Cited in Ludwig Elm, *Hochschule und Neofaschismus*, Berlin (East), 1972, p. 61.

by the United States, the Soviet Union and, above all, Britain and Poland. Such books frequently convey the impression that war was virtually forced on Hitler as an act of self-defence. In this context, reference is frequently made to the 'declaration of war' by the President of the Jewish World Congress, Chaim Weizmann, to Hitler in September 1939 and the book published in 1941 by the American Jew, Theodore N. Kaufman, *Germany must Perish!*. However, these efforts did not achieve large-scale publicity until 1961 in the form of a book by the American historian and Harvard graduate, Prof. David L. Hoggan,[20] with the descriptive title *The War Forced on Us*, which was published by a right-wing extremist West German publishing company and to date has run to fourteen editions. Hoggan lays the main blame for the Second World War, which he considers had the primary aim of destroying Germany, on British politicians, and makes fulsome excuses for Hitler.

The enthusiasm of the revisionists to re-assess historical connections, the reversal of cause and effect and the exaggeration of what are in reality inconsequential documents, is encouraged by the fact that the leaders of the Western powers in the critical years 1938/9 were guilty of indisputable failings and ineptitude, and underestimated Hitler's fanaticism. To deny the holocaust, on the other hand, requires considerable debating skills, cynicism and an almost total lack of scruples. For it did happen, and it was the Germans who perpetrated it. The revisionists base their arguments on the following circumstances: The extermination, which was perfectly organised from a bureaucratic point of view, was never officially recorded as such, the full details were never put into writing, and hardly any witnesses to the mass murder of millions remain. The victims are dead, and murderers do not incriminate themselves. Therefore, although we are conscious of the holocaust and its dimensions, there is no documented proof of individual murders which would stand up in court.

Here are a few examples of anti-Semitic revisionism:

As early as 1950, the French geographer, Prof. Paul Rassinier, expressed doubts as to the existence of the gas chambers and

---

20. Hoggan, who died in 1988, was awarded a prize by the right-wing extremist *Gesellschaft für freie Publizistik* (Society for Free Journalism).

Figure 2.3 'Germany Must Perish'

Germany Must Perish

BY THEODORE N. KAUFMAN

ARGYLE PRESS, NEWARK, NEW JERSEY

Of the thousands of anti-nazi books published within the last few years **GERMANY MUST PERISH** by THEODORE N. KAUFMAN is the *only volume* which struck fear and terror into the hearts and souls of the Nazis. This amazing book so completely unnerved Dr. Goebbels that he denounced it on the front page of every newspaper in Germany and over the entire German radio network! AND—Adolf Hitler's own newspaper, in a frenzied and crazed statement concerning the book declared it was not Kaufman but President Roosevelt who actually wrote **GERMANY MUST PERISH**

demanded proof. In 1963 his book, *Zum Fall Eichmann: Was ist Wahrheit? Oder Die unbelehrbaren Sieger*[21] (The Eichmann Case: What is Truth? Or the victors who never learned), which was published in German, in which the holocaust is described as 'falsification of history' and as 'deception': there was no 'Final Solution' he claims, the atrocities in the concentration camps were perpetrated for the most part by criminal, violent prisoners, acting without orders from their superiors, and there were no gas chambers at all in the extermination camp of Auschwitz-Birkenau. This was followed in 1970 by another book, *Hexen-Einmal-Eins einer Lüge* (Magic Square of a Lie) by Emil Aretz, which presents virtually the same views. In 1973 the neo-Nazi Manfred Roeder published the memoirs of his combattant Thies Christophersen[22] under the title *Die Auschwitz-Lüge* (The Auschwitz Lie). The latter had been in Auschwitz between January and December 1944 and on one occasion was also in the extermination camp of Birkenau, to select workers. Christophersen describes life in the camps as pleasant (he talks of the inmates having 'elegant' clothes and 'perfectly good' shoes, socks and underwear, of the women prisoners having 'lipstick, powder and make-up', and of the inmates even having their own 'brothel'), and his own work gang as a 'jolly crowd' who sang and danced at their work. His report culminates in the conclusion:[23]

> During my time in Auschwitz I never noticed the slightest evidence of mass gassings. The smell of burnt flesh, which is purported to have often hung over the camp, is also an outright lie.

In 1976 the American electrical engineer, Prof. Arthur R. Butz, published his book *The Hoax of the Twentieth Century*, (which appeared in German in 1977 under the title *Der Jahrhundert-Betrug*), in which he exposes the extermination of the Jews as a 'propaganda lie' and claims that Nazi policy towards Jews was aimed at 'forcing all Jews to leave the German sphere of influence

---

21. The French version was published in Paris as early as 1962. To my knowledge, the book has appeared in five editions in West Germany to date.
22. For further information on Christophersen and Roeder, see the section on neo-Nazis in Chapter 4, p. 175.
23. *Die Auschwitz-Lüge. Ein Erlebnisbericht von Thies Christophersen*, Deutsche Bürger-Initiative, Book 2 in a series, Mohrkirch (3rd edition), 1975, p. 33.

in Europe' and their 'resettlement . . . in the East'. The final treatment of the the 'Auschwitz lie' which we shall mention for the time being was written by the former judge Dr Wilhelm Stäglich, *Der Auschwitz-Mythos. Legende oder Wirklichkeit?* (The Auschwitz Myth. Legend or Reality?, 1979). The University of Göttingen withdrew his doctorate as a result of this 'anti-Semitic and contemptible piece of work'. Based on an assessment of the available documentation for the Nazi period, eye-witness reports and memoirs and, finally, the Frankfurt Auschwitz trial (1963–5), the book concludes that 'the Auschwitz myth has its roots in a morass of contradictory legends, and is not based on what really happened'.

The major consequence of West German right-wing extremism's efforts towards revisionism is the fact that glossing over and relativising the Nazi past has long since contaminated established history as well – admittedly in a mitigated form and without any open declaration of political intent.

The Professor of History at Erlangen, Hellmut Diwald, received harsh criticism for his *Geschichte der Deutschen* (History of the Germans), which appeared in 1978. As a result of public pressure, the book, which had a planned print-run of 100,000, and which was published by the respected Propyläen publishing company, had to be re-written. In the chapter 'Die Endlösung' (the 'Final Solution'), Diwald had given the impression that 'central questions' regarding the circumstances of the extermination of the Jews 'still remain unanswered despite all that has been written'. He continues: 'One of the most terrible events of modern times was exploited by deliberate disinformation, deceptions and exaggerations for the purpose of totally discrediting a nation.'

In the first edition, the author accounts for the existence of furnaces in Birkenau as follows:

> Birkenau, which belonged to the Auschwitz complex, served as a camp for those inmates who had been declared unfit to work. This is the reason why the mortality rates in that camp were highest. On 26 July 1942 a disastrous typhoid epidemic broke out in Birkenau. Within just under three months up to twenty thousand people died. That was the reason why there were unusually large facilities for burning corpses in Birkenau.

What is Right-wing Extremism?

Diwald does not tell any direct lies, but instead employs deliberate linguistic ambiguities with the aim of misleading the reader. Only in the second edition do we find the unequivocal statement: 'There is nothing misleading . . . regarding the fact of the systematic extermination of the Jews.' And only here does the editor express appropriate sentiments for the victims of the incomprehensible crime.

In 1986 a newspaper article by the Berlin historian Prof. Ernst Nolte triggered the so-called historians' dispute.[24] This controversy, which was accompanied by extraordinary public interest and which was conducted largely in the media between historians and social scientists, focuses primarily on the unprecedented uniqueness of the holocaust. However, according to a controversial essay by Wehler, 'disposal of the German past' and the 'self-conception of the Federal Republic'[25] lie behind this.

Nolte supports the theory that the extermination of the Jews by the Nazis must be seen in conjunction with the extermination of the bourgeoisie and peasantry in Russia after the revolution, and poses the question that the holocaust might have been a reaction to preceding Bolshevik atrocities:

> Could it be that the National Socialists and Hitler only committed an 'Asian' crime because they saw themselves and people like them as potential or real victims of an 'Asian' crime? Is it not the case that the *Gulag Archipelago* [Solzhenitsyn's 1973 book about the Soviet system of forced labour camps] was more original than Auschwitz? Wasn't Bolshevik 'class murder' the logical and actual forerunner of National Socialist 'racial murder'?

There is no space here for a full account of the debate. However, one last remark (which I hope will see an end to the matter) deserves to be quoted at some length, because I consider it a highly appropriate justification for national consensus when considering our most recent history. At the opening of the 37th convention of historians on 12 October 1988, the West German President, Richard von Weizsäcker, explained:[26]

---

24. *Historikerstreit. Die Dokumentation der Kontroverse um die Einzigartigkeit der nationalsozialistischen Judenvernichtung*, Munich, 1987.
25. Hans-Ulrich Wehler, *Entsorgung der deutschen Vergangenheit? Ein polemischer Essay zum 'Historikerstreit'*, Munich, 1988.
26. *Bulletin des Presse- und Informationsamts der Bundesregierung*, no. 131, 14 October 1988.

Just like any other nation, ours wishes to recognise elements of itself in its past. To look in the mirror of this history really requires considerable strength . . .

The German nation, like other nations, has always suffered under its history, and certainly not only since 1933. But it cannot make anyone else responsible for what happened to it and its neighbours under national socialism. It was led by criminals and allowed itself to be led by criminals. It knows this, particularly where it would rather not.

A course of violence, poverty and death brought about the end of the war. For many people, only then did injustice and sorrow manifest themselves in their full proportions. Only gradually did the full truth emerge. It remains exceedingly difficult to believe. But nevertheless, liberation can only be achieved through the liberating influence of truth and through a total acceptance of that truth.

These are the responsible tasks faced by historians. Nothing that it unearths will reduce the crimes of national socialism . . .

What does it mean to us whether Auschwitz bears comparison to the terrible extermination of other people? Auschwitz remains unique. It was perpetrated by Germans and in the name of Germans. This truth is irrefutable. And it will never be forgotten . . .

Historical truth means . . . taking history upon oneself as one's own. We must do this, if only for the sake of the present.

Right-wing Extremism as a Research Topic

The previous description of the main characteristics of right-wing extremism, its ideology and its general political aims has given an impression of which topic areas and questions should be covered by a scientific analysis of right-wing extremism:

1. The spread of anti-democratic attitudes among the population.

2. The way in which West Germany deals with its national socialist past.

3. The extent and development of right-wing extremist activity (in both organised and unorganised forms).

4. The manifestos and aims of right-wing extremist organisations.

5. The relations between right-wing extremism and those leading organisations in West Germany that have a formative influence on politics.

I have described right-wing extremism as a complex combination of attitudes and behaviour patterns aimed at the abolition or permanent restriction of democratic structures and processes, focusing on the 'national question', in other words, the restoration of the German empire. However, an analysis of right-wing extremism cannot limit itself to an analysis of its manifestations, because action directed against democracy is neither natural, nor acceptable. This raises two further questions:

6. How does right-wing extremism develop, and what determines the success of right-wing extremist organisations?
7. How does the population react to West German right-wing extremism, and what can and should be done to combat it?

From a democratic point of view, causes and countermeasures (in other words, anti-Fascism) naturally form part of any research into right-wing extremism.

3
Repressing and Glossing over the Past
Right-wing Extremism as an Integral Part of West German Political Culture

> The world was almost won by such an ape!
> The nations put him where his kind belong.
> But don't rejoice too soon at your escape –
> The womb he crawled from still is going strong.
> (Brecht, Epilogue to *Arturo Ui*)

This portrayal of right-wing extremism in West Germany begins with a consideration of the circumstances of its development and its socio-political milieu since 1945. Bertolt Brecht's warning, that the social basis for anti-democratic thinking and behaviour has by no means evaporated, must be taken seriously.

In this chapter I shall demonstrate that right-wing extremism forms a permanent and integral part of West German political culture and examine why it is repressed and glossed over. The two basic ways of dealing with both historical and contemporary right-wing extremism are: to repress it psychologically and to gloss over its political significance.

Anti-democratic Attitudes in West Germany

'Fascism does not arrive overnight' is a well-known anti-Fascist slogan. What it means is that Fascism develops in specific socio-economic, ideological and political crisis situations and remains a threat for as long as the factors causing it remain acute. The cartoon (Figure 3.1) ironises the widespread opinion in Germany that national socialism took Germans unawares and through no fault of their own, like a terrible (but now cured)

Figure 3.1 'And then in 1933, lots of brown beings from outer space came and murdered and ravaged everywhere and disappeared from the earth again in 1945.'

Source: Wochenschau, no. 2/80, p. 74

disease. This image is handed down from generation to generation.

'Adolf Hitler was an Italian'

Between October 1976 and April 1977 over 3,000 schoolchildren from a number of West German schools wrote an essay on the topic 'What I have heard about Adolf Hitler'.[1] The results can

---

1. Dieter Boßmann (ed.), 'Was ich über Adolf Hitler gehört habe . . .', *Folgen eines Tabus: Auszüge aus Schüler-Aufsätzen von heute*, Frankfurt, 1977.

confidently be regarded as an important document of West Germany's political culture. Here are a few excerpts:

Karin, 15: 'I haven't heard anything about this topic at school yet.'

Ilona, 15: 'I have never met him face to face.'

Walter, 17: 'Adolf Hitler was born in the twentieth century.'

Guido, 15: 'He was in office for a long time, and was still in office after the war. Then, twenty five years later, he died.'

Joachim, 14: 'Hitler was alive at the time of the Nazis.'

Claudia, 14: 'Adolf Hitler was an Italian.'

Albrecht, 18: 'In about 1875 he made a violent attack on the monarchy, because people were being arrested by the army for no reason.'

Marco, 17: 'He belonged to the NSDAP, which was a radical, left-wing branch of the SPD.'

Wolfgang, 17: 'Before the First World War he joined the Communist Party, then later he founded his own party.'

Katharina, 16: 'Hitler founded the SED'.[2]

Petra, 16: 'I think he was a Nazi, but I don't know what that means.'

Petra, 14: 'Hitler was a member of the CDU.'

Ralf, 18: 'He was a man who worked his way up to become a dictator of the German people.'

Axel, 18: 'He became Chancellor and Head of the Armed Forces after Bismarck's death'.[3]

Hans Peter, 13: 'Everyone had to vote for Hitler, otherwise they were sentenced by the War Courts.'

---

2. The SED (Socialist Unity Party of Germany) was founded in 1946 in the Soviet zone as the result of a merger between the SPD and KPD.

3. Prince Otto von Bismarck was Chancellor from 1871 to 1890; he died in 1898.

Dagmar, 14: 'Hitler was the leader of a Communist party whose policies were similar to those of the GDR.'

Uwe, 17: 'It has to be said, however, that there was peace in Germany while he was in power. There was no hunger and the currency was stable.'

Ulrike, 15: 'Hitler created a lot of jobs by taking the Jews' money and building factories.'

Bernd, 14: 'If you listen to some grandparents, they think he was good.'

What is most remarkable about these young people's comments is their startling ignorance about the national socialist period; this is generally expressed in their absurd ideas about Adolf Hitler. The children have not made up this nonsense; it is obviously based largely on what their parents and grandparents have told them, and they have not been corrected at school. The editor of the documents, Dieter Boßmann, believes that this results from the fact that national socialism is considered a taboo subject. And indeed, there has never been a truly critical examination of the Nazi dictatorship.

Views on National Socialism

In December 1952 the Office of the US High Commissioner for Germany put the following question to 1,200 representatively selected inhabitants of the three Western zones: 'All things considered, was there more good in the ideas of national socialism or more evil'? Approximately half of those questioned (44 per cent) believed that there was 'more good', 39 per cent replied that there was 'more evil', and 17 per cent did not express an opinion.[4]

What explanation is there for this completely uncritical attitude? Did national socialism still have a strong appeal at the beginning of the 1950s?

Let's imagine ourselves at that time. Only seven years had

---

4. *A Year-End Survey of Rightist and Nationalist Sentiments in West Germany*, Office of the US High Commissioner for Germany, Report No. 167, 12 January 1953, p. 8.

elapsed since German Fascism had perished in the ruins of the Second World War. In twelve short years the Nazis had succeeded in destroying the German Empire and plunging the nation into economic and social chaos. Furthermore, the war had cost the lives of over 24 million of the armed forces and 31 million civilians in Europe and Asia. Five to six million European Jews perished in the holocaust. Under the banner of nationalism and the people's community (*Volksgemeinschaft*), the rulers of the 'Thousand Year Empire' had brought immense suffering, poverty and destruction on Europe. The delusion of German world power had cost the Germans dearly. This can be illustrated by some statistics: 12 million servicemen were imprisoned, approximately 11 million Germans lost their homes, and 4.5–6 million people in the three Western zones were bombed out.

In view of the trail of destruction left by the Nazi regime, which was experienced by every German at first hand, there can only be one explanation for the result of the survey quoted: the true character of national socialism did not penetrate the consciousness of the German people even after it had failed and the full extent of its crimes had been revealed (for example, in the Nuremberg trials[5]). There is a lack of sympathy for the millions of victims and no regret for the injustices perpetrated.

Characteristic of the fact that Germans have inadequately addressed their national socialist past is that even twenty-five years later, 26 per cent of West Germans still agree with the statement: 'National socialism was basically a good idea which was just poorly carried out'.[6]

The survey results (Table 3.1) indicate the extent of sympathy for Hitler, if he – as the question is worded – is exonerated of responsibility for the Second World War. In 1978, thirty-three years after national socialism had been defeated, approximately 30 per cent of West Germans still considered him (under the hypothetical conditions described above) to be one of the greatest German statesmen.

Admittedly, sympathy for national socialism has declined

5. See below, p. 72.
6. *Forschungsgruppe Wahlen Mannhein, Politbarometer* 1977, quotation from Martin und Sylvia Greiffenhagen, *Ein schwieriges Vaterland. Zur politischen Kultur Deutschlands*, Munich, 1979, p. 334.

Table 3.1 Hitler: Would he have been one of the greatest German statesmen had it not been for the war? (1955–78)

Question: 'Everything that had been built up between 1933 and 1939 and much, much more was destroyed by the war. Would you say that Hitler would have been one of the greatest German statesmen had it not been for the war?'

	1955	1960	1964	1967	1972	1975	1978
Yes (%)	48	34	29	32	35	38	31
No (%)	36	43	44	52	49	44	55

Source: Institut für Demoskopie.[7]

Table 3.2 Evaluation of the 'Third Reich' (1975–78)

Question: 'A question about Hitler and national socialism. Some people say: apart from the war and the persecution of Jews, the Third Reich wasn't all that bad. Others say: the Third Reich was a bad thing under any circumstances. What is your opinion?'

	1975	1977	1978
The Third Reich was not all that bad (%)	35	38	37
A bad thing under any circumstances (%)	42	40	40
No reply (%)	23	22	23

Source: Institut für Demoskopie.[8]

since the early 1950s. However, the potential for pro-Nazi views in the West German population still exists today, evaluating national socialism in a critical but benevolent light, in other words, only expressing disapproval of its grossest excesses. In the past twenty years the size of this potential has varied between 20 and 40 per cent. Within this range, the individual survey results obviously depend on political events and on the

---

7. Institut für Demoskopie Allensbach, *Demokratie-Verankerung in der Bundesrepublik Deutschland. Eine empirische Untersuchung zum 30jährigen Bestehen der Bundesrepublik*, Allensbach, 1979, p. 96.
8. Ibid., p. 102.

particular question asked. For example, in 1978 'only' 21 per cent of those questioned believed that the Nazi state was *not* an illegal state (in 1977 31 per cent and in 1964 28 per cent).[9] Apparently, one fifth of the population considered the Nazi state to be a 'legal state'.

Pro-Nazi views are by no means confined to those age groups upon which national socialism had a formative influence. It is true that younger people express comparatively more critical views of German Fascism. Nevertheless, one fifth of 16–29-year-olds in 1978 believed that Hitler would have been one of the greatest German statesmen had it not been for the war, that the 'Third Reich' was not really so bad and that the Nazi state cannot be described as an illegal state.[10]

Table 3.3 Sympathies for a man like Hitler (1954–83)

Question: 'If we had the opportunity again – as in 1933 – to vote in an election for or against a man like Hitler, how would you vote?

	1954	1958	1965	1968	1983
For a man like Hitler (%)	15	10	4	6	5
Against a man like Hitler (%)	81	81	80	83	77
No reply (%)	4	9	16	11	18

Source: EMNID.[11]

Nevertheless, in 1983 5 per cent of the population still expressed unreserved support for 'a man like Hitler'. That means that approximately 2.5 million West Germans have – to put it mildly – a completely uncritical image of the Fascist dictatorship. In addition, it is worth noting that the proportion of those questioned who give no reply is increasing.

The SINUS Study

Characteristic of the way in which Germans cope with their national socialist past is the fact that the first extensive scientific

9. Ibid., p. 101.
10. Ibid., p. 103.
11. EMNID-Informationen, 8–9/1968, p. 1, and 10/1983, p. 26.

study of right-wing extremist views in West Germany was not undertaken until thirty-five years after the end of the war. Incidentally, no university in West Germany has a chair for neo-Fascism and there are no research institutes for right-wing extremism. A few historians are involved in the subject on a full-time basis, because in West Germany the dominant opinion is that Fascism is an historical phenomenon, to be studied within the field of history. The comment by the well-known Conservative historian Ernst Nolte, who described the period between the two world wars as the 'epoch' of Fascism, is characteristic of this attitude.[12]

Between May 1979 and April 1980 the SINUS Institute conducted a research project commissioned by the Federal Chancellory regarding right-wing extremist political views in West Germany. On the basis of approximately 7,000 interviews with citizens eligible to vote (aged 18 and above), the researchers established that a potential 13 per cent of those questioned had closed right-wing extremist opinions. Approximately half of these (6 per cent of the population) condone right-wing extremist acts of violence and can be considered potential sympathisers for right-wing terrorist organisations. In addition to the 13 per cent cited, a further 2 per cent are described by the SINUS researchers as the 'right-wing extremist ecology potential', in other words, people who combine elements of the national socialist 'blood and soil' ideology (i.e. the idea that political stability and power depend on unification of race and territory) with modern ecology concepts.[13]

One further important finding of this study is that, in addition to the 13 or 15 per cent with consistent right-wing extremist views mentioned above, a potential 37 per cent of those questioned were shown to have authoritarian but not extremist attitudes. The study describes these individuals as potential 'bridges to the right'.[14] They function as a link between right-wing extremist and democratic positions, and in periods of crisis

12. Cf. Ernst Nolte, *Der Faschismus in seiner Epoche*, Munich, 1963; Nolte, *Die faschistischen Bewegungen*, Munich, 1966. Ernst Nolte is one of the initiators of the so-called 'historians' dispute'. See Chapter 2.
13. *5 Millionen Deutsche: 'Wir sollten wieder einen Führer haben . . .'. Die SINUS-Studie über rechtsextremistische Einstellungen bei den Deutschen*, Reinbek, 1981, pp. 77ff.
14. Ibid., pp. 92ff.

they could form a reserve of supporters or voters of right-wing extremist parties or organisations.

The analysis of the socio-structural characteristics of those with potentially right-wing extremist views (see Table 3.4) shows that young people are comparatively less susceptible than middle-aged and older people. Members of trade unions, on the one hand, and supporters of social democracy (SPD) and liberalism (FDP), on the other, prove to be particularly resistant. No further significant socio-structural characteristics of the right-wing extremist camp are apparent. There is no gender-specific difference, because single women are disproportionately represented in the generation that survived the war. With regards to religion, there are no obvious differences. People with no vocational training, farmers and semi-skilled and unskilled workers are somewhat over-represented. With regards to regional distribution, right-wing extremism is over-represented in Hesse and Bavaria. There are comparatively more right-wing extremists in large villages, small towns and on the suburbs than in Germany as a whole.

One final correlation is revealed by all empirical studies of anti-democratic views: people with potentially right-wing extremist views are generally affiliated to the large democratic parties (80 per cent) and not to right-wing extremist parties. This means that support for right-wing extremist parties is not identical to the size of the right-wing extremist potential. (In West Germany, right-wing extremism is always glossed over, with the argument that right-wing extremist parties have very few voters and even fewer members.)

Anti-Semitic and Xenophobic Attitudes

In 1933, approximately 500,000 Jews (0.8 per cent of the population) were living in Germany; today there are approximately 30,000 (0.05 per cent). The number of Jews in Europe who fell victim to the national socialist policy of extermination lies between 5 and 6 million.

However, anti-Semitism is still quite widespread in West Germany. In a study by the Frankfurt Institute for Social Research in 1950/1, 37 per cent of those questioned were shown to be extremely anti-Semitic, and a further 25 per cent fairly

Table 3.4 Socio-structural characteristics of those with right-wing extremist attitudes in comparison with the population as a whole

	Population as a whole (%)	Those with right-wing extremist views (%)
Age		
18–21	8	4
22–25	7	4
26–29	7	5
30–39	17	13
40–49	18	17
50–59	16	18
60–69	14	20
70 and over	14	19
Sex		
Male	45	44
Female	55	56
Education		
No vocational training	22	26
Vocational training	44	43
'O' levels (equivalent)	22	22
'A' levels (equivalent), degree	12	8
Selected occupations		
Farmers	3	6
Non-qualified white-collar employees	15	13
Qualified white-collar employees	20	17
Managerial staff	5	5
Unskilled workers	5	7
Semi-skilled workers	10	13
Skilled workers	15	11
Religion		
Catholic	46	48
Protestant	47	46
Union Member		
Yes	19	12
No	81	88

continued on page 48

Table 3.4 continued

	Population as a whole (%)	Those with right-wing extremist views (%)
Party preference		
CDU/CSU		
SPD		
FDP		

Source: Data from the SINUS study.

Note:
The table is read as follows: the percentage of 18–21-year-olds in the population eligible to vote is 8 per cent but their percentage among those with potentially right-wing extremist views is only 4 per cent.

anti-Semitic.[15] In 1982, the Cologne sociologist, Alphons Silbermann, published the results of an extensive research project into anti-Semitic prejudices in West Germany: 20 per cent of those questioned could be categorised as strongly anti-Semitic, and a further 50 per cent showed at least traces of anti-Semitic views.[16] The figures are for the year 1974.

The attendant circumstances of the Silbermann study, which the author presents at the beginning of his book, are almost as interesting as the research results themselves. One reason for the enormous time gap between his first application for financial support from the German Research Society and the submission of the final report is that correspondence with the research society and its evaluators alone lasted a total of twenty-nine months. In a statement by the evaluators following completion of the project, Silbermann was told that the 'contents of the results were not surprising' and 'did not impart any new analytical insights'.[17] Pollock and the authors of the SINUS study were also subjected to severe criticism, mainly of their methods.

15. Friedrich Pollock, *Gruppenexperiment*, Frankfurt, 1955.
16. Alphons Silbermann, *Sind wir Antisemiten? Ausmaß und Wirkung eines sozialen Vorurteils in der Bundesrepublik Deutschland*, Cologne, 1982.
17. Ibid., p. 17. In this context I would also refer to the empirical analysis by Panahi in 1979, where the interrelation between nationalism, anti-Semitism and racism is vividly illustrated: Badi Panahi, *Vorurteile*, Frankfurt, 1980.

In February 1988 the Berlin Centre for Research into Anti-Semitism published the following Statistics: 6 per cent of the West German population showed manifest anti-Semitism in the sense of a closed world-view, a further 10–15 per cent expressed overt anti-Semitic prejudices, and a further 15–20 per cent showed anti-Semitic traits in their thinking, without expressing this openly.[18]

Table 3.5 Xenophobia in the Federal Republic of Germany (1982)

	Friendly towards foreigners (%)	Ambivalent (%)	Hostile towards foreigners (%)
Total	29	22	49
Age			
Up to 20	64	14	23
21–24	33	32	35
25–34	38	23	40
35–49	27	26	47
50–64	28	18	54
Over 64	22	15	63
Education			
No vocational training	24	17	60
Vocational training	23	24	53
'O' levels (equivalent)	44	24	33
'A' levels (equivalent), degree	48	25	28
Employment			
Employed	32	25	43
Students	53	17	30
Housewives	26	19	55
Pensioners	20	15	65
Party preference			
FDP	30	34	37
SPD	29	24	47
CDU/CSU	25	21	54

Source: INFAS.[19]

18. *Frankfurter Rundschau*, 4 February 1988, p. 1.
19. Institut für angewandte Sozialwissenschaft, *Meinungen und Einstellungen*

Table 3.6 Attitudes to foreign workers living in ghettoes

Question: 'Do you think it better for foreign workers to live in their own areas, or do you think it better for them to live with Germans on the same estate or in the same block of flats?

	1973	1980	1982
In their own areas (%)	38	35	40
Together with Germans (%)	49	63	60
No reply given (%)	13	3	—

Source: EMNID.

Xenophobic attitudes are likewise fairly widespread in West Germany. At the end of 1981, INFAS established that approximately half the population showed overt signs of hostility towards foreigners.

Xenophobia increases with age and decreases as the level of education rises. Those who expressed pessimistic economic expectations when questioned tend to have a particularly negative attitude towards foreign workers. According to INFAS, people who are already worried about the future are more inclined to assume that the problems caused by immigrants will increase.

The theory that economic problems encourage xenophobia is also supported by an EMNID study.[20] In 1982, when asked, 'Do you think that deporting foreign workers would be the best way to fight unemployment?', 55 per cent of the population replied, 'Yes'. In particular, foreigners are used as scapegoats for the economic crisis. The fact that in West Germany in particular there is a marked tendency for foreigners to live in ghettoes is very divisive (see Table 3.6).

Denying the Past

Although sympathy for national socialism has decreased markedly since 1945, nevertheless a widespread potential for right-

zum Ausländerproblem. Endbericht einer Untersuchung für das Presse- und Informationsamt der Bundesregierung, mimeo manuscript, Bonn–Bad Godesberg, April, 1982.
20. *EMNID-Informationen*, 1–2/1982, pp. 14ff.

wing extremist views exists in West Germany. This potential consists mainly of pro-Nazi, anti-Semitic and xenophobic attitudes, which fluctuate between 20 and 40 per cent. The proportion of the population which has a firm right-wing extremist attitude to life is currently some 15 per cent. To date, the vast majority of those people with potentially right-wing extremist attitudes – with a few exceptions – have tended to be affliated with the large, catch-all parties rather than to right-wing extremist parties. It remains to be seen whether the success of the Republikaner will change this. Alexander and Margarete Mitscherlich, commenting from a socio-psychological point of view, wrote:[21]

> While it is true that after 1945 the Nazi ideology was temporarily rejected, this does not mean that people had managed to establish a safe critical distance from it. A critical analysis of the past would have been required; but this did not occur. Hence fragments of this ideology which could be described as naive, because they are unreflective, have remained completely unchecked.

The Mitscherlichs' central theory is that people manage to reject the feelings of fear, guilt and shame connected with the Nazi past by repressing, or rather denying, national socialism. This is a type of self-defense mechanism to protect the ego from being undermined. For, after all, the Germans had shown the highest admiration and boundless trust in the Führer; they had cheered him enthusiastically; indeed, they had loved him. The Führer had taken the place of the ideal ego. Since everyone – the Mitscherlichs argue – had taken part in the Führer's meaningful life, the Führer himself became a part of every individual and so merged with the masses. Hence those left behind in 1945 felt that their egos had been betrayed. They sought protection, denied the past and defended themselves against disquieting memories: 'The vast majority of Germans are currently experiencing the period of national socialist rule retrospectively, in the manner of an infectious disease which occurs during childhood and spoils things.' The consciousness is directed towards the unreal, towards fantasies, in order to avoid any insight into

---

21. Alexander und Margarete Mitscherlich, *Die Unfähigkeit zu trauern*, Munich, 1977 (new edition), p. 42.

reality and the pain associated with it: 'The Nazi past is made to seem unreal'. People see themselves as the 'victims of evil forces: firstly of the evil Jews, then of the evil Nazis, and finally of the evil Russians. In each case the evil is externalised: it is sought outside and affects the individual from the outside'.[22]

It would be insufficient to interpret the potential for anti-democratic views purely as conscious support of the concepts of authoritarian or Fascist rule. It is equally a result of the refusal to engage in a critical examination of the past which would necessitate separation from the beloved object, Adolf Hitler.

Table 3.7 Feelings of national pride in major European countries (1983)[23]

Question: 'Would you say you are very proud, quite proud, not very proud, or not at all proud to be German (British, French, etc.)?'

National pride	Respondents, by country (%)				
	Germany	France	Britain	Italy	European Community[a]
Strong ('very'/'quite' proud)	56	75	92	84	77
Moderate ('not very' proud)	24	14	5	10	13
Weak ('not at all' proud)	9	5	2	4	5
Don't know/no reply	11	6	1	2	5

a. Ten-nation weighted average.
Source: *Euro-barometer*, no. 19 (June 1983), p. 54.

The many facets of the widespread potential for right-wing extremist views in West Germany can only be understood against the background of German history. Anti-democratic views, right-wing extremist parties and activities exist in all Western European countries. But nowhere else is the burden of the past so oppressive – even for the younger generation. The situation is all the more serious because there has never been an

---

22. Ibid., pp. 25, 34, 60, 71ff.
23. From David P. Conradt, *The German Polity*, New York and London, 1986, p. 52.

Repressing and Glossing over the Past

in-depth critical examination of the past. The most common way of coping with the past is to repress it and deny it, and ignorance is characteristic of the predominant attitude. Hence national socialism still has a formative influence on West Germany's political culture, in the form of the West Germans' troubled relationship with their own history and nation: nowhere in Western Europe is the 'national identity' less pronounced than in West Germany (see Table 3.7).

The Silent, Inexorable Return of the Past

> The silent, gradual, insidious, inexorable return of the past seems to be West Germany's fate. Dressed in both old and new cloaks of justice, individuals occupy the highest positions in administration, justice and associations, whilst dozens of them occupy middle positions. They control the economy – and have done for some time. . . . Tomorrow, they will also provide us with generals.[24]

It is symptomatic of the way in which West Germany deals with its historical past that a politician who had voted for the Enabling Law in 1933 [which abolished parliamentary control and laid the foundations for Nazi rule] was elected the first head of state. On 12 September 1949, Theodor Heuss (Liberal) was elected President with 416 votes, against 312 votes for the SPD chairman Kurt Schumacher. It was not a representative of the anti-Fascist opposition who became head of the Second Republic, but a man who, as a member of the German Reichstag, had voted for the 'Law to Remove Danger from the Nation and the Empire' and had thus encouraged the abolition of parliamentary democracy and the establishment of the Fascist dictatorship. I do not intend to dispute the fact that, after 1945, Theodor Heuss personally rendered outstanding service to the establishment of the civil-democratic, free market and Western-oriented democracy. However, viewed objectively, his appointment is proof of a criminal system being glossed over.

24. Eugen Kogon, 'Beinahe mit dem Rücken an der Wand', in *Frankfurter Hefte*, vol. 9 (1954) pp. 641-5, quotation p. 641. Kogon, a left-wing, Catholic journalist and political scientist, was a prisoner in a concentration camp and a member of the resistance, and has edited one of the standard works on the concentration camps, *Der SS-Staat*.

What crimes are we talking about exactly?

1. After taking power the Nazis abolished all basic rights and terrorised their opponents.
2. Opponents of national socialism, as well as victims of racial and religious persecution, were interned in concentration camps and murdered in their millions. This includes primarily the almost complete annihilation of European Jews.
3. Approximately 100,000 – possibly as many as 150,000 – people were murdered in the course of the euthanasia programme (the execution of 'worthless lives').
4. Task groups from the security police and the security forces, as well as divisions of the Waffen-SS, murdered hundreds of thousands of 'elements considered hostile to the empire and to Germany' in Poland and in the occupied areas of the Soviet Union.
5. Police units were often deployed against partisans with merciless violence and cruelty. Countless villages and farms were burnt down or destroyed as 'retaliatory measures'.
6. Crimes against prisoners-of-war, which were illegal under international law, were mainly committed against Soviet soldiers. For example, all commissioners of the Red Army who were caught were summarily shot. Of the 5.5 million Soviet soldiers who were captured by the Germans, at least 2.6 million died, mainly due to malnutrition and disease, but thousands were shot.[25]

The full extent of Nazi crimes is not known, and one can only attempt to outline them. The exact number of victims and the exact number of those involved in committing the crimes is not known.

Who were 'the culprits'? Who were 'the Nazis'?

In 1943 the NSDAP had approximately 6.5 million members,[26]

---

25. Adalbert Rückerl, *NS-Verbrechen vor Gericht. Versuch einer Vergangenheitsbewältigung*, Heidelberg, 1982, pp. 22ff.
26. Kurt Pätzold and Manfred Weißbecker, *Geschichte der NSDAP 1920–1945*, Cologne, 1981, p. 419, note 17. In total, the NSDAP probably had over 10 million members up to 1945.

while their subsidiary organisations probably had a further 4 million.[27] Together, this comprised approximately one fifth of the German adult population. This one fifth was probably in control of the important offices and positions of state and in society. But there were probably more fellow travellers among them than criminals, although some of these were certainly accomplices.[28] However, the actual criminals did not come from this circle, but from a much broader group. Many crimes were committed by people who were not members of any Nazi organisation (unless one labels the entire power and terror apparatus of the Third Reich a Nazi organisation). Perpetrators, accomplices and 'hangers-on' came from all sectors of the population.

Who is guilty: the person who carries out the crime, or the person who orders it? Should the SS thug who murders Jews on command be punished, or the person who issued the command? Should one also condemn the person who prepares the way for the crime morally, journalistically or politically, who legitimises it or grants it legal protection? Was Theodor Heuss guilty?

This is obviously a very complex question for which there are no straightforward answers or easy solutions. In the following sections we shall show that, regardless of the complexity of moral, political and legal guilt, not even the hardcore of Nazi criminals who were responsible have been called to account.

The Failed Attempt at de-Nazification

The allies, united in their opposition to Hitler, originally unanimously intended to eradicate national socialism completely, following their military victory over Germany, and to bring all Nazis to court.[29] In January 1942, the governments-in-exile of

---

27. Jörg Friedrich, *Die kalte Amnestie. NS-Täter in der Bundesrepublik*, Frankfurt, 1984, p. 190.

28. Four-fifths of all Germans were not former members of a Nazi organisation, so this was possible. Nevertheless, members of the resistance were very few.

29. For information on the victors' general concepts of their policy on Germany, cf. Hans-Peter Schwarz, *Vom Reich zur Bundesrepublik. Deutschland im Widerstreit der außenpolitischen Konzeptionen in den Jahren der Besatzungsherrschaft 1945–1949* (2nd edition) Stuttgart, 1980.

eight countries occupied by Germany (Belgium, Czechoslovakia, France, Greece, Luxembourg, the Netherlands, Poland and Yugoslavia) held a conference in London and declared that the sentencing of the Nazi criminals was one of their most important war objectives. In the course of the year the United States, Great Britain and the Soviet Union also joined this proclamation. In the Moscow Three-Powers Declaration of 30 October 1943, delivered in the name of thirty-two 'United Nations' (the core of the United Nations, which was later founded) the following statement was made:[30]

> The United Kingdom, the United States and the Soviet Union have received proof from many sources of atrocities, massacres and cold-blooded mass executions which have been committed by Hitler's troops in many of the countries they have conquered. . . . The brutalities of Nazi rule are nothing new, and all peoples and countries in their power have suffered under the worst form of terrorist rule. However, what is new is that many of these countries are being won back by the liberating powers and that in their desperation, the retreating Hitlerists and Huns are doubling their merciless atrocities . . .
>
> As soon as any government in Germany is able to call a ceasefire, those German officers, soldiers and members of the Nazi party who were responsible for the atrocities, massacres and executions described above, or who took part in them with their approval, will be sent back to the countries in which their heinous crimes were committed, to be tried and sentenced according to the laws of these liberated countries and the free governments established in them . . .
>
> The above statement excludes the rights of the main German offenders whose offences are not confined to one geographical area; they will be sentenced by a common verdict from the Allied governments.

Hence the allies were not prepared to concede the Germans the opportunity of self-purification. Rather, they had made a firm decision personally to supervise the punishment of Nazi criminals. Each crime was to be sentenced in the country in which it was committed, and an international court was only envisaged for the main war criminals. Although the Moscow Declaration

30. Quotation from Michael Ratz et al., *Die Justiz und die Nazis. Zur Strafverfolgung von Nazismus und Neonazismus seit 1945*, Frankfurt, 1979, pp. 11ff.

Repressing and Glossing over the Past

still placed considerable emphasis on punishing actual crimes, it soon became clear that the allies wanted more than merely to punish Nazi gangsters. They were seeking political purification and de-Nazification, accompanied by deep-seated social changes.

A few months after the end of the war, the 'big three', Churchill, Roosevelt and Stalin, met between 4 and 11 February 1945 in Yalta in the Crimea, and decided upon the formation of the United Nations, the division of Germany (among other things, by means of Poland's 'displacement to the West') and the formation of occupation zones. France was to be invited to participate in the occupation of Germany. Above all, however, they established the guidelines for the treatment of Germany following 'unconditional surrender',[31] as follows:[32]

> The United Kingdom, the United States of America and the USSR will have absolute power with reference to Germany . . .
> It is our unshakeable desire to destroy German militarism and national socialism, and to ensure that Germany is never again in a position to destroy world peace. We are determined to disarm and disband all German troops; . . . to try to sentence all war criminals as quickly as possible, and to obtain compensation in the same proportions as the destruction caused by the Germans; to abolish the national socialist party and national socialist laws, organisations and institutions; to eliminate all national socialist and military influences from public office as well as from the cultural and economic life of the German people; and in accordance with one another, to execute all measures necessary to ensure the future peace and security of the world.
> We do not intend to destroy the German people; but only when national socialism and militarism have been eradicated can the Germans hope to lead a dignified life and to gain a place in the international community.

Three months later, on 8 May 1945, representatives of the Supreme Command of the German army signed documents of unconditional surrender in the headquarters of General

---

31. This demand was made for the first time by President Roosevelt at the Casablanca Conference (14–26 January 1943).
32. Quotation from Helmuth K. G. Rönnefarth and Heinrich Euler, *Konferenzen und Verträge. Vertrags-Ploetz*, Part II, vol. 4A, (2nd edition), Würzburg, 1959, p. 246.

Eisenhower and Marshall Schukow. On 9 May 1945, at one minute past midnight, hostilities in Europe ceased. On 23 May the Dönitz government was arrested. (Hitler had named Grand Admiral Karl Dönitz as his successor as President before committing suicide on 30 April.) On 5 June, the four victorious powers finally assumed supreme power of government. The highest organ of control was the Allied Control Council. Germany was divided into four occupation zones, while Berlin was divided into four sectors. The capital of the 'Empire' was jointly administered by the four victorious powers.

At first the allies did not trust the Germans to abandon militarism and national socialism of their own accord, and even those who had offered resistance to the Hitler regime were not considered as potential partners in the operation. This was due to the theory of the German people's collective guilt, which was advocated particularly staunchly by US President Roosevelt, who died on 12 April 1945. Responsibility for militarism, national socialism, war and inhumanity was conferred wholesale on all Germans. Finance Minister Henry Morgenthau's plan, which aimed to impose draconian penalties on all Germans and turn Germany into an agricultural country, should also be viewed in this context. Although the Morgenthau plan was not an official plank of US policy, its spirit was nevertheless manifested in Directive 1067 of the Joint Chiefs of Staff, which initially determined US occupation policy:[33]

> Germany is not being occupied with the aim of liberation, but as a conquered hostile nation. . . . The allies' main aim is to prevent Germany ever again threatening world peace. Important steps towards achieving this aim are: the elimination of all forms of militarism, the immediate arrest of war criminals so that they can be sentenced . . . and preparations to rebuild German political life on a democratic basis.

Democratisation of German society was to be supported by measures of 're-education'. Particular attention was paid to the education system: by purging the teaching staff in schools and colleges, the allies hoped to guarantee a democratic influence on

---

33. Quotation from Justus Fürstenau, *Entnazifizerung. Ein Kapitel deutscher Nachkriegspolitik*, Neuwied and Berlin, 1969, p. 24.

young people. By licensing all forms of political activity, the founding of political parties and associations and the publishing of newspapers and journals, as well as by censoring the press and radio, the Western occupying forces believed they would be able to suppress any anti-democratic efforts.

Stalin only intended eliminating and sentencing the Nazi elite from politics, the economy and the military, but not the middle and lower officials, provided that they submitted to the new order, and not to take any action at all against the so-called hangers-on. He did not support the collective guilt theory, but was able to distinguish between Nazi activists, opportunists and resistance. He is supposed to have said that 'Hitlers come and go, but the German people and the German state remain'.

Even in the various anti-Fascist resistance groups, both within and outside of Germany, it was believed that Hitler's Fascist organisations had to be broken up and the staff purged. While the more middle-class resistance restricted themselves to justly punishing the truly influential and leading Nazis while abstaining from political justice, the communist and socialist Nazi opponents were primarily concerned with abolishing the social basis of national socialism among major landowners, the economy, the military and the Civil Service. They generally considered Fascism a specific form of bourgeois rule, which could only be smashed by the working class co-operating with the anti-Fascist middle class. Middle-class resistance was often heavily criticised for its motives: by striving only for the re-establishment of a state under the rule of law and a constitution, they were preventing the necessary radical changes in the power structures of the economy and politics, and, as such, were also hindering de-Nazification.

Differing opinions also prevailed among the partners of the anti-Hitler coalition over the question of how the eradication of German Fascism could be set in motion. At the Yalta Conference, no regulations for its implementation had been agreed upon, and therefore in the initial stages, each occupying power proceeded at its own discretion within its own zone.

Stalin was mainly concerned with destroying the social bases of national socialism and establishing a new social order. Moscow communists were convinced that this social order could not yet be of a socialist nature (and they considered it quite wrong to attempt to impose the Soviet system on Germany). They were striving for the completion of the civil-democratic revolution as the first stage on the road to socialism.[34] The planned anti-Fascist, democratic radical changes were aimed at a parliamentary republic with complete civil-democratic rights and freedom for the people. The major property-owners in agriculture and industry were to be expropriated and deprived of power, and those systems of production that were necessary for everyday life were to be nationalised, while other private ownership would remain unaffected.

The Allies Commence de-Nazification

In August 1945, the Soviet military administration began the de-Nazification programme in their zone. Initially, all members of the NSDAP and its subsidiary organisations, all officials and administrative staff, all officers (from lieutenants upwards) and all industrial managers were affected. According to Western estimates, approximately 150,000 people were arrested, sentenced or interned. The number of those who died in the former concentration camp at Buchenwald alone is estimated at 70,000.[35] However, it soon became clear that if they were to continue with the rigid de-Nazification policy, many sectors of public life would collapse, and by autumn 1945 they began distinguishing between activists and hangers-on and to make the latter exempt from sentencing and accountability. This was done in the expectation 'that they would make a complete break from their political past and participate wholeheartedly in the rebuilding of our country'.[36]

Overall, de-Nazification in the Soviet occupation zone was carefully controlled with the aim of gradually replacing the old elites in academia and in the property-owning middle classes with classes that had until then been underprivileged, while at

---

34. For more details, see Dietrich Staritz, *Sozialismus in einem halben Lande. Zur Programmatik und Politik der KPD/SED in der Phase der antifaschistisch-demokratischen Umwälzung in der DDR*, Berlin, 1976, pp. 42ff. At the second SED party conference in 1952, the delegates decided to 'start to create the bases of socialism'.
35. Dietrich Staritz, *Die Gründung der DDR. Von der sowjetischen Besatzungsherrschaft zum sozialistischen Staat*, Munich, 1984, pp. 99ff.
36. Quotation from Fürstenau, *Entnazifizierung*, p. 23.

the same time securing and extending the influence of the KPD and later the SED.[37] This restructuring process was completed in 1948 (the official date of the completion of de-Nazification was 22 February 1948) and had led to the dismissal of approximately 520,000[38] people, a large proportion of whom probably fled to the West.

While de-Nazification in the Soviet occupation zone was confined mainly to the active Nazis and was conducted with the help of German anti-Fascists ('purging committees', 'special purging committees', German courts), in the Western zones, policies were initially determined by the theory of collective guilt. This meant in effect that the German people were not considered as possible allies or associates, and the military were left to cope alone. Under Directive JCS 1067, US troops received an index of organisations and positions whose members or holders were established Nazi activists or sympathisers and who were therefore to be detained. In addition, lists of people said to have committed war crimes were drawn up, and these people were to be arrested immediately ('automatic arrest'). In addition, the directive envisaged the imprisonment of all Nazis, the elimination of the NSDAP and its subsidiary organisations, the confiscation of Nazi property, and the abolition of all laws that had supported unlawful rule. Permission had to be granted by the military government for any form of political activity.

The US de-Nazification programme, which was soon adopted by the two other Western allies – albeit in a mitigated form – was shortsighted and inconsistent. It made too great a demand on the military personnel, who had only an inadequate knowledge of the German situation, and it did not contain any indication of who was to replace those Nazis who had been dismissed. Who were the victorious powers actually carrying out de-Nazification for? And, if all Germans were suspect or guilty, what was going to replace the Nazi rule?

Moreover, in everyday practice the military governments faced the problem that, being the ultimate state power, they were responsible for providing for the population and for overcoming the chaotic mess. At the end of the Second World War

37. In spring 1946 the KPD and the SPD merged to become the SED (Socialist Unity Party of Germany) in the Soviet occupation zone.
38. Staritz, *Die Gründung der DDR*, p. 102.

Table 3.8 Automatic arrest in the three Western zones

	Automatically arrested by 1 January 1947	Released by 1 January 1947
British zone	64,500	34,000 (= 53%)
American zone	95,250	44,244 (= 46%)
French zone	18,963	8,040 (= 42%)

Source: Fürstenau, *Entnazifizierung*, p. 44f.

some 25 million Germans had been bombed out, evacuated or were refugees. In addition some 4 million DPs (Displaced Persons) were flocking back to their home countries from whence the Germans had transported them, mainly as forced labour. Most large towns had been destroyed; transport and communication links had broken down. There was hardly any food or fuel, and almost no accommodation. On the other hand, the black market and crime were flourishing. Under these conditions, which worsened daily with the influx of expellees and refugees, the occupation officers often concentrated their efforts on solving the pressing problems of providing food and rebuilding, and in doing so neglected the primary aim of de-Nazification, despite orders to the contrary. What is more, in dealing with the exigencies of everyday life, they were forced to employ the help of experienced experts without conducting a thorough examination of their political past. Hence it was not uncommon for competent administrative experts with 'dark brown'[39] views to be employed.

However, for the most part, the Western allies, particularly the Americans, devoted themselves with the greatest of care, indeed with over-enthusiasm, to the de-Nazification programme.

An example: By the end of 1946 almost 180,000 people had been subjected to automatic arrest. Almost half of these had to be released because there was no proof that they had taken part in war crimes.

In the case of blue-collar workers, office workers and officials in the Civil Service who either remained in employment or were

---

39. In Germany, the colour brown is synonymous with Fascism because the Nazis wore brown uniforms ('Brown Shirts'), in the same way as the Italian Fascists were called 'Black Shirts'.

reinstated, the military governments used a comprehensive questionnaire with approximately 130 questions demanding detailed information of all qualifications and activities, and membership of associations, political parties, etc. This questionnaire was the most important basis of political purging in Germany. By 1 June 1946 the US military government had received 1,613,000 completed questionnaires which had to be processed. The following assessments were possible:

1. Unconditional dismissal from service.
2. Dismissal from service under certain conditions. (Dismissal recommended.)
3. Dismissal from service under certain conditions.
4. No proof of Nazi activity.
5. Proof of Anti-fascist activity.

On the basis of approximately 1 million processed questionnaires the following judgements were made (figures from March 1946):[40]

– unconditionally dismissed from service: 18 per cent.
– dismissal recommended: 7 per cent.
– dismissal under certain circumstances: 24 per cent.
– no proof of Nazi activity: 50 per cent.
– proof of anti-Fascist activity: 1 per cent.

In September 1945, the Americans decreed Law No. 8, which forbade the employment in a private company or in public service of former members of the NSDAP and its associated organisations unless it was for manual work. This in fact meant that approximately 20 per cent of the working population was banned from employment. Every German who wanted to work had to be subjected to a 'process of individual inquisition' (*Fürstenau*).

40. Fürstenau, *Entnazifizierung*, p. 38.

De-Nazification in the Hands of the Germans

It was impossible to achieve such an extensive programme of de-Nazification without the co-operation of the Germans, and hence West German officials and offices were included simultaneously in the de-Nazification process together with the revival of political life in the Western zones; de-Nazification itself, however, still remained under allied supremacy. On 5 March 1946, the 'Law for the Liberation from National Socialism and Militarism' (Law No. 104) was declared in the US zone of occupation. This law included the following new rules: the number of people involved was not reduced – despite emphatic German wishes to the contrary – but the use of the questionnaire (now known as a registration form) was drastically reduced. From now on, trials were carried out in German 'sentencing chambers', generally without a cross-examination, and appeal chambers were set up as revisionist courts. The *Berufsverbot* (i.e. exclusion from a Civil Service profession by government ruling) remained in force for anything other than manual work.[41]

In October 1946 these orders were extended by Directive No. 38 from the Controlling Council to cover the other two Western zones, though with certain modifications: The British and the French implemented de-Nazification less rigidly than the Americans. They reduced the number of people affected by not insisting on de-Nazification of the 'small party member', and they did not enforce the general *Berufsverbot*. In the British zone, the sentencing chambers were only set up for individual occupational groups and branches of the economy, and their decisions only had recommendatory influence on the military government. They reserved the decision as to who was a main offender and who was incriminated. The French, in any case, only participated in de-Nazification under protest, and concentrated mainly on the Nazi elite.

The West German politicians involved in de-Nazification generally criticised both US rigour and the discrepancies of de-Nazification in the three Western zones (hence creating uncer-

---

41. Erich Schullze. *Gesetz zur Befreiung von Nationalsozialismus und Militarismus vom 5. März 1946 mit Ausführungsvorschriften, Formblättern, der Anweisungen für die Auswerter der Meldebögen und der Rangliste in mehrfarbiger Wiedergabe* (2nd edition), Munich, 1947.

Repressing and Glossing over the Past

tainty as to the legal position). Since they usually viewed the problem from a legal standpoint, they often viewed the concept of an extensive political purge with considerable scepticism. They wanted, if possible, to restrict the circle of those affected to middle and high-level Nazis, and basically only wanted to sentence those Nazis who had violated the laws existing at the time. When the three Western allies put de-Nazification in the hands of the Germans by means of the 'liberation law', the (German) sentencing chambers did everything in their power to deal with the cases of the 'small' Nazis first, in order to reintegrate the majority of those involved into the economy and push ahead with rebuilding society. This brought the accusation of German de-Nazification bureaucracy that they had hooked 'the little fish' and let 'the big ones' get away. And, indeed, for the most part this was true. In his book, Rückerl, the head of the 'Central Office for the *Land* Justice Administrations to Solve National Socialist Crimes', gives a vivid description of the problems faced by the sentencing chambers:[42]

> Functionaries of the Nazi regime who had committed serious crimes during the war in the areas occupied at times by the German army and had not mentioned this fact – understandably – on the questionnaire, usually passed through the de-Nazification procedures relatively unscathed. Even in cases where it became known in the course of the proceedings that the defendant had participated in crimes, for example, murdering Jews in a concentration camp, the sentencing chambers, who at the time, as a result of insufficient knowledge of the situation and a lack of information, frequently did not recognise the severity and extent of the crimes committed, imposed only relatively lenient sentences. On the other hand, it was not uncommon for severe sanctions to be imposed on minor party members who had only joined the NSDAP or one of its associated organisations because they were worried about their families and losing their jobs, and hence had succumbed to pressure from their superiors, and who had only had subordinate positions. The falsification of questionnaires and preferential treatment in the form of handing out so-called 'Persil tokens'[43] were just as common as

---

42. Rückerl, *NS-Verbrechen*, p. 118.
43. As the accused had to exonerate themselves in court, in other words 'wash themselves clean', they endeavoured to find witnesses who could certify that they had offered passive resistance, for example, that they had made

informants. The fact that preferential treatment and informing frequently occurred, not because of political beliefs, but for economic reasons or personal feuds, made the whole affair appear even more dubious. There can be no doubt that 'de-Nazification' at that time politically corrupted part of our society.

Criticism of de-Nazification soon came from the United States. In view of the increasing East–West tensions and the imminent division of Germany, in 1947/8 US policy changed. In the future, rebuilding the country and strengthening economic and political life in West Germany, with the aim of creating an independent state capable of existing by itself, would take priority over de-Nazification.

At the end of 1946, the *Länder* in the US zone (Bavaria, Württemberg-Baden, Hesse and Bremen) and the British zone (Schleswig-Holstein, Lower Saxony, Hamburg and North Rhine-Westphalia) joined to became a bi-zone. In 1947 the bi-zone was placed under the parliamentary control of the Economic Council, with the Executive Committee acting as a co-ordinating body. The Western zones and the Soviet zone became increasingly estranged from one another, both economically and politically. While anti-capitalist structural reforms (e.g. the land reform) occurred in the Eastern zone, the Americans supported a strengthening of the spirit of free enterprise and stalled any intentions on the part of the political left and the unions of nationalising industry. At the London Six Power Conference (February 1948) the future of (West) Germany was discussed for the first time without the participation of the Soviet Union, and preparations were made to extend the bi-zone to a tri-zone to include the zone occupied by the French (with the *Länder* Südwürttemberg-Hohenzollern and Rhineland-Palatinate).[44] As a result, the Soviet Marshall Sokolovski left the meeting of the Allied Control Council in Berlin (20 March 1948), signalling the end of the supreme governing body of the four victorious powers in Germany. At the London conference at the beginning

disparaging remarks about the Nazis. It was often the case that culprits exonerated one another.

44. Initially, the Saarland belonged to the French zone, but in 1946 it was separated off. It received autonomous status, but was incorporated into the French economy and customs area. Following a referendum in 1955, it has been part of Germany again since 1957.

of June 1948, the regional presidents of the three Western zones received permission to call a meeting to draw up a constitution for the three Western zones, which were to be united. Ten days later, on 18 June 1948, the military governments in the three Western zones announced a separate currency reform. The old Reichsmark was replaced by the Deutsche Mark (DM). On 23 June monetary reform took place in the Soviet zone, and in July a new currency was installed there as well: the Deutsche Mark der Deutschen Notenbank (MDN), disparagingly called the Ostmark in the West. The Soviet military administration initially used the currency reform in the Western zones as a reason for stopping the traffic of people and provisions between the Western zones and Berlin, the provision of electricity from the Eastern sector, and deliveries of foodstuffs from their zone. On the night of 23/24 June, the Berlin blockade began (it was lifted on 5 May 1949), and on 26 June the United States and Great Britain set up an air bridge to supply provisions to the three Western sectors of Berlin. For 300 days, British and US planes transported some 6.4 million tons of food, fuel, tools and machinery into the blockaded city. In the meantime, the division of Germany was progressing. On 23 May 1949 the Parliamentary Council announced the Basic Law for the Federal Republic of Germany as a temporary constitution for the state consisting of the Western zones, and on 30 May the German People's Congress in the Eastern zone passed the constitution for the German Democratic Republic. On 14 August 1949, elections took place in the West for the first German Bundestag, the West German parliament.

The events briefly described here form the background to the change in US de-Nazification policy, which occurred in 1947/8. At that time, the number of those in the United States pleading for an immediate halt to the trials in the sentencing chambers – with the exception of those against major criminals – and for an amnesty for all those who were not major criminals, was increasing. This sudden change in direction received severe criticism from the German left, but also annoyed supporters of strict de-Nazification as befits a state under the rule of law. For example, in Bavaria in March 1948[45] a high-ranking official declared:

45. Quotation from Fürstenau, *Entnazifizierung*, p. 95.

It will hardly be possible to stand in front of the nation now and announce an end to the remaining cases in a generous trial, after the way that, to date, following the orders of the occupying powers, the 'little people' have all been called to account and the truly guilty ones are finally about to take their turn.

In autumn 1948, after almost completely dismantling their de-Nazification bureaucracy, the Americans ceased surveillance of de-Nazification. The French and British followed suit later. Following the founding of the Federal Republic, the Bundestag immediately became involved in the question of a uniform final legislative for all *Länder* and finally, on 15 October 1950, passed relevant guidelines. These were then translated into concrete laws in the individual *Länder*, ending with Bavaria in 1954. This, then, concluded – or rather, liquidated – de-Nazification.

The summary of de-Nazification was sobering. Of a total of 3.6 million Germans who had been tried, 175,152 people were classified as guilty or incriminated. Of the 3.6 million trials against supposed or actual Nazis, 95 per cent proved to be 'hangers-on', had their cases dropped or got off altogether.

De-Nazification and the Party Dispute

The fact that, despite the vast bureaucratic resources devoted to it, de-Nazification petered out with few real results and was thus a farce, was also due to the fact that the overwhelming majority of Germans did not want a root-and-branch political purge, and even the trials in the sentencing chambers were soon only approved of by about one third of the population.[46] In 1952, 60 per cent of the population thought that former members of the NSDAP should not be disadvantaged with respect to their promotion chances at work.

Following the Liberation Law, the main German supporters of de-Nazification had been the political parties that were loth to cut themselves off from majority opinion. While, initially, the

46. Until the end of 1946, approximately half of those questioned in the American zone had declared themselves satisfied with the way in which de-Nazification was being carried out. Thereafter, the approval rates sank rapidly: in 1947/8 to approximately one third, and in 1949 to approximately 17 per cent of the population. See *German Views on Denazification*, OMGUS-Information Services Division Germany, Report no. 182, 11 July 1949, Bad Nauheim APO 807.

Table 3.9 Review of de-Nazification in the Western zones (FRG), 1949/50

	Number	Percentage
Number of cases processed	3,660,648	100
Grouping:		
Major criminals	1,667	.05
Incriminated (Nazi activists, militarists, property confiscators)	23,060	0.5
Minor criminals (probation group)	150,425	4.1
Hangers-on	1,005,874	27.5
No case to answer	1,213,873	33.2
Trial stopped[a]	1,265,749	34.6

a. Granted amnesty, innocent, etc.

Source: Fürstenau, *Entnazifierung*, p. 228f.

left (Social Democrats and communists) fought extremely hard for consistent de-Nazification, the bourgeois parties tended to hold back. They rejected democratic-socialist aims linked with left-wing anti-Fascism and defended a pro-Western capitalist, free market economy, thus agreeing in principle with the allies. While the workers' parties viewed Fascism as the ultimate consequence of capitalist production relations, the bourgeois parties were primarily concerned with thwarting any efforts towards socialism. They were mainly concerned with bringing the small clique of leading Nazis to trial, while at the same time integrating the mass of former national socialist supporters into the existing order and winning them over to democracy. One important factor involved is the fact that former party members represented a considerable number of potential voters with a formative influence on power structures in the Western zone state. Hence the bourgeois parties put themselves forward as representing the interests of the 'former members' or the 'victims of de-Nazification', and did so successfully. For the measures of de-Nazification had affected the middle and upper classes[47] more than anyone else; in other words, they had affected the voters and target group of the bourgeois parties rather than those of the SPD and KPD.

47. Fürstenau, *Entnazifizierung*, p. 174, note 47.

Table 3.10 German views on de-Nazification (1952)

Question: 'Do you generally approve or not of former members of the NSDAP today again having the same opportunities for advancement in business and politics as the rest of the Germans?'

	West Germany	British zone	US zone	French zone
Approve (%)	58	59	61	48
Disapprove (%)	29	30	26	31
No opinion (%)	13	11	13	21

	Approve	Disapprove
Sex		
Men	64	29
Women	52	28
Education		
Secondary school	54	31
Higher education	77	18
Income (per month)		
0–299 DM	53	30
300–399 DM	58	33
400 DM and more	72	21
Party preference		
SPD	58	34
CDU/CSU	58	34
Liberals	76	20
Occupation		
Professionals	72	21
Businessmen	68	21
White-collar workers	70	23
Skilled workers	61	29
Semi-Skilled workers	53	34
Farmers	52	30
Unemployed	46	35

Source: *A Year End Survey*, HICOG Report no. 167, p. 20.

Strictly speaking, de-Nazification was closely linked to the question of the future economic and political structures in postwar Germany. However, the influential moderate wing of the SPD considered it unacceptable to combine de-Nazification with socialism. Rather, they represented the opinion that de-Nazification and socialism were two separate things, the former being a matter for the sentencing chambers and the latter being the object of democratic decisions within parliaments. Admittedly, the moderate Social Democrats clung to the belief that de-Nazification must serve to exclude permanently the Nazi elite from political life, but they too began increasingly to emphasise the significance of the way in which justice was meted out at the trials. In doing so, they moved somewhat closer to the bourgeois parties, which, in 1948/9, began to dissociate themselves from the accusation that the legality of de-Nazification was questionable. While they had previously countered the social revolutionary implications of de-Nazification with the argument of legality, this argument was now directed against de-Nazification *per se*. Even social democracy could not close its eyes to the objections that the unequal treatment in the different zones, and the persecution of the hangers-on and minor party members while leading Nazis were spared, was difficult to reconcile with the principles of a state under the rule of law. Moreover, the more public opinion turned against de-Nazification, the more the SPD made heavy weather of the debate regarding the stance of the bourgeois parties, which, in view of the forthcoming Bundestag elections, were now stepping up their calls for an amnesty, a halt to the current trials in the sentencing chambers, and classification of the 'guilty' verdicts. In 1948 the Social Democratic Party leader, Kurt Schumacher, one of the original anti-Fascists and a former inmate of a concentration camp,[48] declared:

> The Social Democratic Party has demanded the toughest sentences imaginable for all the guilty parties. However, the fact that it was possible, understandable and excusable for an individual to slip into this movement is a point which should have been taken into consideration from the outset. By failing to do so adequately and by attempting to load the barbarity of collective guilt onto an entire nation, the truly guilty parties were protected.

The completion of de-Nazification occurred without any noteworthy political resistance. Hence it was also possible to ignore its consequences, which were in any case undramatic.

---

48. Quotation from *Turmwächter der Demokratie. Ein Lebensbild von Kurt Schumacher*, vol. 2: *Reden und Schriften*, Berlin, 1953, p. 141.

Politics Against Democracy

The main consequence was the reinstatement of all officials dismissed after 1945 as a result of de-Nazification. The only exceptions were those few officials who had been declared unacceptable for public service by a sentencing chamber.[49] The net result of this was that all Nazi officials – except for a small group of leading exponents – returned to their jobs as government officials, judges, public prosecutors, teachers, etc.

The Rehabilitation and Protection of Nazi Criminals

The political purge failed as a means of overcoming national socialism, not least because of a lack of support from the West Germans. One common and important argument against de-Nazification is the fact that political purges contradict the principles of a state under the rule of law. After twelve years of illegal rule, rebuilding and proving the worth of a state under the rule of law was much more important, it is argued, than carrying out dubious inquisitions.

One must doubt the credibility of this argument, however, if one evaluates the course and results of the Nazi trials. In contrast to de-Nazification, whereby the entire population was politically screened and every individual was forced to prove his innocence, the Nazi trials were carried out according to criminal law. In a trial before a court of law, the accused must be proved of having committed the crime. One might think this was at least one way in which the West Germans succeeded in purging themselves of national socialism. But this is not the case. Not even the West German courts were consistent in their sentencing of Nazi criminals. I emphasise the word criminals, for the Nazi trials dealt primarily with murder and manslaughter.

The legal prosecution of Nazi criminals began, as decreed by the Moscow Three Powers Declaration in October 1943, in allied and foreign courts. The trials against the German 'major war criminals'[50] took place in Nuremberg from 14 November 1945 to

---

49. The lever for this was Article 131 of the Basic Law and the Law to Control the Legal Circumstances of People Falling under Article 131 of the Basic Law of 11 May 1951. This group of people were described as '131s'.

50. Cf. Joe Heydecker and Johannes Leeb, *Der Nürnberger Prozeß* (2nd edition), Frankfurt, 1979. It was not possible, for example, to prosecute the following Nazis in Nuremberg: Adolf Hitler (committed suicide in April 1945),

Repressing and Glossing over the Past

1 October 1946. Twenty four leading Nazis[51] were charged with the following offences:

1. Preparing a war of aggression.
2. Crimes against peace.
3. War crimes.
4. Crimes against humanity.

Following a ten-month trial the sentences shown in Table 3.11 were passed.

After the main Nuremberg trials a number of other trials were conducted by the four occupying powers and various other states involved (mainly Poland, Yugoslavia, Czechoslovakia). The twelve follow-up trials by US military courts in Nuremberg (May 1946–April 1949) received particular publicity. Further trials took place under the aegis of the Americans in Dachau, Darmstadt and Ludwigsburg. In total, 1,941 people were brought before US military courts, of whom 324 were sentenced to death, 247 to life imprisonment and 946 to fixed terms of imprisonment. The prison sentences were later reduced, and all those sentenced were released by 1958.[52]

In total, British military courts charged 1,085 people, of whom 240 received the death sentence. The prison sentences were generally reduced later, and the last inmates were released by 1957. French military courts sentenced a total of 2,107 people, 104 of whom were sentenced to death. Here again, the final releases occurred in 1957. The number of sentences passed by Soviet military courts is not known, but is definitely many times greater than the total of those passed by Western occupying powers. In Poland, 5,358 Germans are said to have been sentenced for participation in Nazi crimes.

Dr Joseph Goebbels (committed suicide in April 1945) and Heinrich Himmler (committed suicide in May 1945 in British custody).
51. Dr Robert Ley, Organisational Leader of the NSDAP, comitted suicide before the main trial began. The process against the major industrialist Gustav Krupp von Bohlen und Halbach was stopped because he was unable to stand trial; he died in 1950.
52. For information on this and the following, see Rückerl, *NS-Verbrechen*, pp. 95ff. and Ratz, *Justiz*, pp. 41ff.

Table 3.11 Results of the Nuremberg trials

1. Death by hanging

Martin Bormann[a]	*Reichsleiter*, Head of the Nazi Party Chancellory
Dr Hans Frank	Governor-General of Poland
Dr Wilhelm Frick	Minister of the Interior
Hermann Göring[b]	*Reichsmarschall*, Commander in Chief of the Luftwaffe
Alfred Jodl	General, Chief of the OKW [German High Command] Operations Staff
Dr Ernst Kaltenbrunner	SS-General, Chief of the Reich Main Security Office
Wilhelm Keitel	Field Marshall, Chief of OKW
Joachim von Ribbentrop	Foreign Minister
Alfred Rosenberg	Minister for the Occupied Eastern Territories
Franz Sauckel	*Gauleiter*[c] of Thuringia, Head of the Manpower Procurement Programme
Dr Arthur Seyss-Inquart	Commissioner for the Netherlands
Julius Streicher	*Gauleiter* of Franconia, Editor of *Stürmer*

a. Tried *in absentia*.
b. Committed suicide before sentence could be imposed.
c. *Gauleiter*: Head of an administrative district of the Nazi Party.

2. Sentenced to Life Imprisonment

Walther Funk[a]	Minister of the Economy
Rudolf Hess[b]	Hitler's official deputy
Erich Raeder[c]	Grand Admiral, Commander-in-Chief of the Navy

a. Released in 1957 owing to ill-health.
b. Committed suicide in 1987.
c. Released in 1955 owing to ill-health.

3. Sentenced to fixed terms of Imprisonment

Karl Dönitz	Grand Admiral, Raeder's successor as Commander-in-Chief of the Navy, last President of the German Reich: 10 years' imprisonment
Konstantin von Neurath[a]	Foreign Minister, Protector of Bohemia-Moravia: 15 years' imprisonment

Baldur von Schirach	Reichsjugendführer, Leader of Hitler Youth, *Gauleiter* of Vienna: 20 years' imprisonment
Albert Speer	Minister for Munitions: 20 years' imprisonment

a. Pardoned in 1954 owing to ill-health.

4. Acquitted

Hans Fritsche	Leader of the Radio Department in the Ministry for Propaganda
Franz von Papen	Vice-Chancellor, Ambassador to Austria and Turkey
Dr Hjalmar Schacht	President of the Reichsbank, Minister of the Economy

Much criticism has been levelled at these trials – particularly from Germans – which can be summed up by the key words 'victors' justice' or 'revenge justice'. The main objections are as follows: only German war criminals were sentenced, but not the criminals from the other belligerent states, in particular for crimes committed by Soviet soldiers against Germans. Moreover, the Soviet Union had also waged a war of aggression (against Poland and Finland), and had expressly approved the German invasion of Norway. From a legal point of view, this criticism is partly justified, but nevertheless frequently appears quite unconvincing coming from the Germans, since their concern for the perpetrators was much greater than their concern for the victims.

Attitudes changed at the end of the 1940s, as a result of international realignments. With escalating East–West conflict, people began to discuss the question of German participation in defence. The West German government believed that rearmament would only be possible if war criminals could be pardoned and the 'defamation' of the German armed forces ceased, because they would, after all, be needed to form a new army. In 1951, generous amnesties were granted to those condemned by the military courts. Those death sentences that had not already been carried out were commuted to prison sentences, and early releases were ordered. Hence it was not uncommon for leaders of taskforces, who had been found guilty of the murder of hundreds of thousands of people and sentenced to death, to be set free in the mid-1950s. Even commanders of concentration camps were soon released. For example, in 1954 the British released the commander of the Großrosen concentration camp, Johannes Hassebroek, who had been sentenced to life imprisonment.

The main significance of the trials is that they provided an effective reconstruction of Nazi crimes, revealed them to the world, and conveyed an impression of the true extent of the atrocities of which so many Germans professed ignorance or genuinely had no idea. Above all, it became evident that:

> all the murders described as Nazi crimes were in fact cold-blooded mass murders which were conducted utilising all the bureaucratic and technical means available, usually by people who had no relation to their victims and who had never experienced the slightest harm or disturbance from their victims or their fellow countrymen.[53]

Trials in West German Courts

In this sense, the military courts did perform indispensable groundwork for the Nazi trials to be conducted later under German control. However, much time passed before these trials took place. Admittedly, the restrictions imposed on the West German judiciary no longer applied after 1950, but initially only very few inquiries were launched. According to German law, once a crime becomes known, the public prosecutors are only obliged to conduct a trial if the crime was committed in their area of jurisdiction or if the suspect resides there. However, the majority of Nazi crimes were committed outside West Germany. The state-organised mass murder of millions generally took place in Eastern Europe (Poland, the Soviet Union, Czechoslovakia, etc.), and the identity of the perpetrators was not generally known. A particularly serious example of passivity is the Reich Main Security Office, the nucleus of Nazi terror, which was resident in Berlin and for whose crimes the Berlin public prosecutor was responsible. However, between 1950 and 1963 the latter did not undertake any measures to institute trials against members of this office, who in some cases had been known since the Nuremberg trials.

53. Rückerl, NS-Verbrechen, p. 16.

In 1958 the criminal prosecution of Nazi criminals was set in motion almost by accident. In Ulm, a carefully prepared and highly publicised taskforce trial occurred, which revealed just how little the West German judiciary had done in carrying out their duty to punish Nazi injustices. In 1959, the Sozialistische Deutsche Studentenbund (SDS) opened an exhibition in Karlsruhe compiled by a Berlin student, Reinhard M. Strecker, concerning 138 Nazi lawyers who were working in West Germany as judges and public prosecutors, some of them in very high positions. There were even six judges and public prosecutors from the People's Court among them. In December 1959, the synagogue in Cologne was desecrated with Fascist graffiti. This incident sparked off a wave of further right-wing extremist, and in particular anti-Semitic, incidents involving over 1,000 people. This touched the sensibilities of the West German public and forced the political institutions to take action. At the end of 1958, the 'Central Office for the *Land* Justice Administrations to Solve National Socialist Crimes' was established in Ludwigsburg near Stuttgart. From then on – almost fifteen years after the liberation from Fascism – systematic investigations into Nazi crimes and criminals were conducted by the West German judiciary.

However, investigations could only be initiated in the case of murder. All other Nazi crimes came under the statute of limitations[54] until 1960: in 1950 less serious crimes with a maximum sentence of five years' imprisonment became invalid, and in 1955 the ten-year period of the statute of limitations came into force. From 1955 onwards, only cases of murder and manslaughter could be prosecuted, and the latter became invalid under this ruling in 1960. In 1965 the twenty-year period of the statute of limitations for murder would lapse. In the German Bundestag, however, the government was still not ready to abolish the statute of limitations for murder. They simply postponed the beginning of the period of the statute of limitations from 1945 to 1950. Hence in 1969, Members of Parliament were faced with this question once again, and yet again there was no majority in favour of abolishing the statute of limitations. The period of the statute of limitations was extended from 20 to 30

---

54. This means that judicial punishment of a crime is no longer possible once a specific period of time has elapsed. Under German law, murder came under the statute of limitations after twenty years and manslaughter after fifteen.

years. Consequently, in 1979 there was yet another debate in the Bundestag regarding the statute of limitations. Here the decision was taken to abolish the statute of limitations for murder so that Nazi murders can still be investigated for as long as the murderers are still alive, although this problem will obviously resolve itself fairly soon, simply due to age.

The exact number of people who have been sentenced in German or foreign courts for Nazi crimes or war crimes is not known, as no figures are available from the Soviet Union, Czechoslovakia and Yugoslavia. The number is estimated at 70,000.[55]

Table 3.12   Review of the prosecution of Nazi war crimes by (West) German courts, 1945–85

	Number	Percentage
Inquiries initiated	90,921	100
Condemned persons	6,479	7.1
Of these		
Death sentence[a]	12	0.01
Life imprisonment	160	0.2
Fixed term of imprisonment	6,192	6.8
Fined	114	0.1
Cautioned by juvenile court	1	0.0

a. The death sentence was abolished in 1949.

Source: Bundesministerium der Justiz (Federal Ministry for Justice).[56]

For the Nazis' mass murder of millions, the West German judicial authorities were able to track down and sentence exactly 172 murderers. It seems that the state-organised mass murder committed by the Nazis was the perfect murder: 'It showed breathtaking efficiency, and the criminals disappeared into thin air'.[57] It is noteworthy that not a single member of a Special Court or of the People's Court has been sentenced for the murder(s) they committed in view of their part in passing illegal death sentences.

    55. Rückerl, *NS-Verbrechen*, p. 307.
    56. Albrecht Götz, *Bilanz der Verfolgung von NS-Straftaten*, Cologne, 1986, p. 149.
    57. Friedrich, *Amnestie*, p. 353.

Repressing and Glossing over the Past

The lack of enthusiasm of the judicial authorities corresponded with the unpopularity of the prosecution of Nazi crimes among the population. In 1968, 74 per cent agreed with the statement: 'We should at long last stop asking whether individuals held positions of leadership during the Third Reich'.[58] In the 1970s, however, the proportion of those who supported the Nazi trials markedly increased (see Table 3.13).

The high degree of support for prosecution in 1979 was probably the result of impressions created by the broadcasting of the television film *Holocaust*, which gave a vivid portrayal of the fate of the Jews under national socialism in the style of a 'soap opera'. *Holocaust* had a lasting effect on German sentiment and led to intensive discussions regarding the way in which the German people came to terms with their past.

Table 3.13 The prosecution of Nazi crimes in the eyes of the population (1974–79)

Question: 'Recently, discussions have intensified regarding the problem of the prosecution of crimes committed during the period of national socialism. What is your personal opinion on this: Should we continue to prosecute crimes committed during the Nazi era – or should we forget the past once and for all?

	1974	1978	1979
We should continue to prosecute Nazi crimes (%)	25	34	50
We should forget the past (%)	60	64	46
No opinion (%)	15	2	4

Source: EMNID.[59]

Continuity or Discontinuity of the Post-war Elites?

The consequence of the failed attempt at de-Nazification and reluctance to prosecute Nazi crimes is obvious: in all areas of West German society there has been continuity of personnel

58. Agreed strongly: 43 per cent; agreed moderately: 16 per cent; agreed weakly: 15 per cent. Max Kaase, 'Demokratische Einstellungen in der Bundesrepublik Deutschland', in *Sozialwissenschaftliches Jahrbuch für Politik*, vol. 2, Munich and Vienna, 1971, p. 119ff., figures p. 324.
59. *EMNID-Informationen*, 2/1979, pp. 10ff and 11–12/1978, p. 9f.

from the Fascist to the post-Fascist period, which cannot be overlooked. The proportion of Nazis in particular professions, such as teachers, lawyers, the military or in the middle and upper leadership groups, is not actually known. No enquiries have been conducted on this matter in West Germany. Documents are published at regular intervals in East Germany, no doubt with propagandistic ulterior motives and they should therefore be treated with caution. For example, in 1965 the comprehensive *Brown Book* appeared in East Germany containing biographical details of the Nazi history of:

– 21 ministers and secretaries of state.

– 100 generals and admirals in the armed forces.

– 828 senior officials in the judiciary, including public prosecutors and judges.

– 245 senior civil servants in the Foreign Office.

– 297 senior officials in the police and the Office for the Protection of the Constitution.

In particularly serious cases, violent protests erupted in West Germany, for example, against Dr Hans Globke, who had been appointed Secretary of State by the first West German Chancellor, Konrad Adenauer. During the Nazi era Globke had been an official in the Home Office where he had been involved, among other things, in drawing up race laws, and had published a commentary on the 'Law for the Protection of Blood'[60] in 1936. On the whole, however, the West German people accepted the Nazi bias of parts of the social elites without any notable resistance.

In 1956, Lewis J. Edinger of Michigan State University analysed the top positions in politics, administration, interest groups and journalism in West Germany. He came to the following conclusion:[61]

---

60. This law made 'marriages between Jews and nationals with German [!] blood' a punishable offence.
61. Lewis J. Edinger, 'Post-Totalitarian Leadership: Elites in the German Federal Republic', in *American Political Science Review*, vol. LIV (1960), pp. 58ff. Quotation p. 75.

Looking at the elite members in terms of their known or conjectured attitudes towards the totalitarian regime (for example, loyal Nazi party members and military officers), we find that about 24 per cent may be considered to have been supporters of the regime, 57 per cent to have been ambivalent, neutral, or oscillating during the twelve years of Nazi rule, and no more than 19 per cent to have been more or less consistently opposed. Either way, the bulk of the post-totalitarian elite membership was recruited from the ranks of the Germans who, while old enough to care, were ambivalent or neutral towards the regime and were neither among its leaders nor among its major opponents.

How should these figures be interpreted? With reference to the original aims of the allied de-Nazification and re-education policies, one can hardly talk of an anti-Fascist background as far as the top elite is concerned. Moreover, the fact that over half of the leading staff examined by Edinger were politically neutral or ambivalent during the Nazi period does not exactly support a discontinuation of the post-Fascist elites. Likewise, one could hardly expect a new political orientation from this circle of people.

Anti-Communism Instead of Anti-Fascism

After 1945, critical examination of the Nazi past was abandoned in favour of rebuilding the country and integration with the West.

Various factors influenced the Germans in this regard. Feelings of fear, guilt and shame attached to national socialism led to German repression and denial of the Third Reich. Their willingness to undertake a critical reappraisal of the Hitler era was extraordinarily low. Instead of this, people concentrated all their efforts on rebuilding the economy, which was urgently needed and which was seen by German politicians and later also by the allies as their primary objective. In the West, the eradication of poverty, the reconstruction of the capitalist market economy and the economic, political and military integration with the West formed a solid wall in view of developing East–West conflict and the division of Germany that accompanied it. The changed world-political conflicts meant that the Western powers viewed the economic and political consolidation of West Germany as being of paramount importance compared with the old anti-Fascist aims, and the end of the 1940s seemed almost anachronistic. The fact that an inappropriate concept of de-Nazification had failed facilitated the change in direction, which was welcomed by the majority of Germans. They were almost grateful for their new role as the bulwark of the West against the Soviet expansion. For this task – which, after all, corresponded largely with the Germans' self-image before 1945 – converted yesterday's enemy into today's ally and offered him the chance to forge a new self-image by avoiding a self-critical analysis of the past. Compensating anti-Fascism with anti-communism promised international recognition.

Among the Germans, no anti-Fascist consensus existed regarding the evaluation of national socialism and the treatment of the Nazis. De-Nazification soon became caught up in the whirlpool of party disputes regarding fundamental economic and political questions, whereby former hangers-on and activists from the Nazi regime were always seen as potential voters both by the bourgeois parties and the social democrats. These potential voters were very important in the fight between the two major parties (the Christian-Conservative CDU/CSU and the SPD) for political hegemony in West Germany.

The Political Integration of Right-wing Extremism after 1945

The fact that pro-Nazi sympathies were widespread in the immediate post-war era, the failed attempt at de-Nazification, the totally inadequate prosecution of Nazi crimes and last but not the least the serious economic and social problems in postwar Germany, all combined to create optimal conditions for the development of a new right-wing extremism in the Western zones after 1945. Nevertheless, despite certain initial successes, the feared mass nationalist opposition to the formation of a democratic state in the West failed to materialise. This was, initially, a result of the rigid control of political life by the three Western allies, particularly by means of the licensing policy (see below, p. 84). However, the decisive factors were the rapid growth of consensus in West German society, the successful integration strategy of the democratic parties, and the prosperity of the West German economy.

This section deals briefly with the outline conditions for the emergence and development of organised right-wing extremism in the 1950s and 1960s. I shall devote particular attention to two aspects deemed to have a determining influence on the future course of events: the integrative capacity of the bourgeois-democratic parties, and the development of a basic consensus in West German society.

The Military Government's Licensing Policy

The occupation policy of the three Western allies was characterized by two important aims: (1) the elimination of Nazism and militarism; and (2) the reconstruction of political life on a democratic basis. Hence the allies did not only have to prevent supporters of national socialism gaining political influence in post-war Germany, they also had to ensure that the enormous post-war problems – in particular the division of Germany, the hordes of expellees and refugees[62] who were streaming into the three Western zones from the East, the masses of people who had been bombed out, the unemployed and the starving, as well as those subjected to de-Nazification – did not escalate into broad dissatisfaction with the political status qou and develop into a breeding-ground for a new right-wing extremism.

In the early 1950s some 8 million expellees were living in West Germany, approximately 17 per cent of the population. In some *Länder* they made up almost one third of the inhabitants. Furthermore, there were between 4.5 and 6 million victims of bombing, 2.5 million war widows, 1.5 million severely disabled and their dependants, 2 million late returners from POW camps, over 1.5 million unemployed and some 2 million former officials, NSDAP employees and soldiers who had been subjected

---

62. According to current law, the term 'expellee' is used to describe those people who were expelled or have fled into the Federal Republic of Germany or into the Western zones from the eastern territories of the former German Reich on the other side of the Oder and the Neiße or from (southern) eastern European states. 'Refugees' are those people who have come into the Western zones or the Federal Republic of Germany from the Soviet zone of occupation or from the GDR. Hence refugees and expellees are distinguished according to their country of origin.

to de-Nazification ('victims of de-Nazification'). Bearing in mind the results of the US surveys from this period, which had unearthed a wide potential for pro-Nazi attitudes,[63] we can understand why the military governments feared a resurgence of political right-wing extremism.

The Western allies were concerned from the outset to control carefully the development of democratic institutions and structures. First, the NSDAP and its subsidiary organisations and possible successors were banned, and second, all socio-political activities were subject to a licensing requirement and continual strict control. It was self-evident that parties, unions, associations and interest groups could only become active with permission, and at first the military governments only licensed such activities at the local and regional levels. Political parties (with a few exceptions) were only granted a license if they could prove that their manifesto was anti-Fascist/democratic and that their politicians were non-Nazis. Moreover, the occupying powers were concerned to prevent a fragmentation of the party system (as in the Weimar Republic) by only encouraging a few promising parties.

The parties initially licensed were:[64]

1. The Kommunistische Partei Deutschlands (KPD).
2. The Sozialdemokratische Partei Deutschlands (SPD).
3. The Christlich Demokratische Union Deutschlands (CDU)[65] (in all *Länder* except Bavaria).
4. The Christlich-Soziale Union (CSU) in Bavaria.[66]
5. The Freie Demokratische Partei (FDP).[67]

63. See pp. 41-50 above.
64. The parties mentioned here are dealt with in greater detail in Richard Stöss (ed.), *Parteien-Handbuch. Die Parteien der Bundesrepublik Deutschland 1945–1980*, 2 vols, Opladen, 1983/4.
65. The CDU, which is predominantly Catholic/conservative, originally emerged at regional level with various names. A federal organisation was only created in 1950.
66. The CSU, which is highly federalist and conservative, is the sister party of the CDU and exists only in Bavaria.
67. Regionally, the Liberals existed under many different names. In 1948 the various groups emerged into an umbrella organisation for the three Western zones.

Repressing and Glossing over the Past

However, smaller parties, which had only regional support, were also granted licenses, including:

6. The Bayernpartei (BP) as a traditionally-oriented competitor to the CSU.

7. The Deutsche Zentrums-Partei (DZP) as a Catholic competitor to the CDU, particularly in North Rhine-Westphalia.

8. The Deutsche Partei (DP) as a nationalist-Conservative-oriented and Protestant competitor to the CDU, mainly in Lower Saxony.

However, in the American, British and French zones political parties with very anti-democratic objectives were also permitted, as long as former Nazis did not have any decisive influence.

9. In Bavaria (in the American zone), in as early as 1945, the Wirtschaftliche Aufbau-Vereinigung (WAV) was granted a licensed. It represented the dissatisfaction of authoritarian bourgeois groups with the economic and political situation in occupied Germany, and was opposed to the 'liberation law'[68] and the construction of parliamentary/democratic structures. In 1946 it gained seats in the Bavarian Parliament, and in 1949 it entered the Bundestag.

10. In the British zone the Deutsche Konservative Partei–Deutsche Rechtspartei (DKP–DRP), founded in March 1946, obtained a licensed, first at local level, and then throughout the entire zone. It followed the ideological tradition of the authoritarian/conservative DNVP of the Weimar Republic and represented the forerunner of the later Deutsche Reichspartei (DRP), further details of which appear later in this book. It entered the first Bundestag with five seats.

11. In the French zone, in the spring of 1949, the Sammlung zur

---

68. The party chairman, Alfred Loritz, was temporarily responsible for de-Nazification in Bavaria as a Special Minister for Political Liberation and converted this into a 'major rehabilitation process'. Cf. Hans Woller, 'Die Wirtschaftliche Aufbau-Vereinigung', in Stöss, *Parteien-Handbuch*, vol. 2, p. 2473.

Tat/Europäische Volksbewegung (SzT/EVD) was granted a license. While the WAV and the DKP–DRP can be classified as representatives of Old Nationalism, the SzT/EVD followed a policy of New Nationalism. However, it never achieved political success nor managed to win any parliamentary seats.

It is not known why the three Western military governments also granted licenses to right-wing extremist parties. They probably believed that, in this way, they would be able to control better any political right-wing extremism that might take root. The parties were, after all, subject to constant scrutiny and as such were hardly in a position to offer known Nazis any scope for activity.

The admission policy towards expellees became particularly restrictive. All licensed parties were concerned to devote particular attention to the plight of the expellees. However, dissatisfaction among large sections of the expellees regarding their particularly desperate material needs and regarding the Soviet occupation policy in their former homeland soon exploded into the need to form their own parties and interest groups. In addition, the indigenous population often viewed the expellees with mistrust and often even with open rejection, for they themselves barely had enough to live on and hence saw the millions of expellees as troublesome 'immigrants' or 'newcomers' rather than as fellow German nationals. The allies feared a new form of class struggle between the established population and the expellees, and in spring 1946 imposed a ban on expellees forming organisations because they suspected that the expellees in particular represented a large, anti-democratic potential which threatened to disrupt permanently their concept of political democratisation and economic consolidation of the three Western zones.

In time, however, they eased the restrictive licensing policy and allowed the expellees to form interest groups at both the local and regional levels. Political parties, however, were not permitted. Hence the expellees – unless they supported licensed anti-Fascist/democratic parties, of which only approximately half of them did – were forced to seek alternative political means of expressing their dissatisfaction and protest.

They did this – often with other groups of victims – in two ways: on the one hand, they joined with 'independent candidates'[69] in local and *Länder* elections, in some cases with considerable success. On the other, they formed election pacts with right-wing extremist parties in order to gain seats in parliament for their representatives. Politicians from the right-wing extremist parties hoped to gain additional support for their anti-democratic and nationalist efforts by extending their electoral base to include the expellees and victims, and believed that this potential opposition, which was still disorganised and lacking a political-ideological orientation, would be in need of a unified leadership in order to convert their large numbers of supporters into a political force against the 'licensed parties'.

The 1949 Bundestag Elections

At the first Bundestag elections in 1949, these election coalitions and independent candidates gained up to 16 per cent of the vote in those states that were heavily populated with expellees. In Bavaria, factions of the expellees formed an election alliance with the WAV and won 14.4 per cent of the vote. In North Württemberg and North Baden the expellees' independent candidates from the unlicensed 'Notgemeinschaft' won 15.7 and 11.7 per cent of the vote respectively. In Hesse the independents won 11.5 per cent, in Lower Saxony the DKP–DRP,[70] whom the expellees supported, won 8.1 per cent and the independent candidates also won 8.1 per cent. Finally, in Schleswig-Holstein the independents won 7.6 per cent. In total, the right-wing extremist potential outside of the established parties in West Germany comprised 10.5 per cent of the voters (see Table 3.14).

This, however, only resulted in eighteen seats in the Bundestag (out of a total of 402), because the independents, except in one case, failed to achieve the majority of votes in their

---

69. The voting system in West Germany is different from that in Great Britain and comprises a mix of proportional representation and the majority system. Parties are allocated seats in respect of the proportion of votes they have received. It is also possible for individuals to stand for election independently of any party. They are subject to the majority system in the constituency where they stand.
70. The party campaigned here under the name 'Deutsche Rechtspartei'.

Table 3.14 The potential for right-wing extremist opposition in the 1949 Bundestag elections

Votes for independent candidates	893,342
Votes for expellees' and victims' organisations	248,305
Votes for licensed right-wing extremist parties	1,353,830
Total	2,495,477
Percentage of valid votes	10.5%

constituency. Nevertheless, the results of the first Bundestag elections signalled a certain weakness in the party system, which was visible, for example, in the fact that the first Chancellor of West Germany, Konrad Adenauer, was only elected with a one-vote majority. (Opponents say this was his own vote.)

This weakness was caused by several factors: the fragmentation of the party system, the bloc opposition between the bourgeois-democratic parties CDU/CSU, DP and FDP on the one hand and the SPD on the other,[71] and finally, the differences within the *bürgerblock*. In the immediate post-war period, clear discrepancies between the SPD and the bourgeois-democratic parties had already been revealed in their economic and social policies, as well as their foreign policy. The SPD had to assert its concept of democratic socialism, not only against the bourgeois-democratic parties, but also against the intentions of, in particular, the US occupying forces. The CDU/CSU and FDP, on the other hand, with their concepts of a capitalist market economy, albeit protected by a social safety-net, were clearly in line with the US occupying powers and were able to present themselves as the only true friends of the defence forces and as champions of a global anti-communist strategy, which seemed

71. As a result of their virtually unquestioning orientation towards the Soviet policy on Germany and the resulting internal conflicts and purgings as a political alternative, the communists had discredited themselves for the most part, especially as anti-communism was further strengthened in Germany following the East–West division and the intensification of East–West conflict. However, this did not only affect the communists but also the Social Democrats – who were in fact anti-communist – who were unjustly but nevertheless successfully denounced as supporters of communism by the bourgeois parties, who based their accusations of the Social Democratic reformist/anti-capitalist policies and their scepticism on political and, above all, military Western integration.

to be the only way of guaranteeing security for the Western zone state and recognition in the Western alliance. Moreover, reconstruction (not least as a result of US economic aid) was making clear progress, which the bourgeois-democratic parties claimed to be a victory of the market economy over socialism; meanwhile, of course, in the other part of Germany, socialism was faced with considerable problems in reconstructing industry and feeding the Central German people. The SPD's conviction, that once German Fascism had been crushed by the anti-Hitler coalition, socialism would come to the forefront, was increasingly proving to be pure fiction.

Kurt Schumacher, the chairman of the SPD, was firmly convinced that his party would win the first Bundestag elections. However, this hope failed to materialise: the SPD, with 29.2 per cent of the vote, was only 1.8 percentage points behind the CDU/CSU, the strongest party with 31 per cent. The remaining 40 per cent of the vote was distributed between the small parties, who were the decisive factor by which government would in future determine West German politics. From a purely statistical point of view, the left-wing camp (SPD and KPD) received 34.9 per cent of the vote nationwide, while the twelve bourgeois parties together received 61.3 per cent of the vote. Hence fragmentation only involved the bourgeois camp of the party system. The Union parties therefore faced the task of forming a majority capable of governing.

Konrad Adenauer succeeded in forming a government from the CDU/CSU, FDP and DP. This coalition, the *bürgerblock*, only had 46.9 per cent of the vote, but with 52 per cent of the seats (208 out of 402) had an extremely narrow majority of MPs in the first parliament. Between the opposition right-wing extremist MPs (4 per cent), upon whom the *bürgerblock* could not usually rely for support, and the *bürgerblock* votes, there was a contingency of thirty seats (7 per cent) of smaller parties who were partly in opposition, and the *bürgerblock* could only occasionally rely on their support. Hence the first government in West Germany had a very uncertain majority, and in future, the *bürgerblock* would have to do everything possible to achieve unification of the bourgeois camp. Its political future depended upon it.

At the time, this task appeared extraordinarily difficult. The distribution of seats only reflected a distorted picture of the real power structure:

1. The right-wing extremist opposition potential (10.5 per cent of the vote) was only represented by eighteen MPs due to the electoral system, even though they would have been entitled to forty seats from their proportion of the vote.
2. As a result of the allies' licensing policy, no neo-Fascist parties stood for election. Since the obligation to license was due to be abolished after the election, it was to be expected that such parties would then form and would attract a considerable number of voters, such as those who had voted for the *bürgerblock* parties or who had abstained from voting as a protest. The election turnout in 1949 was only 78.5 per cent.
3. This was also true of the expellees. Their attempts to form their own party were obvious, and it could be expected that these expellee parties would attract at least 10 per cent of the votes.

Hence it was vital that the *bürgerblock* unified its camp and concentrated its strength. It had to undertake all conceivable efforts to extend its influence within the bourgeois camp and to prevent organised right-wing extremism receiving support from former Nazis and new right-wing extremists, thus weakening the political influence of the bourgeois government. This meant integration of the old and new right-wing extremists, as well as the expellees, into the *bürgerblock*.

In the founding year of the Federal Republic of Germany, then, the political interests of the dominant bourgeois parties did not exclude the right-wing extremist potential for anti-Fascist reasons. In order to retain their own power and extend it, in order to consolidate the free market economy and secure integration with the West, and in order to prevent the SPD from gaining power, integration and absorption were the obvious choice.

The future of the 'CDU state' depended on whether the anti-democratic potential could be transferred to the *bürgerblock* camp. In political practice, therefore, the party functionaries felt obliged to gloss over the Nazi problem and the new form of right-wing extremism and to concentrate instead on the threat of communism. The integration policy was justified with the claim that they were introducing Nazis to democracy. Glossing over right-wing extremism has since become an integral part of bourgeois integration policy.

The leaders of right-wing extremism soon saw through this strategy. For them it was a question of undermining the Adenauer government and preventing the supposed henchmen of the occupying powers, the 'licensed parties', the supposed betrayers of national unity, from strengthening their position and pushing ahead with the sell-out of Germany. The right-wing extremists were fighting for 'internal reconciliation' and national reunification.

In 1949 within the bourgeois camp, a determined battle began between the *bürgerblock* and the nationalist opposition for those potential voters whose attitudes towards the recently formed Federal Republic of Germany ranged from critical to disapproving. I shall discuss this rivalry in the following chapter.

First, we shall consider why this competition was won by the *bürgerblock*. This was not immediately obvious at the time. Conditions for the success of right-wing extremism seemed reasonably favourable:

1. No critical analysis of national socialism took place.

2. Among the people, pro-Nazi attitudes were widespread.

3. The process of de-Nazification had just been halted.

4. The war criminals were confident of a pardon.

5. Those officials that had been removed from office could count on soon being reinstated.

The extreme threat to the *bürgerblock* of a further fragmentation of the bourgeois camp was illustrated just a few months after the Bundestag elections. The licensing barrier had barely been lifted when a large number of new parties appeared from nowhere. On 2 October 1949, the neo-Fascist Sozialistische Reichspartei (SRP) was formed, and won 11 per cent of the votes in the 1951 Landtag elections in Lower Saxony. At the beginning of December 1949, the Deutsche Gemeinschaft (DG) was formed, whose initial successes were mainly in southern Germany and which can be classified as New Nationalism. In an alliance with expellee groups, it managed to gain seats in two *Land* parliaments in 1950. On 8 January 1950, the expellee politician Waldemar Kraft founded the Block der Heimatvertriebenen und Entrechteten (BHE),[72] which in the same year achieved 23.4 per cent of the vote in the Schleswig-Holstein Landtag elections. Two weeks later, the Deutsche Reichspartei (DRP) was launched, the loyal proponent of Old Nationalism, which in 1964 merged with the Nationaldemokratische Partei Deutschlands (NPD), a party that still exists today.

From Bloc Opposition to Basic Consensus

The victor of this development, of which only a brief outline is given, was Adenauer, and its consequence is frequently termed the 'CDU state'. This refers to an economically prosperous and politically stable order without serious social conflicts – a contrast to the Weimar Republic. A glance at the results of the Bundestag elections up to 1961 (see Table 3.15) reveals two things: the *bürgerblock* was able to increase its support among the voters to a considerable extent, while at the same time, within the *bürgerblock* , a process of concentration towards the CDU/CSU occurred; they were driving out the minor *bürgerblock* parties.

In 1961 there were only three parties represented in the Bundestag – the CDU/CSU, the FDP and the SPD. The small *bürgerblock* parties only ever had seats for a limited period of time in one or the other *Land* parliaments – they had completely lost their influence at the federal level. This was also true of the right-wing extremist parties. The CDU/CSU, and to a certain extent the FDP as well, had completely absorbed the bourgeois opposition potential and eradicated the right-wing extremist strongholds.

The growing political stability which had emerged on the basis of a booming economy is characterised by two factors which distinguish the Federal Republic, not only from the Wei-

---

72. As from 1952, the party was called Gesamtdeutscher Block/Block der Heimatvertriebenen und Entrechteten (GB/BHE).

Table 3.15 *Bürgerblock* votes in the Bundestag elections, 1949–61

Election	Proportion of votes	Proportion of Seats	CDU/CSU proportion of *bürgerblock* votes
1949	46.9	51.7	66.1
1953	63.9	68.3	70.8
1957	61.3	65.9	81.9
1961	58.1	61.9	78.0

mar Republic but also from a large number of Western European countries. I am referring to a *constitutional consensus* regarding the formal rules in parliamentary democracy, which by the end of the 1950s had expanded to a *popular consensus* regarding the internal and foreign policy foundations of the Federal Republic of Germany.

Constitutional consensus is the prerequisite for a functioning democracy. All Western democracies that are rich in tradition are characterised by this type of consensus, which emerged from the bourgeois-democratic revolutions of the nineteenth century. This was not true of Germany. The first democratic republic was not based on constitutional consensus. On the contrary, the Weimar constitution was very controversial and was fought passionately. Only with the establishment of the constitutional consensus towards the end of the 1940s and the beginning of the 1950s did West Germany manage to join the democratic states of the Western world. The fact that such a stable system (critics even talk of a 'hyper-stable' system) was able to develop from this is again due to a national trait which is also found in the Scandinavian states: a consensus regarding the decisive political questions of the republic which is shared by the overwhelming majority of the population.

As the overwhelming political stability in West Germany forms a decisive barrier to success for the nationalist opposition, it would be useful to define the terms 'constitutional consensus' and 'basic consensus'.

When the Basic Law was passed and the Western zone state formed in 1949, a political and legal consensus was achieved between the relevant political forces, which for the time being comprised the following elements:

1. The provisional recognition of the fact that the republic was a 'part-state' with the aim of reunification; in the face of worsening East–West conflict, a pro-Western foreign policy and a basic ideology of anti-communism.

2. The democratic-pluralist character of the political order; overcoming the centralism of the Weimar Republic and the Third Reich by including federalist elements in the structure of the state; limitation of the representative function of local parliaments[73] – which apparently encouraged political instability – in favour of extending governmental power; 'authoritarian democracy' by balancing interest pluralism which was oriented towards the common weal with a 'strong' state; protection from internal and external enemies of the state (defence of the constitution).[74]

3. A bias towards political compromise by means of a parliamentary system which mediates decision-making and rejects extra-parliamentary pressure because it contradicts the system.

This type of consensus was able to develop in the Western zones after 1945 despite all the differences of opinion in everyday political questions because:

1. The disastrous economic and social consequences of the Second World War forced the entire population to work together for reconstruction, and blurred social conflicts.

---

73. The Weimar constitution conceived parliament as the most accurate reflection possible of political forces in the population. As a result of proportional representation, minor parties received parliamentary seats for a minimum of votes. Hence the parliaments were full of small parties, rendering the formation of stable governments extremely difficult. For this reason, the Federal Republic introduced restrictive clauses into its voting system. For example, parties have to achieve a certain percentage of votes (between 5 and 10 per cent) and/or win several constituencies directly in order to be considered in the allocation of seats. Hence, restrictive clauses make it difficult for minor parties to achieve parliamentary success and ensure that only the major parties sit in parliament.

74. West Germany's Basic Law contains rulings which make it possible to ban anti-constitutional parties and associations. For example, in 1952 the neo-Fascist SRP and in 1956 the KPD were banned. The KPD ban made it clear that this type of ruling could also be used against opponents who are politically unpopular.

2. Due to the division of Germany, the reactionary pro-Prussian forces had lost their territorial basis to a considerable extent, while at the same time political Catholicism (which was based in the south-west, was anti-Prussian and more Western/anti-Bolshevist than nationalist) had become considerably more important.
3. With the loss of middle and eastern Germany, the main strongholds of the left-wing workers' movement had been lost, and SPD policy was now more heavily influenced by their south-western, social reformist wing than pre-1933.
4. The Western allies first took over political power and imposed the restoration of capitalism and pluralist democracy (as far as this was necessary) in their zones.
5. The majority of the bourgeois classes were keen to overcome political fragmentation in order to prevent socialist forces from gaining power.
6. Following its defeat in the fight against Fascism, the workers' movement was now representing anti-Fascist/democratic and reformist demands and supported parliamentary democracy.

This meant that, in essence, the most important historical and conceptional pre-requisites had been established in political and legal terms, and towards the end of the 1950s, this led to the social anchoring of a basic consensus, the details of which were open to discussion. In addition to the authoritarian-democratic representative system, this consensus comprises three elements:

1. The capitulation and division of Germany, the changed international power structures and the development of the Cold War eliminated the conditions for a nationalist, sovereign or where possible even military/aggressive West German foreign policy. Western integration – which by no means excluded a flexible policy towards the East – was a necessary condition for the re-establishment of capitalism and the development of the 'economic miracle' in the 1950s. Hence, nationalism as a foreign policy strategy aiming for territorial changes (but not as an integration ideology) had become an anachronism. West Germany's contribution to defence in the North Atlantic

Alliance, which is seen as indispensable to the military security of the West as a whole, is closely related to integration with the West.

2. The 'social market economy' is based on the private ownership of the means of production and guarantees the free movement of capital, as well as government structural aid or income benefits to the middle class. Through this, through a new economic concept, a balancing out of interests between capital and the middle class within the framework of capitalist production conditions has become possible. By formally permitting socialisation under the constitutional law (socialist demands are formally covered by the constitutional consensus), this concept was also open to the consensus of the large majority of the workers' movement.

3. Active state social policy to maintain and strengthen the welfare state is recognised as a necessary and integral part of the economic order. This is conceived of as a class compromise, which as a whole is aimed at guaranteeing a high degree of employment and social security for the needy (the unemployed, the handicapped) by optimal accumulation conditions for society as a whole ('continual growth') and by means of a 'social net' to soften the blow of the unequal distribution of income and opportunities caused by capitalism.

However, it was only the rapid economic upturn in the 1950s, frequently described as an 'economic miracle', which made it possible for the economic and social components of the basic consensus to become reality. This upturn offered all social classes optimum opportunities to increase their wealth, employment and living conditions, facilitated the gradual elimination of the old middle class in a process that was cushioned by a social welfare state and was hence largely conflict-free; and also offered expellees satisfactory conditions for economic and social integration. Moreover, the consciousness and values of growing sections of the population spanned classes and social strata and encouraged consensus because they were dominated by anti-communism and an orientation towards growth and wealth. The orientation towards promotion and consumerism largely surpassed political interests and even the need for political participation. The desire for peace, order and minimal conflict and party dispute characterised the political attitudes of the population, the majority of whom were clearly tired of ideological arguments. All this was favourable to the relative autonomy of the state and political institutions.

The developments in the 1950s outlined here were increasingly reducing the bloc opposition between the bourgeois parties and the Social Democrats. The economic and foreign policy of the 'CDU state' was gaining increasing recognition within the workers' movement. The SPD, traditionally faithful to the constitution, had only achieved around 30 per cent of the vote in the 1949, 1953 and 1957 Bundestag elections, and had reason to fear being trapped in their '30 per cent tower' because there was very little voter movement between the *bürgerblock* and the Social Democrats. Hence the party gradually gave up its policy of 'constructive opposition' in order to penetrate the reserve of middle-class voters. At their 1959 party conference in Bad Godesberg, they adapted their manifesto to the political facts that had been created by the *bürgerblock* and hence abolished the traditional gulf between social-reformist practice and socialist theory. The change in direction, frequently described as conformist, bore its first fruits in the 1961 Bundestag elections, when they achieved 36.2 per cent of the vote; the upward trend culminated in 1972 when the SPD become the strongest party in the German Bundestag, with 45.8 per cent of the vote. From an historical perspective, the SPD's movement away from liberal and democratic socialism at the end of the 1950s contributed to the completion of the basic consensus.

The nature of this consensus, which guaranteed enormous political stability, lies in the fact that it represents more than simply a political class alliance based on parliamentary democracy. It indicates a broad social recognition of the economic, political and ideological bases of society, which can only be explained against the background of specific German historical experience. The typical West German feeling in the 1950s and 1960s that 'we are somebody again' is explained in psychological terms by the Mitscherlichs:[75]

---

75. Alexander and Margarete Mitscherlich, *Die Unfähigkeit zu trauern*, pp. 18ff.

From being a reactionary, aggressive nation under national socialism we changed into an apolitical, conservative nation. . . . We have only developed a small amount of psychological interest for the motives which allowed us to become the supporters of a Führer who led us to the greatest material and moral catastrophe in our history – which from a logical point of view ought to be our most crucial problem of recognition – and we have only been marginally interested in rebuilding our society. Instead, we have concentrated all our energy on a spirit of enterprise to rebuild what had been destroyed, engendering admiration and envy, and on the extension and modernisation of our industrial potential even down to kitchen fittings. The exclusivity of this effort cannot be overlooked; it has gradually allowed the political life of our country to solidify increasingly into administrative routine. . . . The restitution of the economy was our hobby horse; however, the establishment of a democratic state was only forced upon by the victors . . .

Fragile Stability?

The political integration of post-war right-wing extremism guaranteed the *bürgerblock* political hegemony and contributed considerably to the high degree of stability in the Federal Republic of Germany. As such, it is justifiably attributed to the success of the Adenauer government.

The integration strategy, however, prevented a critical evaluation of both the past and the present. Since integration of the old Nazis and new right-wing extremists was understood as a measure for buttressing the state and as an act of reconciliation on the part of the people, no true distance from national socialism was ever established. The 'transfer of Nazi votes to the democratic parties'[76] had been successful, the spirit of the times, characterised by repressing and playing down the past and an orientation towards consumerism and promotion, did much to encourage the development, or continuation, of anti-democratic, in particular pro-Nazi, anti-Semitic and xenophobic views.

To date, this latent right-wing extremism has for the most part been contained within the bourgeois-democratic parties, and has only resulted in partial and temporary success of the right-wing extremist parties and organisations. However, the fact

76. Friedrich, *Amnestie*, p. 239.

must not be overlooked that the wide divergence between latent and manifest right-wing extremism puts pressure on the political stability of West Germany and represents a permanent challenge to democracy. The parties' capacity for integration is, after all, based on specific social conditions, which are by no means always fulfilled: a prosperous economy satisfying all needs as equally as possible, social justice and security and finally, basic consensus. Crises and inequality in the socio-economic system, together with a reduction in the integrative powers of the 'catch-all parties', also encourage organised right-wing extremism. This has been shown in the past by the example of the NPD, which between 1966 and 1969 was able to achieve considerable parliamentary success. It is also illustrated today in the surprising success of the Republikaner. The absence of a democratically founded 'national identity' is also beneficial to right-wing extremism, which represents one of the most serious consequences of repressing and glossing over national socialism.

4
The Development of Organised Right-wing Extremism

After considering the conditions under which post-war extremism emerged and its socio-political milieu, we shall now consider the policies of right-wing extremism[1] and its relations to the bourgeois-democratic camp after 1945. The aim of this chapter, however, is not solely to describe contemporary history. I shall primarily consider the question of the internal conditions for the success of right-wing extremism.

When analysing success, conventionally, a distinction is made between *external* and *internal* factors. I have already mentioned the following as being external factors which limit the success of right-wing extremism: a prosperous economy, society's ability to form a consensus, and – based on this – the capacity of the democratic institutions, in particular that of the bourgeois parties, to integrate. However, even in West Germany, economic crises and political conflicts occur periodically, reducing the integrative performance of the established parties and offering right-wing extremism a window of opportunity. However, it must be possible for these opportunities to be used, which leads us on to the internal factors. Right-wing extremist parties and organisations, for their part, face the task of fulfilling organisational, personnel and conceptual requirements in order to mobilise the dissatisfaction of the people to their advantage.

1. Background literature in English: for the period up to the end of the 1950s the voluminous standard work by Kurt P. Tauber is recommended: *Beyond Eagle and Swastika. German Nationalism since 1945*, 2 vols, Middletown, 1967. A short introduction is to be found in Richard Stöss, 'The Problem of Right-Wing Extremism in West Germany', in *West European Politics*, vol. 11, no. 2, April 1988, pp. 34–46 (special issue on right-wing extremism in Western Europe, ed. Klaus von Beyme). Background literature in German: Peter Dudek and Hans-Gerd Jaschke, *Entstehung und Entwicklung des Rechtsextremismus in der Bundesrepublik*, 2 vols. Opladen, 1984; Richard Stöss (ed.), *Parteien-Handbuch. Die Parteien der Bundesrepublik Deutschland 1945–1980*, 2 vols, Opladen, 1983/4.

The Development of Organised Right-wing Extremism

Above all, they are required to develop attractive ideological and political alternatives to the repertoire of the established institutions in order to recruit new members, supporters and voters.

Overview of Development

Generally, the development of West German right-wing extremism is divided into two main stages, with 1965 considered to be the turning-point. According to Lutz Niethammer, until then the so-called 'post-Fascists' influenced events, that is, people who had received their political socialisation during the era of national socialism and 'were united by camaraderie and memories of the Third Reich'. After 1965, activists increasingly came to the forefront who were not tainted with national socialism but who had grown up in the era of the 'Cold War' and had been influenced politically by the 'CDU state'. Niethammer describes this generation as the 'neo-Fascists'.[2] In accordance with the terminology used here, I distinguish between 'post-war extremism' and 'new extremism'.

The stage of post-war extremism can be divided into three phases: until approximately 1952 it profited to a certain extent from the many social, economic and political problems of social collapse, characterised by the smashing of the Nazi system, the occupation policy, the division of Germany and the founding of the Federal Republic of Germany. By the 1953 Bundestag elections, the *bürgerblock* policy achieved its first success. The reconstruction efforts led to economic prosperity, and the new order established itself and developed considerable social integrative forces which gradually undermined right-wing extremism.

Fragmentation, organisational and personal rivalries and social isolation became characteristic of the nationalist opposition. Their voter potential shrank to a small hardcore of antidemocratic outsiders. At the beginning of the 1960s, steps towards developing a new ideology and policy *vis-à-vis* their allies aimed at reforming the nationalist opposition were taken. The organisational requirements for the political success of the new

---

2. Lutz Niethammer, *Angepaßter Faschismus. Politische Praxis der NPD*, Frankfurt, 1969.

right-wing extremism in the second half of the 1970s were fulfilled in 1964/5.

The first major economic crisis, the decline of the *bürgerblock* and the Grand Coalition of CDU/CSU and SPD, initiated the second stage of development. It can be divided into four phases: between 1966 and 1969 the NPD, which had been founded in 1964, experienced a rapid upturn: it gained seats in seven *Land* parliaments and in 1969 it came close to winning seats in the Bundestag. The second phase was characterised by defeat, decline and the agony of the National Democrats, while at the same time right-wing youth extremism was developing at the extra-parliamentary level. The political climate in West Germany became particularly harsh as a result of the confrontation between the social-liberal federal government and the CDU/CSU opposition, and this encouraged the development of violence in the framework of the campaign against the treaties with the East. After 1977/8 the violence escalated into right-wing terrorism, which was carried out primarily by youth groups and was inspired by neo-Nazi sentiments. Until the mid-1980s, neo-Nazis were organisationally weakened and politically disillusioned after being banned and their leaders imprisoned. The final phase began in 1986. At the end of the 1970s and beginning of the 1980s a process of internal, organisational and programmatic consolidation developed within the NPD. At the same time, however, a serious competitor developed in the form of the DVU. Since 1986, both organisations have been co-operating in elections and have achieved good election results in comparison with the 1970s. In 1987 they even achieved parliamentary success for the first time. In 1989, a new party, which was scarcely tainted with the odium of neo-Fascism, – the six-year-old Republikaner – achieved the real breakthrough. Practically from a standing position, the party – which officially is not considered as right-wing extremist – was able to mobilise an enormous voter potential. In Berlin they entered parliament with 7.5 per cent of the second vote (with 11 seats) and in the European elections they achieved 7.1 per cent nationwide (with 6 seats).

There are no precise figures regarding the strength of the right-wing extremist camp after 1945. Only the Federal and *Land* Ministries for the Interior have such data and have been pub-

Table 4.1 Phases of development of organised right-wing extremism, 1945–88

1. *Post-war right-wing extremism*
1945–1952 Development and initial successes, caused by historical continuity and specific post-war problems.
1953–1961 Decline and organisational fragmentation as a result of the growing integrative power of the socio-political system (particularly of the governing *bürgerblock*).
1962–1965 New orientation in terms of concepts and policy towards their allies.

2. *New right-wing extremism*
1966–1969 Upswing of the NPD in view of the collapse of the *bürgerblock* and the first major economic crisis.
1970–1976 Repolarisation within the party system; collapse and agony of the NPD; increase in the willingness of youth right-wing extremism to use violence.
1977–1985 Emergence and subsequent disappearance of a neo-Nazi wave of terrorism; simultaneous reconsolidation of the NPD, which however was surpassed by the DVU in terms of membership.
Co-operation between the DVU and NPD in elections, with moderate successes; rise of the Republikaner.

lishing them since the early 1960s. However, the data are ascertained according to political points of view: the decisive factor is which organisations are classified as right-wing extremist and included in the count. In addition, the annual statistics are largely based on estimates of the membership figures of the individual organisations (although this is consolidated by informants). These types of estimate are generally subject to subjective factors. On the whole, it can be assumed that the official figures are generally too low and that the level of the trend is higher. Nevertheless, the official statistics do represent an accurate reflection of the development of organised right-wing extremism.

Until 1964 there was a decline in the membership figures from 76,000 (in 1954) to just under 21,000. This decline was the expression of the integration of post-war right-wing extremism. In the mid-1960s, a new wave of right-wing extremism emerged

Figure 4.1 Development of the membership of organised right-wing extremism, 1954–87

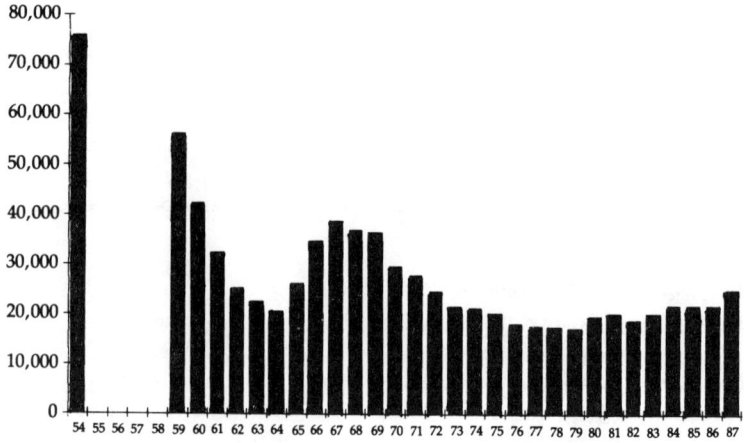

Source: Federal Ministry for the Interior

which at its peak (in 1967) comprised some 39,000 organised members. This increase in members benefited the NPD almost exclusively. Between 1965 and 1975 it was the hegemonial power within the nationalist opposition.

The downward trend after 1969 would have been even sharper had there not been an increase in youth right-wing extremism in the 1970s. Since 1980, total membership has increased somewhat, which is the result of increases among the neo-Nazis and in the DVU.

The development of the right-wing extremist parties was heavily influenced by Old Nationalism. The 'Harzburger Front' alliance predominated, in other words, the merging of authoritarian/conservative and (neo-)Fascist forces as represented by the traditional line of the DRP-DKP/DRP/NPD. Neo-Fascist parties (SRP, FAP[3]), on the other hand, were of subordinate importance, probably as a result of the ever-present threat of being banned.

Following a certain degree of initial success, New Nationalist parties (DG/AUD) since 1952 have led a shadowy existence at the periphery of the right-wing extremist party spectrum. In

3. Freiheitliche Deutsche Arbeiterpartei.

Figure 4.2 Development of the membership of organised right-wing extremism in comparison with the NPD, 1965–87

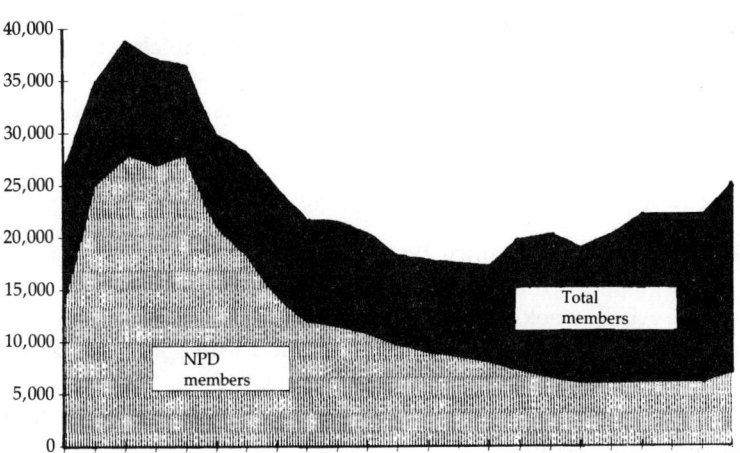

Source: Federal Ministry for the Interior

1980, the small AUD was disbanded. Their members turned primarily to the Greens, and their former leader, August Haußleiter, even temporarily became one of the three party chairmen of the Ecology Party. In the extra-parliamentary field, from the beginning of the 1970s, a nationalist-revolutionary New Right had begun to emerge which, although exercising a certain ideological influence on the parties of Old Nationalism, did not itself found any parties.

An important indicator of the resonance of right-wing extremism is the evolution of the press. After initial increases in circulation (until 1967), the trend was generally downward. This may be a result of the lessening importance of right-wing extremist parties, because the work of the press was initially strongly influenced by the parties. The mouthpieces of the DRP/NPD are:

- *Das Ziel* (1952–4).
- [Der] *Reichsruf* (1954–64).
- *Deutsche Nachrichten* (1965–73).
- *Deutsche Stimme* (after 1976).

Politics Against Democracy

In 1974/5 the NPD could not afford its own party mouthpiece, and a joint venture with the right-wing extremist publisher and millionaire, Dr Gerhard Frey, failed. Since 1976, the *Deutsche Stimme* has appeared monthly, with a current circulation of 150,000.

The New Nationalist parties (DG/AUD) distribute (or distributed) the following newspapers:

- [Die] *Deutsche Gemeinschaft* (1951–79).

- *Die Unabhängigen* (since 1967).

The AUD weekly magazine *Die Unabhängigen* is currently published for faithful supporters of the former DG and AUD chairman Haußleiter. Since 1979, the paper can also be purchased under the name *Die Grünen*. Both papers are identical in terms of their content.

In total, right-wing extremist publications in 1987 amounted to eighty-six titles with an annual circulation of some 10 million copies. Non-party newspapers and journals predominate. The paper with the largest circulation is currently the *Deutsche National-Zeitung*, which is part of Frey's publishing house. Approximately 100,000 copies of this are on the market every week.

Post-war Right-wing Extremism (1945–65)

The Old Nationalists Reorganise

The geographical home of Old Nationalism is the Prussian and protestant north of Germany. After 1945, however, the traditional areas east of the Elbe fell under Soviet occupation so that efforts to form a successor organisation to the DNVP concentrated on Schleswig-Holstein, Hamburg, Lower Saxony and Westphalia. The British military government was in command here, and they showed themselves perfectly willing to permit the existence of nationalist conservative parties.

Shortly after the end of the war, former DNVP functionaries set about drawing together remaining old supporters for a new party, which was to be called the Deutsche Konservative Partei (DKP). Initially, this was conducted independently at the local

The Development of Organised Right-wing Extremism

Figure 4.3 Development of right-wing extremist parties, 1945–88

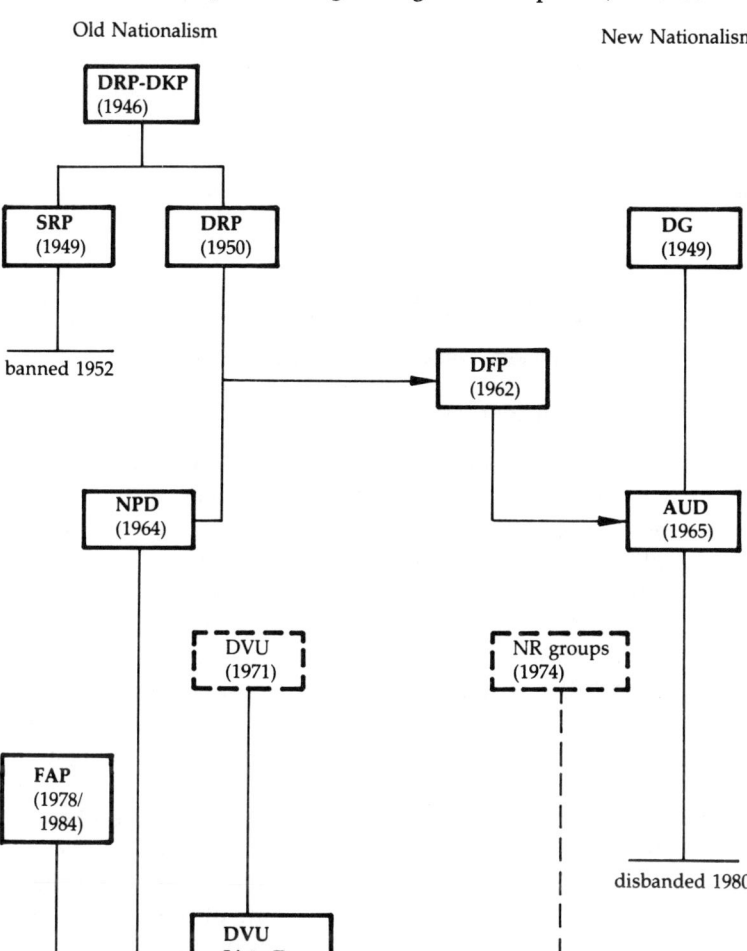

level. At the same time, members and supporters of *volkisch* and anti-Semitic groups from the Weimar Republic were undertaking similar efforts, which, in February 1946, led to the founding of the Deutsche Aufbau-Partei (DAP). In March 1946, the DKP and DAP merged to form the DKP–DRP, with the *Land* associations allowed to select one of the two names.

Figure 4.4 Development of extreme right-wing journalism, 1961–87

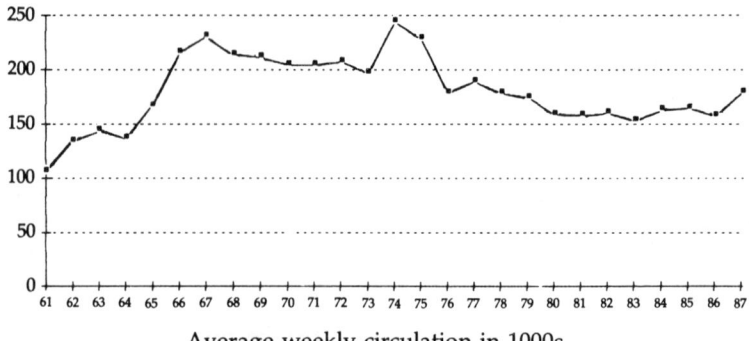

Average weekly circulation in 1000s

Source: Federal Ministry for the Interior

The DKP – DRP soon became a 'refuge for all types of right-wing extremists',[4] who argued over the political course the party should take. The main motive of all those involved was to merge all parties right of the CDU into a 'major right-wing party'. While the DNVP traditionalists were keen on an alliance with the CDU/CSU in order to prevent a victory by the SPD, the radical forces demanded a clear distinction from parties who did not represent the nationalist interests of the German people. Their hatred was concentrated on the CDU/CSU, whom they accused of sacrificing national unity for the sake of integration with the West.

After approximately 1948, radical and particularly neo-Fascist nationalists extended their influence, particularly in the DRP in Lower Saxony. People whose views were more nationalist/conservative felt excluded by this and some of them joined the FDP, while the majority joined the Deutsche Partei (DP). The DP, on the whole, was not a right-wing extremist party. It represented the anti-Prussian,[5] federalist and Protestant middle class which hated the German nationalists and had little

4. Horst W. Schmollinger, 'Die Deutsche Konservative Partei-Deutsche Rechtspartei', in Stöss, *Parteien-Handbuch*, vol. 1, p. 982.
5. Until 1837 the kingdom of Hannover was ruled by the same house as England. However, the union was a purely formal affair. For example George II, during his sixty-year reign, did not visit his homeland once. In 1866, Hannover was annexed by Prussia, causing strong anti-Prussian feeling among the people, which took root again after 1945.

sympathy for political Catholicism.[6] The DP represented an economic and social policy, which was protectionist towards the middle class and, as such, opposed to liberal capitalism. Through this and their initial strategy of independence from the CDU they had a certain attraction for right-wing extremist circles.

This was not true, of course, of the radical nationalists who had taken refuge in the DRP in Lower Saxony because they could not obtain permission from the British occupying forces to found their own party. This group, led by Dr Fritz Dorls (who had been an NSDAP member since 1929), Dr Gerhard Krüger (member of the SA from 1926 and member of the NSDAP from 1928), Dr Justus Krause (who like Dorls was initially a CDU member) and Fritz Rößler[7] (member of the NSDAP from 1930), succeeded in repressing the influence of the moderate DRP fraction, led by Leonhard Schlüter and Adolf von Thadden (later chairman of the DRP and the NPD). For the 1949 Bundestag elections they managed to secure the help and support of former prominent Nazis, including Otto Ernst Remer, who had been promoted to colonel and later to general for special 'services' in suppressing the conspiracy [against Hitler] of 20 July 1944. Their propaganda, which in some cases was blatantly pro-Nazi, brought the DRP 8.1 per cent of the vote in the first Bundestag election in Lower Saxony and five seats in the Bundestag (including seats for Dorls, Rößler or Richter, and Thadden) while the other *Land* organisations of the DKP–DRP were unable to achieve any parliamentary success.

This, together with the fact that the allied licensing conditions had expired, accelerated the decline of the party. The main beneficiary was the DP, which had received 17.8 per cent of the vote in Lower Saxony (twelve seats in the Bundestag) and also had respectable results in Schleswig-Holstein (three seats), Bremen and Hamburg (one seat each). Hence for the time being the dream of a 'major right-wing party' was over. The remaining

6. At Landtag elections in Lower Saxony, the CDU was initially only marginally more successful than the DP: in 1947, they achieved 19.9 per cent of the vote and the DP 17.9 per cent.
7. Rößler lived under the false name of Dr Franz Richter until his cover was blown in 1952. With a forged c.v. he had also managed to deceive the de-Nazification authorities.

members of the DKP–DRP were not at all pleased with the DP for their orientation towards the *bürgerblock* and then the alliance with the CDU/CSU, but for their part continued to argue about the correct path to national unity. The neo-Fascists abused their internal party opponents as being social reactionaries and monarchists and demanded 'faith in their nationalist and social convictions'. The dispute ended on 2 October 1949 with the expulsion from the party of the group led by Dorls, Krüger and Remer, who on the same day founded the Sozialistische Reichspartei (SRP). The rump of the party in Lower Saxony merged with the small NDP[8] in Hessen to the Deutsche Reichspartei (DRP) in mid-January 1950, but initially they stood in the shadows of the successful SRP.

Characterised by their undisguised Nazi propaganda, the SRP experienced a rapid rise. In 1951, they had over 10,000 members and entered the Lower Saxony Landtag with sixteen seats (11 per cent of the vote) and a further eight seats in the Bremen parliament (7.7 per cent of the vote). They were particularly successful in places where the NSDAP had already achieved good election results. In Lower Saxony, for example, the SRP achieved an absolute majority in thirty-five local governments and were the largest party in 375 local governments. Electoral analyses have revealed that the SRP recruited approximately half of its voters from the bourgeois-democratic camp (DP, CDU, FDP). Neo-fascism was hence threatening to shatter the *bürgerblock's* power position.

How the vote was divided in Lower Saxony illustrates this problem: in 1947 the bourgeois camp was split and hardly capable of forming a majority. The SPD was the strongest party because its social policies appealed to expellees; moreover, because of its attitude towards reunification, it probably also appealed to right-wing extremist voters. In 1949, for the first time, separate election alternatives were available to the expellees and the right-wing extremists with the Independents and the DRP. There were limits to the losses experienced by the CDU/DP/FDP, but the SPD were the real losers in the election. In 1951, a 'true' expellee party (the BHE) and the neo-Fascist

---

8. The Nationaldemokratische Partei (NDP) operated in Hesse between 1945 and 1950 but was not licensed at *Land* level.

Table 4.2 Election results in Lower Saxony, 1947–53

Party	LTE[a] 1947	BTE[b] 1949	LTE 1951	BTE 1953
CDU	19.9	17.6		35.2
DP	17.9	17.8		11.9
CDU + DP[c]	[37.8]	[35.4]	23.8	[47.1]
FDP	8.8	7.5	8.4	6.9
Bürgerblock[d]	[46.6]	[42.9]	[32.2]	[54.0]
BHE	—	—	14.9	10.8
Others	4.1	4.4	3.3	0.5
DRP + SRP + Independent candidates	0.3	16.2	14.1	3.5
SPD + KPD	49.0	36.5	35.5	31.2
Total	100	100	100	100

a. LTE = Landtag election.
b. BTE = Bundestag election.
c. At times, the CDU and DP worked together in the *Niederdeutsche Union* (NU).
d. CDU + DP + FDP.

SRP appeared for the first time. Their electoral successes were at the cost of the *bürgerblock* parties, who were forced to accept dramatic losses. While in 1949 the *bürgerblock* still had reason to be pleased about the SPD losses, it was now in a situation where it had been so stripped of voters that it urgently needed to extend its social base.

The ban on the SRP had an important influence on further developments in Lower Saxony. According to Article 21 of the Basic Law, 'Parties which, by reason of their aims or the behaviour of their adherents, seek to impair or abolish the free democratic basic order or to endanger the existence of the Federal Republic of Germany' may be declared unconstitutional by the Federal Constitutional Court and disbanded.

On this basis, in November 1951, the federal government applied for proceedings to be initiated at the Federal Constitutional Court,[9] which in October 1952, ordered the abolition of the party. In the Bundestag elections in the following year, the *bürgerblock* parties achieved an absolute majority from gains

---

9. At the same time a similar trial was introduced against the KPD, which in 1956 was declared unconstitutional and disbanded.

mainly from right-wing extremists but also from expellees, and the CDU became the dominant force in the *bürgerblock*.

The verdict on the SRP as an anti-constitutional party contains the following statement:

> It is not accused of being involved with former national socialists, but of attracting those who are fixed in their ideas, who have remained true to themselves, not in order to gain positive forces for democracy but in order to maintain and disseminate national socialist ideas.

The SRP had nothing but contempt for the Western zone state:[10]

> Like a freshly painted Coca-Cola stall next to a burnt-out, but still enormous, fundamentally indestructible building from 1,200 years of German Empire history – this is how the Bonn government is viewed by the German people next to the Empire which has been crushed by superior strength. Next to the empire which defended Europe against Bolshevism to the bitter end – and for this was slaughtered by the two suicidal allies of Moscow under the sign of Yalta.

And:[11]

> The German claim to the totality of the Reich which is the result of history and culture, human rights and international law, is inalienable.

The SRP manifesto embodied not only the ideology of the continued existence of the German Reich, but also justification of national socialism as a regime that apparently had aimed to protect Europe against Bolshevism and had not received any recognition for this historic mission. On the contrary: according to the SRP viewpoint, the Western powers supported Soviet plans for the suppression of the German empire, even though this was contrary to their actual interests. Hence the task of the SRP was seen as being to fight the external enemies of the empire and their internal henchmen (e.g. 'licensed parties') and to restore the wounded community spirit:[12]

10. Deutsche Opposition, 19/1951, p. 4.
11. Taken from the SRP 'Aktionsprogramm' in 1949, point 1.
12. SRP 1949 Aktionsprogramm, point 6.

The Development of Organised Right-wing Extremism

The disastrous splitting of the German nation into east and west, north and south, nationals and expellees, propertied and unpropertied, employers and employees, church-goers and free thinkers, Catholics and Protestants, must be overcome. Instead, the German problem imperiously demands the common wishes and action of all Germans to increase our creative forces and our capacity for reconstruction and mastering our common fate.

The party described its economic and social demands with expressions such as 'German Socialism', 'People's Socialism' or 'Reich Socialism'. By this they meant the capitalist-organised community of all workers, who, as the NSDAP manifesto had demanded in its time, should be protected from major capital:[13]

The SRP declares its support for the concept of personal initiative and private property ownership in the sense of obligation and responsibility of the individual towards the nation as a whole in the interest of the greatest possible development of our economy. . . . Economic monopolies and concentrations of power which endanger the community must be prevented. The participation of all workers in the economic yield of production must be controlled by law.

Beneficiaries of the ban on the SRP, which had hardly been demanded for anti-Fascist motives, were the *bürgerblock*, and not the DRP (which likewise belonged to the Old Right). The DRP had been founded in January 1950 in Kassel in Lower Saxony (and did not have to defend itself before the Federal Constitutional Court against the accusation of anti-constitutionality). The DRP differed from the SRP in that it represented the more authoritarian/conservative variety of Old Nationalism, while the SRP continued the Nazi tradition and in part advocated neo-Fascist concepts. Following the ban on the SRP, many of their functionaries turned to the DRP (e.g. Dr Krüger), so that the party was enriched by an influential but never dominant (neo-) Fascist wing ('Harzburger Front' Organisation).[14] Nevertheless, the inheritance of former SRP voters remained low. The DRP found support mainly in northern Germany, particularly in Lower Saxony, but it did not succeed in taking up the successes of the old Deutsche Rechtspartei or the SRP (see Table 4.3).

13. SRP 1949 Aktionsprogramm, point 8.
14. See chapter 2.

Table 4.3 DRP election results, 1950–63

Elections	Year	Number of votes	%	Seats
Bundestag	1953	295,739	1.1	—
	1957	308,564	1.0	—
	1961	262,977	0.8	—
Land Parliaments				
Bavaria	1958	56,864	0.6	—
Bremen	1959	14,689	3.8	—
Hamburg	1953	7,466	0.7	—
	1957	4,109	0.4	—
	1961	9,045	0.9	—
Hesse	1950[a]	1,989	0.1	—
	1958	16,178	0.6	—
Lower Saxony	1951	74,017	2.2	3
	1955	126,692	3.8	6
	1959	122,062	3.6	—
	1963	52,785	1.5	—
North Rhine-Westphalia	1950	107,104	1.7	—
	1958	43,299	0.5	—
Rhineland-Palatinate	1951	7,185	0.5	—
	1959	87,349	5.1	1
	1963	56,155	3.2	—
Saarland	1960	3,325	0.6	—
Schleswig-Holstein	1950	37,115	2.8	—
	1954	17,318	1.5	—
	1958	12,950	1.1	—

a. Stood together with the Nationaldemokratische Partei as the NDP/DRP.

In contrast to the SRP, the DRP avoided stating its ideological foundation and converting it into propaganda. No doubt in fear of an imminent ban, they restricted themselves to criticising existing conditions and assiduously mourned the lost empire. The party considered its raison d'être to be cultivating the 'Reich myth':[15]

Our main duty is to remain faithful to the Reich.

15. Dudek and Jaschke, *Rechtsextremismus*, vol 1, p. 215.

The Development of Organised Right-wing Extremism

> Our main aim is to recreate the German Reich with Berlin as its capital.
>
> Acording to its history, the structure of its economy and the intellectual attitude of its people, Germany belongs to the occidental Christian sphere of culture. Defending our country against a Bolshevist tidal wave is a question of life and death to us.[16]

Politically, the DRP was concerned with becoming the melting-pot of all nationalist-minded people who were dissatisfied with the *bürgerblock* policy. In many respects, their propaganda was similar to the criticisms made by nationalist opposition to the Weimar Republic before 1933, and authoritarian and elitist German nationalism also characterised the mentality of DRP supporters to a large extent. Under its leaders Hans-Heinrich Scheffer, Wilhelm Meinberg, Alexander Andrae and Adolf von Thadden, the party consisted mainly of middle-class people with a pro-Western view who favoured rearmament, as long as the national interests of Germany and, above all, the 'honour of the German soldier' remained protected (see Appendix 1).

The DRP was, therefore, clearly close to the *bürgerblock* in terms of its policy. However, this did not make it any easier for it to steal votes from the *bürgerblock*. The opposite is true. Because they lacked an independent profile, their ties to their own voters were reduced.

A New Right is Established

The formation of a New Right in the West German party system is very closely connected to the journalist August Haußleiter, (born 1905), who, although he had not been a committed national socialist during the Third Reich, was also not a democrat. Haußleiter belonged to the tradition of the 'Conservative revolution',[17] a movement of intellectuals that fought the Weimar Republic as the academic forerunners of the Nazis, without

---

16. Ibid., p. 215f.
17. Cf. Kurt Sontheimer, *Antidemokratisches Denken in der Weimarer Republik*, Munich, 1962 (new edition, 1968); Klemens von Klemperer, *Germany's New Conservatism. Its History and Dilemma in the Twentieth Century*, Princeton, NJ, 1957.

identifying with the NSDAP policy in all respects. A former comrade-in-arms of Haußleiter, Gerhard Opitz, characterised his party chairman as follows: he is one of those people who 'considered the Nazis to be much too loud, much too vulgar, much too ignorant and much too uneducated, and he was terrified of the dynamism of unleashed nationalism'.[18]

In 1946, Haußleiter joined the CSU in Bavaria and became one of their co-founders in Upper Franconia. He soon advanced to become deputy party chairman, representing the Protestant wing in the Catholic-influenced CSU and – in opposition to the CDU/CSU course of Western integration – belonging to the reunification wing of the CDU/CSU. As a result of his growing political isolation within the CSU, and following the founding of the separate Western zone state in autumn 1949, Haußleiter left the party in order to create a new organisational platform for his neutralist programme of German national autonomy.

In contrast to Old Nationalism, he did not orient himself around the historical model of the German Reich but was concerned with founding a new nationalism:

> Whatever else people may think about national socialism, one thing is sure: it was the expression of and one stage in a sociological development, of an evolutionary and revolutionary social process. It did not answer the questions which our century faces, but it did – in an enormous crisis – make these questions visible. In this, general human development, national fate and national tragedy became confused and culminated in a fateful muddle, as is always the case in history. We cannot return to Weimar and we cannot return to the NSDAP, but we have to recognise the new tasks we face. The NSDAP was the glaring antithesis to Weimar. Now, however, the hour is ripe for new, true syntheses. People who cling incorrigibly to Weimar seem just as corrupt as those who cling incorrigibly to the NSDAP, to its external form and its mistakes. Both are reactionaries in the deepest sense of the word.[19]

In this, Haußleiter distanced himself equally from the *bürgerblock* parties and from those of Old Nationalism, and soon entered into a dual political confrontation from which he and his

---

18. Quotation from Richard Stöss, *Vom Nationalismus zum Umweltschutz*, Opladen, 1980, p. 67.
19. *Die Deutsche Gemeinschaft. Informationsdienst (IDG)*, 14/1952.

small entourage of supporters had little chance of emerging as victors.

The national question for all Germany was the focal point of Haußleiter's political intentions. He wanted to work Germany into a 'European peace plan,' to a bloc in the middle between East and West. With this type of concept of neutralism he was rejecting both a policy of Western integration (that of the *bürgerblock*) and a vision of an occidental anti-Bolshevist German Reich as expounded by Old Nationalists.

In this sense he was concerned to unify the potential for opposition in terms of ideology and policy, which had become visible in the first Bundestag elections. In particular, he considered that the 'war generation' and 'those deprived of social rights' (and, again, the expellees) were the predestined social base for a policy of new nationalism. Shortly after the Bundestag election, in September 1949, representatives of various groups and organisations of expellees, victims of bombings and war victims, voters' associations and right-wing extremist parties met in Frankfurt and formed a co-ordinating committee for the entire area of West Germany. As they could not come to an agreement with regard to founding a national party, in December 1949 Haußleiter formed the Deutsche Gemeinschaft (DG) (directly after the lifting of the licensing rule) together with the expellee[20] and victims' groups. Initially organised only in Bavaria, in spring 1950 the Notgemeinschaft in Württemberg-Baden, the Unabhängige Deutsche Gemeinschaft (UDG) in Hesse and temporarily the Tatgemeinschaft freier Deutscher (TfD) in North Rhine-Westphalia joined the DG. In the *Länder* of Lower Saxony and Schleswig-Holstein, where large numbers of expellees had been accepted, however, the DG did not have any support worth mentioning. Initially, the party was primarily a southern German organisation, whose success was also dependent on whether it could gain a foothold in northern Germany. Hence its task was twofold: on the one hand, it had to consolidate its organisation in southern Germany and recruit supporters and members among the expellees, victims and the right-wing extremist potential. On the other, it had to break

---

20. Haußleiter's later wife, Dr Renate Malluche, was at that time one of the main representatives of the Notgemeinschaft (NG) for Bavarian expellees.

through its regional restriction and gain influence in the important expellee areas of northern Germany and among the Old Right there.

The New Right between the Bürgerblock and the Old Right

One can assume that in the first Bundestag election, the *bürgerblock* had completely exhausted its voter potential among the expellees. In 1949, all the signs indicated that the remaining expellees were pressing for autonomous political organisations. Moreover, those who – like the DG – concluded from this that a party of expellees must necessarily be nationalist and directed against the order that was being established in West Germany, were overlooking the fact that the situation of the expellees was not only characterised by demands for the recreation of German unity ('the right of domicile in the East') but also by current economic and social interests in the areas where they had settled ('the right to a decent life in the West'). While the initiators of the DG were convinced that the solution to the expellee problem was linked to social revival in a nationalist sense, those politicians in particular who were active in the expellee interest groups stressed the urgency for an economic and social policy directed at the distribution struggle in order to ease the crisis of the expellees in their new homes. Both concepts were hardly reconcilable with one another. While the anti-democratic/nationalist concept was diametrically opposed to the policy of the *bürgerblock*, a policy concerned with the interests of the expellees was aimed at co-operation (albeit from a distance) and compromise with the aim of economic and social integration. The decision for or against a party representing the interests of the expellees was hence objectively also a decision for or against the Western zone state governed by the *bürgerblock*.

At the September convention in Frankfurt, this question, among others, was under debate. For example, representatives of the refugees' co-operative in Schleswig-Holstein had spoken in favour of forming a party to represent their interests and, therefore, did not join the co-ordinating committee. In January 1950, representatives of various expellee groups in Schleswig-Holstein formed the BHE (mentioned above) as a party specifically to represent their interests in the coming Landtag elections (in July 1950); it achieved surprising electoral success (23.4 per cent of the vote and fifteen seats) and entered a *bürgerblock* government (together with the CDU, FDP and DP). The BHE chairman, Waldemar Kraft (former NSDAP member and chief stormtrooper in the SS), became the deputy Minister President and Minister of Finance, his colleague, Hans Adolf Asbach (likewise a former NSDAP member, member of the SA and section leader in the Deutsche Arbeitsfront), became Minister for Employment, Social Affairs and Expellees.

The success of this policy of representing the interests of the expellees inspired Kraft to extend the BHE immediately to other *Länder*, so that it automatically competed with New Nationalism. The DG had been taken completely by surprise by the development in Schleswig-Holstein and concentrated all its efforts on blocking the spread of the interest party.

In Hesse, representatives of the interest party concept called an inaugural meeting in Frankfurt in August 1950. The majority of the UDG voted against Haußleiter and joined the BHE. In Lower Saxony the initiative came from members of the TfD and other expellee groups, who, in autumn 1950, founded a *Land* BHE association. Before the Landtag election in Lower Saxony in May 1951, the BHE and DG formed an election pact, which gave the DG one place on the BHE list of candidates (which received a total of twenty-one seats). There was a particularly fierce dispute in Bavaria, where Landtag elections were fixed for November 1950. Haußleiter's DG soon experienced competition from expellee politicians, who, like Kraft, gave priority to a policy of representing the interests of the expellees over a policy of nationalist opposition, for example, the leading Nazi politician of the time and later national chairman of the BHE (1954/5) and Federal Minister for Expellees (1953–60), Dr Theodor Oberländer. However, Haußleiter endeavoured to bring all the groups and initiatives together for the election and eventually achieved an election alliance (BHE–DG), which achieved 12.3 per cent of the vote and twenty-six seats (including six for the DG). Haußleiter, who had already entered the Bavarian Landtag in 1946 for the CSU, again gained a seat and became Chairman of the DG parliamentary party. In Württemberg-Baden, the DG leadership initially succeeded in combining the sociopolitical line with the nationalist line by distancing themselves somewhat from the Bavarian headquarters. However, following the 1950 Landtag elections, which gave the DG 14.7 per cent of the vote and sixteen seats, disputes erupted between the supporters of a policy oriented towards expellee interests and those of a nationalist opposition policy. Before elections to the *Land* parliament of the newly-created *Land* of Baden-Württemberg[21] took place, a split had occurred. The DG failed to overcome the 5 per cent hurdle, while the BHE achieved 6.3 per cent of the vote and six seats.

Hence until 1952, for the expellees, the principle of a party representing their interests had triumphed over the principle of a nationalist opposition party. As the initial major successes of the BHE seemed to justify this approach, for opportunist reasons many right-wing extremists then turned to the BHE, which, regardless of occasional coalitions with the SPD in some *Länder*, advanced to become a political supporter of the *bürgerblock* and eventually entered a federal *bürgerblock* government in 1953.

However, the DG was not discouraged by this defeat and immediately set about consolidating the remains of the party by conducting a 'nationalist rally' strategy. In this, it increasingly cultivated extreme nationalist-chauvinist and quasi-Fascist agitation, by means of which it was convinced it would break into the right-wing vote of Old Nationalism and the Deutsche Partei (DP) and the BHE. Above all, it was concerned to gain a foothold as the successor organisation to the banned SRP in northern Germany, and unscrupulously adapted its propaganda to suit the neo-Fascist potential voters it wanted to attract. In addition, SRP cadres were keeping a look-out for an organisation for their supporters in order to enable them to continue working underground. The southern German DG seemed ideal, because the SRP functionaries would have unlimited freedom in their regional catchment area. With Haußleiter's knowldege and probably his approval, SRP cadres penetrated the DG in Lower Saxony, North Rhine-Westphalia and Hesse and took over the regional organisations there. This caused a number of *Land* Ministries for the Interior to produce orders to ban (e.g. in

---

21. Formed in 1952 from the American-occupied Württemberg-Baden and the French-occupied *Länder* South Baden and South Württemberg-Hohenzollern.

Rhineland-Palatinate, Lower Saxony and Hesse), all of which the DG opposed unsuccessfully. In view of the forthcoming Bundestag election it hastily attempted to obtain approval to refound the party in Hesse and Lower Saxony, where it made sure that it did not take on any more leading SRP supporters. On the whole, the adventure with the SRP probably further weakened the DG, especially since in the right-wing extremist camp opinion was becoming increasingly widespread that the *bürgerblock* parties and the BHE provided safer cover (and, moreover, better political influence) than the right-wing extremist parties.

As previously stated, the *bürgerblock* (out of necessity) was concerned to extend its voter base and had its sights set particularly on the supporters of the anti-democratic parties. It was important to the minor *bürgerblock* parties to consolidate their position against the hegemonial efforts of the CDU/CSU. Hence, before the Bundestag elections, it was not a question of extending the basis of the bloc as a whole; every individual party was also striving to increase its number of voters at the cost of the others and to strengthen its position within the bloc. In the FDP, DP and BHE, right-wing extremist and nationalist circles planned to become a platform for a 'national rally' by including right-wing extremist organisations. Those *Land* associations of the FDP with leanings to the right in Hesse and North Rhine-Westphalia had been negotiating since autumn 1952 with the *Land* associations of the DP over this type of project in order to strengthen the weight of nationalist voices within the *bürgerblock* against Adenauer's uncompromising policy of Western integration; while the BHE was also intensifying its efforts to attract nationalist voters. In November 1952, it had added the words 'Gesamtdeutscher Block' (all-German bloc) to its name in order to indicate that, in addition to its policy of representing interests, it also had nationalist concerns ('the right of domicile in the East'), especially as the right wing of the BHE had long been pressing for greater emphasis on the question of reunification.

Former Nazis were also involved in these campaigns, because they realised that the influence of a nationalist opposition would be more effective by working together with nationalist-liberal and nationalist-conservative like-minded people than by being active in sectarian right-wing extremist organisations. In particular, the FDP in North Rhine-Westphalia, Hesse and Lower Saxony was deliberately infiltrated by circles of former Nazis. Much press attention was devoted to the so-called 'Naumann circle',[22] which managed, by means of a clever personnel policy, to occupy important functionary posts in the FDP in North Rhine-Westphalia with its supporters. In January 1953, the British military authorities arrested the leading figures in the Naumann circle. The official press announcement read as follows:[23]

> Under orders from the British High Commissioner, Sir Ivone Kirkpatrick, on Thursday night [15 January 1953] British security authorities unexpectedly arrested seven former leading members of the NSDAP who are accused of having planned to seize power again in West Germany. Chancellor Dr Adenauer was informed the evening before by Kirkpatrick. The action was carried out exclusively by the English without using the German police . . .
> Kirkpatrick said [to the German Press Agency] that the organisation led by Naumann had systematically tried to infiltrate democratic parties, in particular the FDP, the DP and the BHE, in order to usurp them and thus prepare a cold-blooded *coup d'état* . . .
> Kirkpatrick explained his direct intervention by saying that the federal government would not have been able, according to the laws and regulations which apply to it, to step in as resolutely and unhesitatingly as the English were able to according to the regulations contained in the occupation statute . . .

In retrospect, the High Commissioner's fears regarding the existence of a national socialist underground movement and a planned *coup* were grossly exaggerated, and there were probably no realistic plans to overthrow the West German government. In any case, the legal prosecution of the Naumann group soon petered out. Probably, the Adenauer government was not in the least concerned with sentencing the Nazi circle (this was shown by their half-hearted support of de-Nazification and the

22. Dr Werner Naumann had joined the NSDAP in 1928 and became State Secretary in the Reich Ministry for Propaganda. He was even seen by Hitler as a future Minister for Propaganda. However, the end of the war prevented this career move.
23. Quotation from Friedrich Grimm, *Unrecht im Rechtsstaat. Tatsachen und Dokumente zur politischen Justiz, dargestellt am Fall Naumann*, Tübingen, 1957, p. 17f. Grimm was Naumann's defence lawyer.

prosecution of Nazi criminals). What was of concern to them, however, was to check any attempts that could lead to blocking or at least delaying the policy of Western integration by nationalist disruptive action. The arrest of the Naumann circle was a political action, intended to restrict the right wing of the small *bürgerblock* parties and in particular the former (or unrepentant) Nazis who operated there, whose help they relied on in view of their uncertain majority and whom they more or less courted as voters and members. It suddenly became clear to all those involved that a nationalist rally within the *bürgerblock* against Adenauer's policy was also directed against the political interests of the Western occupying powers and hence had no prospect of success. Kirkpatrick's message was understood. The prominent Nazis in the small *bürgerblock* parties either had to show their loyalty or else step back into the lower ranks. They still wished to recruit the support of voters with nationalist views, but nationalist factions were considered undesirable.

In the 1953 Bundestag election campaign, therefore, they went all out to 'blow their own trumpet'. However, only the *bürgerblock* profited from this chauvinist political climate. The southern German DG and the northern German DRP, in the meantime, fought one another doggedly on the same territorial and ideological ground for the same groups of voters. Any attempt by the two parties to work together, which would have been necessary in order to overcome the restrictive clause, failed, mainly because of Haußleiter, who firmly rejected an election alliance with the DRP.

In autumn 1952, DG representatives negotiated with the Deutsche Soziale Bewegung (DSB), led by Karl-Heinz Priester, who had parted company with his friends in the Hesse NDP in 1949 and temporarily joined the SRP. In 1951 he founded the DSB with a small group of supporters in Hesse and Lower Saxony. Eventually, in the winter of 1952, the DSB joined forces with the DG and provided Haußleiter with new organisational bases in the north, which he desperately needed due to banning orders. The DRP immediately retaliated and joined forces with the Franconian groups of the Deutscher Block (DB), which was very successful in certain areas, particularly in Protestant northern Bavaria. The DB was led by Karl Meißner, who was initially favourably disposed towards co-operation with the DRP.

However, when his Franconian party colleagues founded the *Reichsblock* in May 1953, which was *de facto* a 'southern version of the DRP',[24] supported by the DRP, Meißner withdrew and negotiated with Haußleiter. The latter urgently needed support after the DRP had established itself in Bavaria, and he agreed to an election alliance. Similarly, in May 1953, Haußleiter and Meißner called for the founding of the Dachverband der Nationalen Sammlung (DNS) which set itself up as an electoral party in July. The 620 delegates of the three main constituent parties (DG, DB, DSB), and apparently a further seventy small right-wing extremist groups, were counting on an imminent exodus into the nationalist camp and a good election result; results were predicted of 11–14 per cent in Bavaria and 8 per cent in West Germany as a whole.

The second Bundestag elections produced the following results (compared with the 1949 results):

- CDU/CSU   45.2   (31.0)
- FDP   9.5   (11.9)
- DP   3.2[25] (4.0)
- GB/BHE   5.9
- DNS   0.3
- DRP   1.1
- SPD   28.8   (29.2)
- KPD   2.2   (5.7)

Adenauer was the victor. In spite of the losses in its small parties, the *bürgerblock* emerged from the election visibly strengthened and formed a government in coalition with the BHE. The unification of the bourgeois camp was thus completed under the aegis of the CDU/CSU.

The DG and its alliance partners were able to mobilise just under 71,000 votes for themselves, while the DRP mobilised just under 300,000 voters. The right-wing extremist voter potential

---

24. Representatives of the Reichsblock stood for the 1953 Bundestag elections on the DRP list and later merged with it.

had been captured by the established bourgeois parties, and organised right-wing extremism shrank to insignificance. Not only had the DG not succeeded in becoming the nucleus of a rally of the decimated right-wing camp, but even in its *Land* of origin, Bavaria, it had been defeated by the DRP. There the DNS had achieved only 0.6 per cent of the votes but the DRP 1.5 percent. The DRP had now become the strongest force within West German right-wing extremism.

The Anachronism of Nationalist Opposition

So far we have explained the loss of significance of the right-wing extremist parties primarily in terms of the growing capacity of the *bürgerblock* parties to integrate. We shall now examine the conceptional factors within the right-wing extremist camp that were responsible for this development, and why it was Old Nationalism and not New Nationalism that set the tone.

If one analyses the manifesto and political practice of the DRP and the DG, it soon becomes apparent that neither party had an attractive, realistic alternative to counter the policy of the *bürgerblock*. This was particularly true of the nationalist question: the consequences of the Second World War, in particular the emergence of the East–West conflict, the fear of communism and finally the way in which Germany had been stripped of power and divided, had led to the yielding of nationalist state thought and behaviour in favour of the formation of international blocs and bloc disputes, and not only among the West Germans. However, under the specific post-war conditions it was particularly the West Germans who were prepared to sacrifice national sovereignty in favour of integration into the Western bloc. In this, problems such as the political and economic internal structure of the bloc, the relations of the individual states to the community of states, the equality of West Germany and dialogue with communist states (particularly with East Germany) formed the nucleus of current nationalist efforts, although they did not completely abandon the question of

25. The DP had not succeeded in overcoming the 5 per cent hurdle. Since they received the majority in ten constituencies, however, they were again able to re-enter the Bundestag (with fifteen seats).

reunification. It was embedded in the framework of East–West discussions and, realistically, was only seen as being solvable in this context.

In Germany, after 1945, a classic nation-state policy was an anachronism, and the right-wing extremist parties were acutely aware of this, particularly as they did not have any practical suggestions for reunification. It could not be achieved solely by nationalist resentment, polemics against de-Nazification and re-education, and criticism of the occupying powers and the 'licensed parties'. Moreover, in the phase of reconstruction, material interests (economic growth, full employment, consumerism) had high priority. These totally justified needs were misunderstood by the nationalists as contempt for ideal values, and they did not make the effort to adapt their bourgeois concepts of economic order to the conditions that prevailed in a modern, industrialised society. In this respect also, their views were characterised by anachronism. On the whole, the nationalist opposition lacked a viable alternative to the *bürgerblock* in terms of a programme of policies capable of upsetting its capacity for integration. If one also takes into account the high degree of fragmentation within the right-wing extremist camp and the violent rivalries among the egoistic leaders of the minor parties, it then becomes clear why the overwhelming majority of people with potentially right-wing extremist attitudes turned to the *bürgerblock* parties, and only a small hardcore of fanatic nationalists was unwaveringly convinced of the necessity and ultimate success of an independent nationalist opposition. The fact that Old Nationalism was more successful than New Nationalism with these remaining diehards is primarily due to the relatively greater attractiveness of Old Nationalism, as shown by the fact that the DRP was twice as large as the DG.[26] In spite of the orientation of both parties towards former and unrepentant Nazis, in the 1953 Bundestag election campaign the latter represented a neutralist policy directed against remilitarisation, while the DRP (as previously mentioned) presented pro-Western and militarist arguments. While the DRP defended the (supposed or actual) threat to the prop-

26. In 1953 the DRP had some 1,000 members, while the DG probably had 500. In the following years the DRP reached a maximum of 4,500 members and the DG 2,000.

erty and status interests of the predominantly nationalist middle class, the DG initially represented the new immigrants, who were impoverished and searching for social roots, still alien in their new home and considering themselves to be disadvantaged by the established economic and political structures. While the DRP saw itself as a nationalist competitor to the *bürgerblock* parties, with whom they in fact had many things in common in terms of foreign and defence policy questions, the DG consciously played the role of root-and-branch opposition to the *bürgerblock*. Hence the DRP may have been more attractive to the voters because it probably had a greater understanding of how to embody the 'values' which were so meaningful for right-wing extremists, such as Reich, *Deutschtum*, military discipline, obedience, etc., and how to foster the resentment that still existed. In addition, their foreign policy concept corresponded more to the anti-Bolshevist attitude of right-wing extremism than to the nationalist neutralism of the DG, which tended to arouse uncertainty by neglecting the current property and status interests of the old-established bourgeoisie.

A comparison of the election results of the two parties (Tables 4.3 and 4.4) shows that the hegemony of the Old Right within the nationalist camp prevailed until the mid-1960s. In Lower Saxony, their *Land* of origin, the DRP was represented in the Landtag until 1959. In the same year, they succeeded for the last time in overcoming the 5 per cent hurdle and gaining parliamentary seats (in Rhineland-Palatinate). Once the DG had lost its basis of expellee voters, it lived the precarious existence of a minor party, even in southern Germany, from where it had originated.

The 'Doldrum Years'

The years between 1953 and 1961 have been referred to in literature as the 'doldrum years'[27] of right-wing extremism. Indeed, the wave of nationalist sentiment, which had become apparent during the early post-war years, had almost completely subsided by 1953. The consolidation of the domestic and foreign policy bases of West Germany ensured the growing stabilisation of the political order and formed a barrier to the

---

27. Hans Frederik, *Die Rechtsradikalen*, Munich-Inning, p. 30.

Table 4.4 DG election results, 1950–64

Elections	Year	Number of votes	%	Seats
Bundestag	[1953[a]	70,726	0.3	—]
	1957	17,490	0.1	—
	1961	27,308	0.1	—
Land parliaments				
Württemberg-Baden	1950	212,431	14.7	16
Baden-Württemberg	1952	89,459	3.3	—
	1956	11,747	0.4	—
	1960	5,326	0.2	—
	1964	10,322	0.3	—
Bavaria	[1950[b]	1,136,148	12.3	26]
	1954[c]	54,522	0.6	—
	1958	31,919	0.3	—
	1962	30,663	0.3	—
Hamburg	1957	485	0.1	—
	1961	784	0.1	—
Hesse	1958	1,093	0.1	—
	1962	1,433	0.1	—
Lower Saxony	1959	2,775	0.1	—
	1963	2,190	0.1	—
North Rhine-Westphalia	1958	220	0.0	—
	1962	4,917	0.1	—
Rhineland-Palatinate	1951	4,864	0.3	—
	1959	2,453	0.1	—
	1963	4,062	0.2	—
Schleswig-Holstein	1962	1,043	0.1	—

a. Dachverband der Nationalen Sammlung (DNS).
b. Deutscher Gemeinschaftsblock der Heimatvertriebenen und Entrechteten (BHE-DG); the BHE received twenty seats, the DG six.
c. Bayerischer Rechtsblock (BR).

success of anti-democratic (and anti-capitalist) parties. The two right-wing extremist parties (DRP and DG) wrongly believed that this process of stabilisation was connected to a lack of legitimacy, which they believed they would be able to exploit for their own political purposes. They were mainly concerned with the following problem areas:

1. A clear dissatisfaction among the people with the developing division of Germany.
2. The on-going crisis among the (mainly rural) middle class.
3. The growing dominance of the CDU/CSU within the *bürgerblock* and the problems faced by the small *bürgerblock* parties.

Once their course of adapting to the mentality of the Old Right voters had failed, the DG set about defining their programme of New Nationalism in terms of both foreign policy and economic policy. With reference to the nationalist revolutionary liberation struggles of the colonial nations, they spoke of a 'dawning of the age of the nation-state' and compared the anti-imperialist struggle of the peoples of the Third World with their own struggle for German unity, which was primarily directed against the United States and the Soviet Union. Neutrality, non-alignment and anti-imperialism became their central foreign policy demands (see Appendix 2) which they condensed to a plan of 'federal re-formation of the European centre' in 1956. This plan proposed the merging of West Germany, East Germany and Austria on a neutral basis. Economically, they demanded 'modern German socialism', by which they meant co-operative and/or partnership relations, both at company level and in the economy in general, as well as protection of the middle classes against unjustified monopoly demands.

Neutralist plans were also propagated by the DRP after 1954/5, particularly in their Lower Saxony branch. However, these aims had always been disputed in the party and were soon to lead to violent internal disputes. In contrast to the DG, the DRP neutralists supported 'armed' neutrality and demanded direct reunification negotiations with the Soviet Union, which contradicted the anti-imperialist concerns of the DG. In spite of the fact that the two parties agreed in principle about the non-aligned status of a future all-German state, conflicts worsened in the 1950s and culminated in a 'brotherhood struggle'.

Agreement over the key question of the way to achieve reunification was initially perceived by both parties and instigated attempts towards reconciliation at the regional level. Negotiations between the two party leaderships regarding a fusion between the DRP and DG failed, however, again due to Haußleiter's obstinacy, whereupon both before and after the 1957 Bundestag elections, DG groups split away at *Land* level and, in some cases, particularly in Baden-Württemberg, joined the DRP.

In 1957 a brochure was published attacking the DRP in a spiteful and slanderous manner. This pamphlet, written by a certain Karl Staudinger, but which from its style and 'voice' had clearly been written by Haußleiter, insinuated that the neutralist DRP was acting under orders from Moscow, and accused Adolf von Thadden of having worked for the Polish secret service. Even to committed right-wing extremists, Haußleiter had gone too far this time and had become unelectable. Just under 18,000 votes for the DG in the 1957 Bundestag election was the price he had to pay. The DRP (whose overall result was just under 310,000 votes, or 1 per cent) achieved 25,000 in both Bavaria and Baden-Württemberg alone, and had again clearly outstripped its opponent in southern Germany.

From the 'Third Force' to the Nationaldemokratische Sammlung

The strategy of the right-wing extremist parties was also considerably influenced by political relations within the *bürgerblock*: as early as 1955/6 the GB/BHE had argued over the question of Adenauer's policy on Germany and integration with the West. The group, led by Kraft and Oberländer (the so-called 'K. O.–Gruppe'), clung to the CDU/CSU's foreign policy course and left the party. The BHE, whose behaviour was becoming increasingly nationalistic, terminated the coalition, put themselves into the opposition in the Bundestag and concentrated its external image on demands for a 'right of domicile in the East'. The FDP also had to withstand one section leaving the party: in 1956, the unquestioning advocates of a Western integration policy founded the Freie Volkspartei (FVP), which was primarily oriented towards big business and which remained in the federal government, while the FDP, concerned about remaining independent from the CDU/CSU, was forced to leave. The FVP, which was organisationally weak but financially strong, merged with the DP before the 1957 Bundestag elections; the DP again succeeded in entering the Bundestag by gaining some direct mandates. However, the BHE just failed the 5 per cent hurdle because, in contrast to the DP, it was unable to win the required three constituencies directly.

Despite emphasising its national concerns and although it had distanced itself from the CDU/CSU, the BHE did not succeed in obtaining lasting commitment from its supporters. As a party that represented the social and economic interests of the expellees, the BHE symbolised the initial dissatisfaction of a large proportion of the expellees with the federal government's integration policy and their pessimistic expectations for the future. With the indisputable economic and social policy success of representing the political interests of the expellees, by being able to secure the best possible living conditions for its clients in the course of the 1950s, it was continually destroying its own basis for existence. The BHE was making itself superfluous by virtue of its own success. Only a handful of generally revanchist expellees who did not wish to associate themselves with the division of Germany and who, verbally at least, clung to the thought of returning to their old homeland, remained in the party.

The problems faced by the minor *bürgerblock* parties, and the fact that in 1957 the CDU/CSU had obtained the absolute majority of seats in the Bundestag, strengthened the right-wing extremist parties' hopes that they would be able to profit from the supposed collapse of the 'middle' in the party system. Within the DRP, Meinberg and von Thadden in particular supported a policy of collaboration with the minor *bürgerblock* parties who had been weakend by the CDU/CSU. For example, in the Lower Saxony Landtag, DRP members of parliament and the FDP–BHE alliance co-operated temporarily. This 'bourgeois' course, however, aroused severe criticism from the DRP neutralists, who rejected co-operation with pro-Western parties. Conversely, the DRP's neutralist course, which had become officially binding but which was nevertheless controversial, prevented a longer-term alliance with the FDP, DP and BHE. This 'third force' eventually failed because, shortly before the 1961 Bundestag election, the BHE and DP merged to form the Gesamtdeutsche Partei (GDP), but this failed to halt their decline.[28] However, the DRP neutralists considered this fusion

28. The alliance only lasted a short time. Following the defeat in the 1961

to be an affirmation of their policy. In 1960, they succeeded in occupying the executive of the DRP with Prof Heinrich Kunstmann, Dr Oskar Lutz and Werner Gebhardt, while the representatives of a pro-Western course (Meinberg, von Thadden, Otto Hess and Waldemar Schütz) only had seats in the party leadership but continued to control the party machinery and the party press.

In the 1961 Bundestag election, the DRP's voter potential shrank even further (to 0.8 per cent), which the group, led by Meinberg and von Thadden, blamed on the neutralist course taken by the party leadership under Kunstmann. (Apparently, they did not see anything inconsistent in this argument.) At the DRP party conference in Northeim (in December 1961), the split finally occurred: at the elections to select a party chairman, Kunstmann was defeated by his rival von Thadden by 251 votes to 277. The Thadden opponents then left the party, and in January 1962 founded the neutralist Deutsche Freiheits-Partei (DFP). The path was thus cleared for a pro-Western foreign policy in the DRP and for the realisation of the concept of a 'third force' with the remains of the former *bürgerblock* parties (who rejected neutralist ideas). This *'Nationaldemokratische Sammlung'* had become possible, not least because the fusion of the BHE and DP in the Bundestag election had failed, and the *bürgerblock* had become condensed to the CDU/CSU and the DFP. The liberals, as the only bourgeois party outside the CDU/CSU, had been able to secure a small but reliable group of voters.

The fact that the DRP's attempts after 1962 to form a *Nationaldemokratische Sammlung* were making progress was also due to the change in East–West constellations. Once the US President, John F. Kennedy, took office (in January 1961), relations between the United States and the Soviet Union entered a phase of disengagement, which was accelerated by the crises in Cuba and Berlin. Kennedy did act harshly towards the Soviet Union

---

Bundestag election (2.8 per cent, no seats), the majority of former DP supporters withdrew again and the GDP literally represented the successor organisation to the BHE. For some time it was still represented in some *Land* parliaments, but since 1966 has disappeared from the political arena. Two parties emerged from the bankrupt estate of the DP in 1962: one new DP, led by Friedrich Thielen, and a Deutschnationale Volkspartei (DNVP), led by Heinrich Faßbender.

over the Cuba crisis, but this posture was only aimed at maintaining the existing power relations. The President wanted to prevent a change in the status quo, but otherwise wanted relaxed relations with the Eastern bloc, supporting his concept of the coexistence of blocs. West German foreign policy, and in particular Konrad Adenauer, viewed international détente with mistrust, and feared that the superpowers would come to an agreement at the cost of German demands for reunification. The French President, Charles de Gaulle, who had been in office since the end of 1958, viewed the US proposals particularly critically and supported plans to strengthen Europe (under French leadership) against the United States. Adenauer supported him in this, laying the foundations for German–French reconciliation. 'Gaullism' hence implied an economically, politically and militarily strong and independent Europe as a self-confident force existing side-by-side with the United States and the Soviet Union. While nationalist and authoritarian-conservative circles were particularly fond of adopting de Gaulle's ideas ('Gaullists'), liberal and socialist-minded politicians preferred to support Kennedy's vision of an international détente policy ('Atlanticists').

After the neutralists had split from the DRP, the party, now led by the Prussian conservative Adolf von Thadden, supported a policy oriented around the Gaullist model, thus producing a foreign policy concept which its envisaged alliance partners, the rump of the DP and BHE, would be prepared to discuss. Within the CDU/CSU, too, there were heated debates between Gaullists (led by Adenauer)[29] and Atlanticists (led by the Foreign Affairs Minister Gerhard Schröder, who had been in office since 1961). The DRP position was thus granted a certain renown if it could quote Adenauer as an authority if necessary. And it was counting on attracting voters from the CDU/CSU, where the Atlanticists seemed to be gaining control.

Hence by modifying its manifesto, the DRP became:

> 'gradually acceptable to all middle-class and nationalist circles who for many years had supported the right-wing-oriented governing parties but, as a result of the collapse of the old DP and the imminent

---

29. In 1963, Adenauer was replaced as Federal Chancellor by Ludwig Erhard, who had been in office as Finance Minister from 1949 and who belonged to the Atlanticists.

collapse of the BHE (the fusion with the Gesamtdeutsche Partei had remained unsuccessful), were now 'homeless' in a political sense.'[30]

The DRP's policy of gathering support produced its first success in 1963: in Bremen, representatives of the DRP and BHE were standing as candidates on the DP list under Friedrich Thielen (the so-called 'Bremer Liste') and won 5.2 per cent of the vote, resulting in four parliamentary seats. In Baden-Württemberg, representatives of the DRP and other small nationalist groups joined the GDP lists, which had since become completely insignificant, under the leadership of Wilhelm Gutmann. They only achieved 1.8 per cent in the 1964 Landtag elections, but this nevertheless indicated the breadth of the future alliance.

On 28 November 1964, on Thielen's initiative, the Nationaldemokratische Partei Deutschlands (NPD) was founded in Bremen. In addition to the DRP, the main participants were the DP in Bremen, the rump of the GDP and BHE, the DP, and a number of smaller groups, including the Deutschnationale Volkspartei (DNVP) (founded in 1962). The NPD, led by Thielen (former chairman of the DP), Thadden (formerly of the DRP), Gutmann (formerly of the GDP) and Faßbender (formerly of the DNVP) only achieved 2 per cent of the vote in the 1965 Bundestag elections, but a short time later it achieved a rapid upswing due to a favourable political climate.

The Gesamtdeutsche Unabhängigkeitsbewegung

Following the 1961 Bundestag elections, New Nationalists endeavoured to concentrate the efforts of the nationalist and neutralist forces. The 'doldrum years' had affected the DG particularly badly, and Haußleiter was forced to make it known that they were prepared to co-operate with like-minded groups. He became aware of potential alliance partners, not only in the nationalist camp, but also in the democratic, all-German-minded middle class.

Following the so-called 'Godesberg change' within the SPD,

---

30. Fred H. Richards, *Die NPD. Alternative oder Wiederkehr?*, Munich/Vienna, 1967, p. 38.

the DG was convinced that it could no longer expect 'any serious opposition from the German left' to the 'Adenauer state', and it increasingly presented itself as the only true opposition to the authoritarian tendencies of the CDU state. It hoped to improve its chances of resolving the German question because of its concept of all-German independence and non-alignment with the two superpowers in the current international climate of détente. Consequently, it supported a balance of power between the Americans and the Soviets, and polemicised strongly against the advocates of a 'Gaullist' course in the DRP and the CDU/CSU: De Gaulle, they said, had never been a European but a supporter of 'Great France', whose aim was to 'follow Richelieu's policy consistently and add the annexation of Bonn to the conquering of Strasbourg'.[31]

Thus the vision of a nationalist, neutral and détente-oriented 'all-German independence movement' emerged, which was to co-operate with two other small groups: the Deutsche Freiheits-Partei (DFP), which had been founded in 1962 and was led by Kunstmann, Lutz and Scheffer,[32] and the Vereiningung Deutsche Nationalversammlung (VDNV).

The VDNV had been founded in January 1961 by Wolf Schenke, a long-time pioneer of nationalist neutralism in the Federal Republic of Germany. The former FDP Member of Parliament, Hermann Schwann, was chairman. The association saw itself as a pressure group for *rapprochement* between the two German states, and it considered that conditions were favourable for the realisation of the plan of reunification as a result of global co-operation between the superpowers. This plan saw the formation of an all-German national assembly as the first step towards the unification of East and West Germany.

In mid-May 1965, the Aktionsgemeinschaft Unabhängiger Deutscher (AUD) was formed as a umbrella organisation of the DG, DFP and parts of the VDNV. At the founding party conference (in July 1965), Schwann was elected chairman, and Haußleiter and Lutz were elected his deputies. At the Bundestag elections a few months later, however, the party did not

---

31. As mentioned in chapter 2, Alsace-Lorraine was annexed by France following the First World War.

32. A leading role was also played by some former SRP functionaries, such as Werner Gebhardt and Dr Gerhard Krüger.

achieve the success they had expected, only obtaining some 50,000 votes (0.2 per cent). In the following years, too, it was to be unsuccessful in stepping out of the shadow of the NPD. (see Appendix Document 3)

The Decline of the Right-Wing Extremist Support Organisations

Post-war right-wing extremism had to achieve at least two things in targeting its voters:

1. It had to convince those social groups that had been particularly affected, uprooted or disoriented by the smashing of national socialism, the division of Germany and the allied occupation policy, and that had produced the military and political supporters of the Nazi system, of its nationalist or, rather, anti-democratic, policy.
2. It had to appeal to young people in order to ensure long-term recruitment from the succeeding generation.

Despite some initial successes, it did not succeed in doing this. The giant potential consisting of former soldiers in Hitler's armed forces, ex-supporters of Hitler and young people who had been born and brought up in the Third Reich and its interest groups were soon engulfed by the CDU state and showed increasingly fewer preferences for right-wing extremist parties and organisations.

First, let us look back briefly at the soldiers' organisations. Since the original war aims of the anti-Hitler coalition consisted of destroying Nazism and militarism, the 17 million men of the former armed forces[33] (particularly the 500,000 or so officers) were initially particular targets of the de-Nazification policy, viewed as they were as the personification of militarism in Germany. In a similar way to the expellees, soldiers were subject to a special ban on forming organisations, because people were afraid that mass dissatisfaction would lead to a right-wing extremist mass movement. When the ban on political organisations was lifted in December 1949, soldiers' associations ap-

33. Including members of the Waffen-SS.

The Development of Organised Right-wing Extremism

peared from nowhere in large numbers. It is estimated that some 1,000 organisations represented some half a million members.[34] Their primary organisational goal was the abolition of poverty, concentrating particularly on the fight for pensions and maintenance allowances which had initially been withheld from the soldiers.[35] The soldiers' organisations, however, also devoted their efforts to 'preserving tradition' and 'recreating the honour of the professional soldier', since they felt particularly defamed by de-Nazification and the war trials. In addition to social concerns, political motives were also significant, and to a large extent these converged with the criticisms levelled by right-wing extremism at the occupation policy and at the founding of West Germany. These represented potential links for organised right-wing extremism's target group work.

The leading functionaries of the major soldiers' organisations were generally concerned to control the organisational muddle by forming umbrella organisations; on the whole, they succeeded in either integrating or pushing aside nationalist groups and factions. In July 1950 the Bund versorgungsberechtigter ehemaliger Wehrmachtsangehöriger und deren Hinterbliebener (BvW) was formed, which represented the interests of some 60,000 people entitled to pensions.[36] A further step towards organisational unity was the formation, one year later, of the Verband deutscher Soldaten (VdS), which saw the merger, initially of eight, later of thirty-one organisations, including the BvW and the 'Kyffhäuserbund'.[37] Finally, in 1957, the Ring deutscher Soldatenverbände (RdS) was founded, which represented other organisations as well as the VdS. Hence, fragmentation was counteracted to a certain extent, but was not completely abolished at this juncture.

One important disputed political issue was whether former members of the Waffen-SS should be recognised as regular soldiers. Within BvW organisations, this claim was initially

---

34. Dudek and Jaschke, *Rechtsextremismus*, pp. 79ff.
35. For further details, see Georg Meyer, 'Soldaten ohne Armee. Berufssoldaten im Kampf um Standesehre und Versorgung', in Martin Broszat, Klaus-Dietmar Henke and Hans Woller (eds), *Von Stalingrad zur Währungsreform. Zur Sozialgeschichte des Umbruchs in Deutschland*, Munich, 1988, pp. 683ff.
36. In 1984, there were still 1.7 million war pensioners in West Germany.
37. The Kyffhäuserbund was founded in 1900 as an association to protect military tradition and comradeship. It was re-founded in 1952.

rejected by the majority,[38] and hence after 1951 former SS members organised themselves to form the Hilfsgemeinschaft auf Gegenseitigkeit der ehemaligen Angehörigen der Waffen-SS (HIAG). In November 1953, regional HIAG groups formed a 'federal contact office', which in April 1959 eventually became the 'Bundesverband der Soldaten der ehemaligen Wafffen-SS', which merged with the VdS in 1962. The organisation then had a maximum of 20,000 members (some sources even talk of 40,000), and today it represents the only politically active right-wing extremist[39] soldiers' organisation, which provokes anti-fascist counter-demonstrations because of its spectacular rallies and demonstrations.

The 'Stahlhelm-Bund der Frontsoldaten' (Stahlhelm League of Front-Line Soldiers), which had been re-founded in 1951, can also be considered to be right-wing extremist. It had been a supporting organisation of the DNVP in the Weimar Republic, and was ultimately a forerunner to the Nazis. Supposedly some 70,000 members at the beginning of the 1950s (although, in my opinion, this figure is considerably exaggerated) the organisation, which today contains a high proportion of old people and is organisationally exhausted (since 1973 it has called itself 'Stahlhelm-Kampfbund für Europa') cultivates mainly Prussian/militarist feelings of resentment.

The former soldiers' organisations considered themselves to be politically neutral. This also applied to overtly right-wing extremist organisations. Only the DG undertook the attempt in 1953 (which failed) to form their own soldiers' organisation (the *Graue Front*). The DRP acted more prudently. It avoided founding this type of organisation and respected the political neutrality of the existing organisations, which sometimes included DRP members and functionaries in leading positions.

The historical development of the soldiers' organisations, the majority of which cannot be classified in the right-wing extremist camp but which nevertheless cultivate anti-democratic

38. The fact that the SS had been declared an illegal organisation by the International Military Tribunal in Nuremberg, while the German High Command and the general staff had been exonerated from the accusation of being an illegal organisation, is an additional factor.
39. Since 1983 the HIAG is no longer included by the Ministry for the Interior in reports from the Office for the Defence of the Constitution as a right-wing extremist organisation.

thought to a considerable extent, is characterised by the change in the Western allies' war aims; in other words, by the plans to rearm the Federal Republic of Germany only shortly after it had been constituted. Since it was not possible to remilitarise against the wishes of the former soldiers, the occupying forces and the federal government had to prevent fundamental opposition to the policy of the Adenauer government from gaining influence in these organisations. Consequently, a course of integration was introduced, which envisaged a satisfactory solution to the question of pensions and allowances, as well as generous amnesties for those who had been sentenced. By means of shrewd tactical moves towards the major organisations and interventions into their personnel policy, these could at least be manoeuvred into the role of a loyal opposition. Soon part of the former officer corps and their teams could be integrated into the federal army. Hence the policy succeeded largely in isolating and removing those sections of the soldiers' organisations that were critical of the system, while politically embracing the majority, which was prepared to co-operate. In January 1960, the German army founded its own reservist organisation, further reducing the influence of the soldiers' organisations. The high proportion of old people and lack of young recruits accelerated their collapse and marginalisation.

Today, only the HIAG, whose membership has declined rapidly, is capable of staging any noteworthy activities. This is mainly because members of the Waffen-SS cultivate their Nazi traditions with elitist *esprit de corps*, and pursue the trivialisation of national socialism and the justification of their own deeds with particular passion. However, the fact that connections are occasionally unearthed between the HIAG and the German army results from the combination of suppressing and playing down the past described above.

One further important target group of post-war right-wing extremism were the so-called 'victims of de-Nazification'. Although de-Nazification had commenced in 1949/50, and its measures were completed by the end of the 1950s at the latest, as soon as the ban on political activity (at the end of 1949) had been lifted, affected people everywhere joined forces in order to fight for a swift end to, and extensive review of, the verdicts and sentences passed by the sentencing chambers. Following supra-regional fusions, in April 1955 the Bundesverband ehemaliger Internierter und Entnazifizierungsgeschädigter (Federal Association of Former Internees and Victims of De-Nazification) was founded as an umbrella organisation of the many organisations and societies. The association represented some 20,000 members and was mainly concerned with social and legal advice, as well as compensation for the 'victims of de-Nazification'. In addition, one particularly important goal of the organisation was to 'establish historical truth':

> We are mainly concerned with stemming the flood of lies from the initial post-war years with regard to the political development of the NSDAP and the Third Reich, to report false accounts and explain certain historical processes, which to date have only been insufficiently known or which need to be scrutinised due to biased documents and opinions, mainly produced by sections of the allies. However, it is particularly important to research the atrocities of the post-war era which . . . bear no relation to the crimes that occurred at the time of the Third Reich.[40]

The campaign by the association to end the 'defamation' of former Nazis was the decisive source for right-wing extremist historical revisionism, which is still conducted today with particular energy and which denied Germany's sole guilt for the Second World War (the so-called 'war guilt lie') and the holocaust (the so-called 'Auschwitz lie') in a flood of publications.

The organisations of 'de-Nazification victims' continued to insist on their party political neutrality, and to a certain extent this was true. However, these associations attracted a particularly large number of unrepentant Nazis and the right-wing extremist parties viewed them as important supporting organisations. Hence, at that time in neo-Nazi circles, the SRP's success was largely considered to be a result of the dissatisfaction with regard to de-Nazification, and the DRP and DG likewise devoted themselves intensively to this question during the run-up to the 1953 Bundestag elections. If one brings oneself up to date with the actual results of de-Nazification,[41] it becomes clear why

---

40. *Die Brücke*, vol. 4, 1957, no. 15, p. 4.
41. See chapter 3, pp. 69ff.

The Development of Organised Right-wing Extremism

these organisations did not survive long, especially as the vast majority of the small number declared guilty or incriminated soon returned to office and regained their social standing, or were at least able to make an adequate living in the land of economic miracles. At the beginning of the 1960s, the integration process had come to an end and the associations had become completely insignificant.

The nationalist opposition was particularly keen to organise youth. Great confusion reigns over the membership numbers of right-wing extremist youth organisations in the 1950s. Officially, the total number for the year 1959 is given as 2,300 (see Figure 4.7); this, however, is vastly underestimated. The mass media in 1958/9 quoted figures of between 40,000 and 70,000, which were likewise unrealistic. In academic literature, the figures given range between 30,000 and 40,000,[42] but these figures seem to me to be too high. I estimate the total membership number at its peak (around 1955) to be a maximum 20,000 young people. In 1965, 1,000 are said to have been still active.

The post-war boom was due mainly to the activities of former leaders of the Hitler-Jugend (HJ), which had been disbanded by the allies, or former activists in the bourgeois youth movement. Hence an organisational confusion of nationalist, *völkisch*, *bündisch* and military-patriotic groups soon emerged. Politically neutral associations were predominant; the right-wing extremist parties tended to have little success with their younger generations. This was true of the Junge Deutsche Gemeinschaft (JDG) of the DG as well as for the Reichsjugend (Reich Youth) and the Junge Kameradschaft (Young Comradeship) of the DRP. Only the Jugendbund Adler (JBA) of the Deutscher Block (DB) had a respectable number of supporters at the beginning of the 1950s (approximately 5,000 young people), which, however, had shrunk to some 500 members by the mid-1960s.

In June 1954, there was temporarily a certain concentration of forces following the formation of the Kameradschaftsring nationaler Jugendverbände (KNJ). The main participants were the Wiking Jugend (WJ), which had been founded in 1952, the JBA, which had existed since 1950 under the leadership of Richard Etzel, as well as the Arbeitsgemeinschaft nationaler

---

42. Dudek and Jaschke, *Rechtsextremismus*, vol. 1, p. 133.

Jugendbünde Österreichs (ANJÖ). The latter consisted mainly of the Bund Heimattreuer Jugend Österreichs (BHJ), which had been trying to form branches in West Germany since the mid-1950s. In 1960 these merged to form the federal organisation Bund Heimattreuer Jugend (BHJ). One year previously, the KNJ had hit a serious crisis due to the departure of the JBA. At the same time, neutralist circles had founded the Jungdeutschlandbund (JDB), so that the overall process of fragmentation continued. In 1958/9 the ANJÖ/BHJ groups in Austria were banned, and in 1962 disputes between rival factions of the West German BHJ led to several regional organisations disbanding. The remains of the BHJ did reorganise in September 1962, but a continuation of the KNJ was unthinkable. This was also due to the fact that since the mid-1950s, the WJ had been suffering from periodic internal disputes and splits. The formation of the Freundeskreis der Nationalen Jugend (Friends of Nationalist Youth) in 1963 failed to halt the organisational exhaustion of the JBA, WJ and BHJ and their high proportion of old people.

The causes of the decline of right-wing extremist youth organisations did not lie solely in the hopeless fragmentation of their associations and societies and the rivalries between their leaders. On the whole, young people in post-war Germany showed little inclination to organise themselves, indeed to become politically involved at all. There was a surprisingly quick adaptation to the adult world, characterised by achievement, consumerism and political apathy. The values and concepts of order held by the nationalist opposition were extraordinarily unattractive to a youth which tended towards scepticism and which pragmatically concentrated on overcoming the problems of everyday life in the post-war era.

New Right-wing Extremism (1966–88)

The End of the Post-war Era

With the formation of basic consensus at the end of the 1950s, the days of the *bürgerblock* were numbered. The first indications that bloc opposition was disbanding became apparent in the 1961 Bundestag elections, when the SPD was able to win votes from the *bürgerblock* camp for the first time and thus break out of their '30 per cent tower'.

In 1961 the three-party system at federal level was established. The *bürgerblock* now only consisted of two parties: the CDU/CSU had admittedly lost their absolute majority in the Bundestag but was still the predominant force in the bloc, while the FDP played the role of junior partner and was able to increase its proportion of the vote from 7.7 per cent in 1957 to 12.8 per cent and returned to the government coalition in a stronger position. The long-drawn-out coalition negotiations, which culminated in the novelty of a coalition contract, revealed clear splits within the *bürgerblock*. The Liberals had decided on a government alliance with the CDU, but without Adenauer, but were then forced reluctantly to come to terms with the continued Chancellorship of the CDU chairman, albeit limited to two years. Within the CDU/CSU, heated disputes erupted regarding who was to be his successor, accompanied by internal political conflicts (e.g. the so-called '*Spiegel* crisis'*) and foreign policy disputes ('Atlanticists' versus 'Gaullists'). Subsequently, the SPD and FDP began to move closer together. Both parties discovered similarities, particularly in the area of foreign policy, and were co-operating more and more frequently in everyday political affairs.

The total collapse of the *bürgerblock* occurred when the first major economic crisis hit the Federal Republic of Germany. In 1966/7, a clear economic downturn and deep-rooted structural weaknesses in certain branches of industry (e.g. coal, iron, steel and textiles) coincided with a considerable government economic deficit. It was asking too much of the *bürgerblock*'s neo-Liberal economic policy to solve these problems, and as a result of the financial crisis, the government, which had been led by Ludwig Erhard, collapsed, and in December 1966 a 'Grand Coalition' was formed, consisting of the CDU/CSU and the SPD. The end of the 'CDU state' marked the end of the post-war era. Relations had 'normalised', and West German politics was now forced to modernise, adapt and act on actual problem

---

* *Editor's note*: An unauthorised raid in 1962 on the offices of the Hamburg weekly, *Der Spiegel*, raised the issue of parliamentary control and a guarantee of constitutional rights within West Germany.

constellations rather than the consequences of the historical guilt burden.

The absence of opposition in the three-party system – the small FDP was the sole representative of opposition in the Bundestag – led to the emergence of fundamental oppositional forces at the periphery: a new right-wing extremism on the one hand, and an extra-parliamentary, radical-democratic and mainly socialist movement on the other.[43] The upturn in right-wing extremism was caused first by the economic crisis; and second, by the disbanding of the *bürgerblock*, the political merging of the CDU/CSU with the Social Democrats, whom they had previously condemned as being 'enslaved by Moscow', and by the FDP's swing to the left during their period in opposition. As the FDP's power to integrate the nationalist-liberal middle class declined, the CDU/CSU's attraction for right-wing and right-wing extremist voters, who were suspicious of socialism, betrayal of national unity and compliance with communism in the SPD's reform policies, was also reduced. In particular, Willy Brandt's *Ostpolitik*, with its orientation towards détente (Brandt was Minister for Foreign Affairs and later became Chancellor), met with profound distrust, followed quickly by violent opposition among the West German right, who viewed the policy primarily as a means of minimising Soviet imperialism and weakening the desire for military defence.

Hence a vacuum had emerged at the right fringe of the political spectrum, which the Nationaldemokratische Partei Deutschlands (NPD) was able to fill, helped as it was by the economic crisis.

The Rise of the NPD

Between 1966 and 1969, right-wing extremism experienced an upturn previously unknown in the Federal Republic.[44] The

---

43. The reasons for the emergence of an extra-parliamentary opposition (APO) were very varied in nature and cannot be discussed here individually. Generation-specific problems combined with fundamental criticism of the authoritarian structures of society, of the lack of democratic-socialist political opposition, of the SPD for being a 'doctor at the bedside of capitalism' and of imperialism (particularly US imperialism).

44. Reinhard Kühnl, Rainer Riling and Christine Sager, *Die NPD. Struktur, Idologie und Funktion einer neofaschistischen Paratei*, Frankfurt, 1969.

The Development of Organised Right-wing Extremism

NPD entered seven *Land* parliaments with between 5.8 and 9.8 per cent of the vote, and in the 1969 Bundestag elections achieved 4.3 per cent of the vote (see Table 4.5), by far the best election result of any right-wing party since 1949.

This success was made possible largely because the NPD manifesto appeared to continue Adenauer's authoritarian inheritance and hostility to détente. No bourgeois party acted so consistently during the Grand Coalition against the new *Ostpolitik*, against extra-parliamentary opposition and against social democracy as the NPD, which surrounded itself in the aura of conforming to the constitution. Even more than the CSU, the National Democrats presented themselves as the middle-class and anti-Bolshevist stable power in Germany, and as the advocates of the claim for sole West German representation for all-German interests, and of a policy of strength and messianic liberation towards the people of Eastern Europe. By these means, they won the acclaim of the middle-class supporters of the right wing of the former *bürgerblock* parties, while at the same time appealing successfully to the socio-psychological fears of broad social classes – including the working class – caused by the economic crisis in the traditional industrial economic regions.

Initially, the NPD did not have an autonomous manifesto, and certainly no uniform party ideology. Their diffuse conglomeration of demands was an expression of inner-party heterogeneity, which was consolidated by organisational growth (see Figure 4.5). Externally, they were concerned to achieve an image of being nationalist-conservative and faithful to the constitution, in order to avoid a possible ban and to win broad sections of voters from the old *bürgerblock* camp. The party chairman, Friedrich Thielen, served as an advertisement for this legalistic and middle-class, property-owning course. Thielen, a concrete manufacturer from Bremen, had come from the CDU to the NPD via the DP, and had never been a member of the NSDAP. However, former Nazis dominated the upper echelons of the party, and hence the first serious inner-party conflict ended in 1967 with Thielen being expelled from the party and Adolf von Thadden[45] being elected as his successor.

45. Thadden always denied having been a member of the NSDAP. Appa-

Table 4.5 NPD election results, 1965–88

Elections		Year	Number of votes	%	Seats
European Parliament		1984	198,633	0.8	—
Bundestag		1965	664,193	2.0	—
		1969	1,422,010	4.3	—
		1972	207,465	0.6	—
		1976	122,661	0.3	—
		1980	68,096	0.2	—
		1983	91,095	0.2	—
		1987	227,054	0.6	—
Land Parliaments					
Baden-Württemberg		1968	381,569	9.8	12
		1976	42,927	0.9	—
		1980	2,341	0.1	—
		1988	101,889	2.1	—
Bavaria		1966	781,813	7.4	15
		1970	325,646	2.9	—
		1974	121,745	1.1	—
		1978	66,926	0.6	—
		1982	69,656	0.6	—
		1986	58,165	0.5	—
Bremen		1967	35,894	8.8	8
		1971	12,561	2.8	—
		1975	4,781	1.1	—
		1979	1,602	0.4	—
Hamburg		1966	36,654	3.9	—
		1970	27,312	2.7	—
		1974	7,992	0.8	—
		1978	3,231	0.3	—
	(June)	1982[a]	6,221	0.7	—
	(Dec.)	1982[a]	2,804	0.3	—
		1986[a]	6,585	0.7	—
		1987[a]	3,826	0.4	—
Hesse		1966	224,674	7.9	8
		1970	94,531	3.0	—
		1974	32,713	1.0	—
		1978	12,507	0.4	—
		1983	27,076	0.8	—

Table 4.5 continued

Elections	Year	Number of votes	%	Seats
Lower Saxony	1967	249,197	7.0	10
	1970	124,675	3.2	—
	1974	27,581	0.6	—
	1978	17,613	0.4	—
North Rhine-Westphalia	1970	94,043	1.1	—
	1975	36,281	0.4	—
Rhineland-Palatinate	1967	127,680	6.9	4
	1971	53,882	2.7	—
	1975	22,942	1.1	—
	1979	14,915	0.7	—
	1983	3,656	0.1	—
	1987	18,227	0.8	—
Saarland	1970	22,020	3.4	—
	1975	4,774	0.7	—
	1985	4,659	0.7	—
Schleswig-Holstein	1967	72,093	5.8	4
	1971	18,822	1.3	—
	1975	8,123	0.5	—
	1979	2,825	0.2	—
	1988	19,154	1.2	—

a. Hamburger Liste für Ausländerstopp (HLA).

Initially, however, crises such as these did little harm to the party. The series of spectacular electoral successes had begun at the end of 1966 in Hesse (7.9 per cent of the vote, eight seats) and Bavaria (7.4 per cent, fifteen seats) and reached its peak in 1968 in Baden-Württemberg with 9.8 per cent of the vote and twelve seats. In total, the party achieved sixty-one seats in Landtag parliaments and some 600 representatives in local and regional governments. Therefore, they were counting on entering the German Bundestag in 1969: the predictions of opinion research organisations initially ranged between 10 and 15 per cent and later between 6 and 8 per cent of the vote, and

rently, though, he was after 1939: Dudek and Jaschke, *Rechtsextremismus*, vol. 1, p. 320.

Figure 4.5 Development of NPD membership, 1964–87

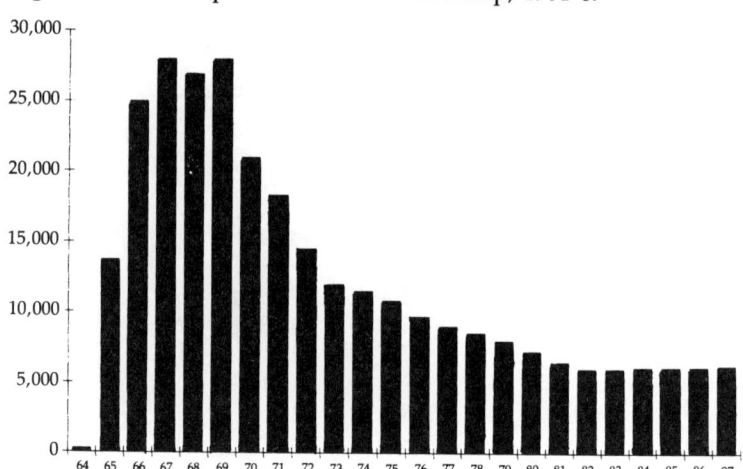

Source: Federal Ministry for the Interior

estimated that they would obtain up to 75 seats.

The militant disputes between NPD supporters and anti-Fascists, which had been taking place since 1966, culminated in the Bundestag election campaign. In particular the *Ordnerdienst* (security service) of the NPD, a violent gang of thugs, continued to ensure negative headlines, discrediting the party in the eyes of the nationalist-conservative electorate, who favoured peace and civil order. In one case, the federal representative of the *Ordnerdienst*, Klaus Kolley, even fired at political opponents with a pistol.

With reference to press reports, Dudek and Jaschke[46] wrote the following report regarding an NPD meeting in Frankfurt:

> On Friday 25 July 1969, at an election meeting in the Cantate Room in Frankfurt . . . militant riots took place . . . The entrance to the Cantate Room had already been blocked by a 'sit-in' hours before the conference began. When the head of the NPD *Ordnerdienst*, Körber, gave the command to take control of the entrance under any circumstances, the men, wearing crash helmets, attacked the demonstrators recklessly, and also set a dog on them. The demonstrators responded with stones and gunfire. The fighting continued when the confer-

46. Ibid., p. 336f.

ence began in the Cantate Room, during which forty demonstrators vociferously prevented the NPD speaker from speaking and were then both verbally and physically attacked by NPD supporters.

The events, in which numerous people from both sides were injured, continued to dominate political discussions for days to come.

The extent to which public indignation, both at home and abroad, regarding the resurgence of right-wing extremism contributed to the fact that the NPD finally failed to enter the Bundestag is unknown. Although the political significance of such anti-Fascist sentiments should not be underestimated, nevertheless other factors are responsible for the downfall of the party from 1969 onwards. But more of that later.

In 1969, the NPD, with some 1.5 million voters, had succeeded in making deep inroads among the supporters of bourgeois-democratic parties in particular. They achieved their success mainly in the rural Protestant regions, where economic power was weak, but they also achieved considerable gains among the Catholic electorate. The party appealed mainly to men, with women vastly under-represented. Regarding its age structure, the generation that had consciously experienced national socialism predominated. With regards to the social composition of its voters, the property-owning middle class and the new middle class were dominant. Expellees were also particularly inclined towards the NPD. It was also in a position to recruit support from manual workers (usually those who were not trade union members). Their regional strongholds were Mid-Franconia, Upper Hesse, the eastern part of Lower Saxony and Schleswig-Holstein, indicating clear parallels to the strongholds of the NSDAP before 1933. In the industrial regions of North Rhine-Westphalia, Baden-Württemberg and the Saarland, the NPD (like the NSDAP before it) found comparatively little support.

The fact that the NPD served as a focal party for those that were economically and socially disadvantaged or dissatisfied from various social strata can be seen from the social composition of its membership (see Table 4.6). The social heterogeneity of its supporters and target groups was characteristic of the rapid upswing of the party, but caused diffuseness in terms of

Table 4.6 NPD members by occupation and social class, 1966–70

	1966	1967	1968	1969	1970
Academics	6	4	5	5	5
Self-employed	25	27	29	28	32
Civil servants	7	6	6	5	4
White-collar employees	18	17	15	15	11
Manual workers in medium-sized companies	14	16	18	20	19
Industrial manual workers	13	16	14	14	15
Housewives	6	5	5	5	6
Pensioners	11	9	8	8	8
No profession					
Total	100	100	100	100	100

All figures are percentages.
Source: Federal Ministry for the Interior.

its ideology and long-term plans, and a lack of unity, which served to encourage the advent of collapse after 1969.

The Collapse of the NPD and Resistance to the Social-Liberal Coalition

The decisive outcome of the 1969 Bundestag election was the formation of the social-liberal coalition of the SPD and FDP under the Chancellorship of Willy Brandt. At the beginning of the year, the SPD and FDP had come to an agreement to elect Gustav Heinemann as the first Social Democratic head of state in the Federal Republic of Germany.

In 1968 the economic situation in West Germany had improved again, and the reformist policy of the Grand Coalition, which was largely influenced by the SPD, brought about its first successes. However, now that the crisis strategy function of the 'mass merger' between the CDU/CSU and SPD was over, conflict between the unequal alliance partners re-emerged stronger than ever. In particular, *Ostpolitik* and the economic and social policies became sources of conflict between the CDU/CSU and the Social Democrats and soon dominated the Bundestag election campaign as well. While the SPD and FDP were emphatically innovatory, presenting programmes for reform and promising

The Development of Organised Right-wing Extremism

greater democracy, the CDU/CSU sought recourse to traditional anti-socialist prejudices, which in view of almost three years of co-operation with the SPD was hardly convincing, producing an anachronistic effect in view of the widespread expectations among the people for reform. The SPD achieved 42.7 per cent of the vote, thus passing the 40 per cent mark for the first time. The FDP, as a result of its swing to the left after 1967/8, was only just able to overcome the 5 per cent barrier (5.8 per cent), but overall it was sufficient for the social-liberal coalition to achieve a parliamentary majority, albeit a narrow one (twelve seats) (see Table 4.7).

The tendencies towards repolarisation, which had become apparent during the election campaign, continued with renewed intensity after 1969. The CDU/CSU found themselves in opposition for the first time at federal level and, following a political swing to the right, took up their old place in the party system. By putting up a vehement opposition to the Federal government's new *Ostpolitik*[47] and its reform plans they were again able to fill the vacuum that had been left when they entered the Grand Coalition, which had facilitated the NPD's temporary upward trend. In the following period, the CDU/CSU attracted some four-fifths of the NPD's voters, literally taking the ground from under their feet.

After the Bundestag elections, the NPD entered a deep internal crisis.[48] Until then party cohesion had been based on the need for unity in order not to jeopardise electoral success; following electoral defeat, internal conflicts emerged at full force. Controversial subjects were the plans and tactics of the nationalist opposition in general, and in particular, the problem of the appropriate form of resistance to the 'sell-out of Germany' by the Brandt government's *Ostpolitik*. The success of the NPD leadership under Adolf von Thadden had come to an abrupt halt. Critics of his rather nationalist-conservative and emphatically legalistic, property-owning, middle-class and 'Gaullist'

---

47. Stages in the policy of détente were the 'Moscow Pact' (1970) with the Soviet Union, the 'Warsaw Pact' (1970) with Poland, the 'Traffic Treaty' and the 'Basic Treaty' (both in 1972) with East Germany and the 'Prague Pact' (1973) with Czechoslovakia.
48. Cf. also Horst W. Schmollinger, 'Die Nationaldemokratische Partei Deutschlands', in Stöss, *Parteien-Handbuch*, vol. 2, pp. 1922ff.

European-nationalist course rapidly achieved considerable internal party influence and they soon succeeded in overthrowing the senior representative of West German right-wing extremism and splitting the party. They were split over the question of how to prevent the imminent downfall of the party and the supposed anti-nationalist and socialist policy of the SPD–FDP coalition: one militant wing supported and practised illegal methods and formed the nucleus for the Nazi combat groups which formed in the mid-1970s and which employed terrorist methods. A more leftist wing, which was dominated by intellectuals, was working on the renewal of the theoretical bases of right-wing extremism, consciously referring to the concepts of New Nationalism. Finally, those nationalist-conservative forces who were striving for co-operation with the right wings of the CDU and CSU became independent.

The NPD leadership was concerned to halt the process of decline by means of extra-parliamentary opposition to the federal government's policy of drawing up a treaty with the GDR. This right-wing extra-parliamentary opposition was intended to combine all factions of the nationalist camp and also to infiltrate nationalist middle-class circles, particularly the expellee associations. Initially, they were successful: in October 1970, the 'Aktion Widerstand' (Action Resistance) was formed and a rally was held in Würzburg in which thirty-four right-wing or right-wing extremist organisations are said to have taken part. Afterwards, a banned demonstration march was staged in the centre of the town, which, according to the organisers, swelled to 5,000 participants and was accompanied by a large number of violent riots. The new style of the right-wing militant group annoyed Thadden's group, who had been in favour of peaceful, legal demonstrations, and it was now forced to distance itself from particularly offensive slogans ('Shoot Brandt') and violent excesses.

Hence the 'Aktion Widerstand' proved to be a flop in terms of its original intentions and was quite incapable of preventing the NPD's decline. On the contrary, it accelerated it. At the beginning of 1971, the NPD withdrew from the action group, in March decided that it was incompatible to be a member of the NPD and a member of the militant combat groups and, at its party conference in November 1971, in Holzminden, decided

The Development of Organised Right-wing Extremism

that party work was to take precedence over activities within the framework of non-party organisations and alliances. Moreover, the initiative for the campaign against the treaties with the East and for replacing the federal government with a new style *bürgerblock* had since been deferred to the CDU/CSU. The latter were able to reach the head of an opposition movement to the social-liberal coalition by means of shrewd (direct and indirect) support to promote the emergence of a right-wing opposition alliance, causing the government's parliamentary majority to collapse temporarily. This process started with the FDP. Its left-wing liberal course was attracting increasing criticism from its right wing, which was hoping for an alliance with the CDU/CSU. Opponents of the party chairman Walter Scheel's policy in mid-1970 combined with representatives of expellee organisations to form the Nationalliberale Aktion (NLA), which later became the Deutsche Union (DU). In autumn 1970, several FDP members of parliament left the party and switched mainly to the CDU or CSU. They were followed by further opponents of governmental policy up to 1972 (including some from the SPD camp) so that in mid-1972, the coalition lost its majority in the Bundestag and had to call new elections.

The election campaign took place in a highly emotional and politicised climate. Confrontation and polarisation took on proportions previously unknown in West Germany. The CDU/CSU and their satellites conducted a campaign against the SPD and FDP supported by money and advertising from employers' associations and special support groups funded by industry and business. The campaign is said to have cost some DM 55 million. Slander, defamation, deception and falsehoods were commonplace. One particularly spiteful advertising campaign was aimed at personally disparaging the Federal Chancellor. The mouthpiece of the CSU, *Bayernkurier*, spoke demogogically of the 'last free elections' in West Germany unless the current government was removed.

The results of the Bundestag elections represented a clear victory for the social-liberal coalition. For the first time, the SPD became the strongest party (with 45.8 per cent) and the FDP improved its performance to 8.4 per cent. Its left-wing–liberal course had now been impressively confirmed (see Table 4.7).

Table 4.7 Election results of the Bundestag parties, 1969–87

Elections	CDU/CSU	FDP	Greens	SPD
SPD–FDP coalition				
1969	46.1	5.8	—	42.7
1972	44.9	8.4	—	45.8
1976	48.6	7.9	—	42.6
1980	44.5	10.6	1.5	42.9
CDU/CSU–FDP coalition				
1983	48.8	7.0	5.6	38.2
1987	44.3	9.1	8.3	37.0

In the following years too, attempts were continually made to undermine the SPD–FDP coalition by founding parties which leaned to the right. For example, in Berlin the Bund Freies Deutschland (BFD), which was led, *inter alia*, by conservative Social Democrats and Unionists, the Deutsch-Soziale Union (DSU), which was active in North Rhine-Westphalia, and the Aktionsgemeinschaft Vierte Partei (AVP), which has been active nationwide since 1975. These parties, which were generally founded as a result of calls from the CSU chairman, Franz Josef Strauß, did not achieve any noteworthy electoral successes, but were able to mobilise anonymous financial resources and polemicise against the social-liberal federal government more spitefully than their mentors would have been able to, playing the role of CDU/CSU 'reservists'. By causing political polarisation, moreover, they strengthened the integrative powers of the CDU/CSU, hence preventing right-wing extremist parties from profiting from the heated political climate.

The strategy preferred by the right wing of the CDU/CSU, led by the CSU chairman Strauß, of confrontation, obstruction and emotional appeal, also characterised the 1976 Bundestag election campaign, when it was suggested that the electorate's choice was a question of 'freedom or socialism'. The opposition did manage to secure additional votes as a result of this strategy, but although the SPD had to accept some losses, the opposition were nevertheless unsuccessful in bringing about a change in power. The Strauß faction laid the blame for this on the 'insipid' course taken by the party chairman and main candidate for

The Development of Organised Right-wing Extremism

Chancellor, Helmut Kohl, and now concentrated all their efforts on electing the CSU chairman, who since 1978 had also held the office of Bavarian prime minister, to become the new Chancellor candidate, and did so successfully. Strauß led the CDU/CSU into the 1980 Bundestag election campaign and was again forced to accept that his strategy of polarisation – especially as he himself was striving for the highest office of government – did not benefit his party but his hated opponent. Although the social-liberal coalition had been deeply affected by growing mass unemployment, violent ecological mass demonstrations and the rise of the 'Greens' and was internally divided, it again managed to achieve a viable working relationship against its common enemy. External pressure facilitated temporary stabilisation of the collapsing alliance and its electoral supporters: the CDU/CSU lost votes, the FDP won votes and the SPD stagnated (see Table 4.7).

Under these conditions the NPD had no chance whatsoever of retaining members and supporters, let alone of repeating something of its electoral successes during the second half of the 1960s. It could not even profit from the economic crisis,[49] which set in in 1974/5 and went considerably deeper than the recession of 1966/7. In the 1972 Bundestag elections it had already slipped to 0.6 per cent of the vote, and in the three following federal elections its electoral support was further reduced to 0.3 per cent and finally 0.2 per cent.

However, it was not only external factors that were responsible for its downfall, but also collapse from within. At the party conference in Holzminden in November 1971 (see above, p. 152), which was accompanied by upheaval and violence, serious disputes erupted regarding the course being taken by the party majority, led by Adolf von Thadden. The faction of his critics was led by the Bavarian *Land* chairman and member of the *Land* parliament Siegfried Pöhlmann, who denounced the

---

49. At the beginning of 1974, the government coalition entered into a period of political turbulence when Chancellor Brandt was forced to resign over a spy scandal and was replaced by Helmut Schmidt. This 'changeover', in fact, represented a political caesura. Brandt's reform policy, blocked by the economic crisis and the solid opposition from the CDU/CSU, employers' associations and the Catholic Church, now gave way to a pragmatic line under Schmidt, who avoided social reform and was content 'to govern the state decently'.

legalistic, parliamentary and middle-class property-owning policy of the party chairman and demanded that 'an image be created for the party by sensational actions'. In addition, he demanded a new orientation in the party programme, particularly in socio-political matters. The frustrated Thadden justified his course, complained about the internal conflict within the party, which he said had become impossible to lead, and eventually resigned from his post. Martin Mußgnug, from Baden-Württemberg, a member of the Thadden camp, was elected his successor (he still leads the party today). Pöhlmann was defeated, left the NPD together with his supporters shortly afterwards, and in January 1972 founded the short-lived Aktion Neue Rechte (ANR). Its 400 members formed a heterogeneous political spectrum, ranging from militant neo-Nazis to intellectual visionaries of a New Nationalism.

The NPD was exhausted organisationally, and in the following years eked out an unenthusiastic and inactive existence. In 1976 Mußgnug demanded internal renewal of the party, which admittedly was rather hesitant and initially only involved questions of content. When revising the party programme, they reverted in part to the ideas of New Nationalism. For example, they departed from the old-fashioned demand for reunification and spoke of a new unification of the German Reich (see Appendix 3). In 1982, the NPD officially renounced its pro-Western line and demanded that the FRG and the GDR leave NATO and the Warsaw Pact respectively. Since then they have seen themselves as 'the only party which represents the ideas of a reunified, non-aligned Germany'. In economic and social policy, too, the party propagated theories of the New Right:

> We are anti-capitalists. We are against Eastern state capitalism and Western liberal capitalism because we support a new social order in the framework of the German nation. . . . We have to allow the German worker to participate in the property, risk and yield of the German economy, in order to lead him, through this, to the German nation and to allow him to become a free citizen in this country.[50]

Important innovative input in their programme in the

---

50. Quotation from Report by the Office for the Defence of the Constitution 1985, Bonn 1986, p. 149.

Table 4.8 Development of membership of the Junge Nationaldemokraten, 1970–87

Year	Number	Year	Number
1970	1,100	1980	1,000
1972	1,100	1981	750
1973	1,400	1982	500
1974	1,300	1983	500
1975	1,300	1984	550
1976	1,800	1985	550
1977	1,500	1986	600
1978	1,500	1987	750
1979	1,400		

Source: Federal Ministry for the Interior.

1970s came from the youth organisation of the NPD, the Junge Nationaldemokraten (JN). In the 1960s, the party had initially made heavy weather of constructing a youth organisation. It did not achieve any real success until 1968. By 1976, the membership of the JN had risen to 1,800; but by 1982, had sunk again to 500 (see Table 4.8). In 1973/4 the JN became involved with the nationalist-revolutionary New Right (see below pp. 161–5 for further details) and advocated nationalist/anti-imperialist theories (see Appendix 4). However, it soon revealed clear sympathies for the militant neo-Nazi groups, who recruited some of their younger members from the youth organisation of the NPD. In 1977, the JN sought programmatic links with the citizens' initiatives and ecology movement, which was becoming more influential by speaking out against the construction of further atomic power stations in West Germany, and the JN adopted an 'ecological manifesto' which, one year later, also found its way into the programme of its parent party. Finally, in 1979, 'theories of socialism', in the sense of a Third Path between capitalism and communism, were worked out and agreed.

The further development of the NPD after 1979 was characterised by its campaign against immigrants ('Stop the immigrants – Germany belongs to the Germans'). With the growth of mass unemployment in West Germany, a xenophobic climate had emerged (see Table 3.5) which the NPD thought it would be able to capitalise on for its own political ends. In January 1980, party members in North Rhine-Westphalia founded the 'Bürgerinitiative Ausländerstopp' (Citizens' Action Group to Stop Foreign Immigration), which collected signatures for a referendum and for a petition to the Bundestag. In 1982, the Hamburger Liste für Ausländerstopp (HLA) was founded, which has since participated in parliamentary elections in the Hanseatic town in place of the NPD (see Table 4.5). At the same time, at the local government elections in Schleswig-Holstein the 'Kieler Liste für Ausländerbegrenzung' (Kiel List to Reduce Foreign Immigration), which was controlled by the NPD, was founded and achieved 3.8 per cent of the vote in their catchment area. Incidentally, similar attempts at founding groups in Hesse and Bavaria failed.

The programmatic renewal of the NPD and its campaign against immigrants (see Appendix 5) did not prevent it from losing members, nor did it recruit any new groups of voters. However, it did contribute to the internal consolidation of the party and facilitated a mood of new departures in the second half of the 1980s.

The Development of New Nationalism since 1965

In contrast to the NPD, New Nationalism as represented by the Aktionsgemeinschaft Unabhängiger Deutscher (AUD) was not able to profit politically from the collapse of the *bürgerblock*, the loss of integration of the major parties and the 1966/7 economic crisis.

Following the AUD's failure in the 1965 Bundestag elections, some of the party's 2,500 members switched to the NPD. Internal conflict between the supporters of the founding partners the DG and the DFP further weakened the party, which in 1967 attempted to join the extra-parliamentary opposition and function as its party-political arm ('a reconnaissance group for extra-parliamentary opposition in parliament'). Apart from the fact that at that time there was no sympathy at all in the extra-parliamentary opposition movement for political parties (after all, the movement considered itself to be in opposition to political parties), co-operation with nationalist organisations was out of the question. Consequently, the project of a Demokratische

The Development of Organised Right-wing Extremism

Table 4.9 AUD election results, 1965–78

Elections	Year	Number of votes	%	Seats
Bundestag	1965	52,637	0.2	–
	1976	22,202	0.1	–
Land Parliaments				
Baden-Württemberg	1968	11,030	0.3	–
Berlin	1967	15,507	1.1	–
	1971	9,136	0.6	–
Hamburg	1974	521	0.0	–
	1978	592	0.1	–
Lower Saxony	1978	1,293	0.0	–

Union (DU) at the 1969 Bundestag elections failed. And the AUD's 'left-wing course', which had been led by Haußleiter since 1969, was again expressed in membership losses. 'Currying favour with the extra-parliamentary opposition' and the alliance with the 'left-wing clowns' was hardly welcomed with open arms, not only among the extra-parliamentary opposition but also within the AUD. The majority of Haußleiter's supporters wanted to have nothing to do with the 'rebellious youth', and would not be convinced by Haußleiter that the nationalist and the extra-parliamentary opposition were ultimately both fighting against the same system. A dispute also broke out regarding the evaluation of the social-liberal coalition's détente policy within the AUD: while the group led by Haußleiter hoped it would be a step towards normalising relations between the two German states and hence towards national unity, his opponents criticised recognition of the GDR as cementing the division of Germany.

In 1970 the AUD had reached an organisational low: it still had 500 members, however. These loyal followers of the party chairman again started to search for a new social base, which they thought they would soon find in the movement of citizens' action groups, opponents of atomic power and ecologists. The AUD's self-image had now changed from a 'party of youth' to a 'party for the protection of life'. Its attempt to become the parliamentary arm of this new movement again failed, however. This was because the movement was moving towards founding

159

a party from within. Since 1978, Green or Alternative Lists had been founded at regional and *Land* level all over the country, which in January 1980 merged to form the federal party, 'Die Grünen'. Members and functionaries of the AUD were also involved in this founding process,[51] and initially were able to form a link between the more left-wing eco-socialist forces and more right-wing, conservative nature lovers. At the founding party conference, however, they were forced to disband their party if they wanted to continue their work together (the so-called 'incompatibility resolution'). Following a ballot among the AUD members, this occurred in November 1980.

Haußleiter, in recognition of his role as a mediator, was elected by the delegates as one of the three co-chairmen of the Greens, but in June 1980 was forced to resign because details of his right-wing extremist past became known and made headlines in the press. However, he continued to work actively 'at the grass-roots' and, in 1986, was elected to the Bavarian Landtag as a Green Member of Parliament. However, for health reasons, he was unable to take up the office. He died on 8 July 1989.

The self-disbanding of the AUD in 1980 meant the admission that, organisationally, New Nationalism, which had emerged as the conceptual variant of post-war right-wing extremism, had failed. This admission was also influenced by the fact that during the second development stage of West German right-wing extremism ('New Right-wing Extremism', after 1966), again in the bosom of the Old Right, nationalist-revolutionary groups had emerged, which appeared considerably more radical than the DG/AUD. They in turn appeared moderate by comparison, and, with their pseudo-left-wing style, were temporarily able to exercise a certain influence within the ecology and alternative movements. In ideological terms, however, the DG/

---

51. The AUD was not the only right-wing extremist group that sought to gain influence in the new party. The initial heterogeneity, the self-image of grass-roots democracy and the partly neutralist, partly all-German overtones in the Greens' discussion of their manifesto made it possible for various small groups from the area of Old and New Right temporarily to infiltrate them unnoticed. Their influence, however, was minimal, and a sensitivity towards right-wing extremist forces soon developed among the Greens. In the mid-1980s the majority of infiltrated right-wing extremists had either left or been forced to leave the party.

The Development of Organised Right-wing Extremism

AUD was the predecessor of the New Right groups: they supplied the main elements of their domestic and foreign policy demands. But with one difference: while the DG/AUD was oriented towards a nation-state, nationalist revolutionaries preferred the image of European nationalism. However, both fathers and grandsons were unanimous in the fact that the national question not only applied to divided Germany, but also included Austria.

The nationalist-revolutionary New Right, which at its peak of development organised some 1,000 members, is a product of the post-war generation. It consists of small circles of highly qualified intellectuals, who grew up in the period of reconstruction and the economic miracle, and who are particularly critical of technology and consumerism. In this respect, they hardly differ from left-wing intellectuals, but the main difference is that they consider the 'colonialisation' of Germany and the lack of German national identity to be the root of all evils.

The impetus for the emergence of New Right groups came from journals: first, the *Nation Europa*, published since 1951, containing controversial discussions regarding the problem of nationalism, then in 1964 *Fragmente* and *Junges Forum*. This was followed by small regional groups: mainly Hamburg, Berlin, Bochum and Munich. Many of these 'basis groups' took part in the militant activities of the 'Aktion Widerstand', almost all of them were involved in the founding of the Aktion Neue Rechte (ANR) in January 1972. The nationalist revolutionaries hoped to be able to influence the politically heterogeneous ANR from a programmatic point of view. The leading nationalist revolutionary, Henning Eichberg, is said to have drawn up the declaration of principles, which contains the following passage (see Appendix 6):

Modern nationalism is anti-imperialist
Modern nationalism in Germany is the policy of liberation. We employ the policy of unification of Germany against the beneficiaries of 1945, against the dividers [of Germany] and bureaucrats. Unification of Germany entails fighting the status quo, fighting the small state policy and the cementing of crazy borders. The Yalta system, 'murder at the wall', the division of territory must disappear, together with all those who try and justify it today.

> The solution to the national question in Germany cannot be separated from the fight against Soviet imperialism. We counter the capitulation policy of the treaties of Moscow and Warsaw with the solidarity of all repressed peoples.
> Our aim is a 'nation Europe' as a political unit. . . . The Europe of European socialism is the Europe of the people. A nation Europe as a major power in equal partnership with the United States is the only protection against the imperialism of the aggressive, peace-hating Soviet Union.

Central ideological elements of New Nationalism had entered the ANR party programme in the key words 'socialism'[52] and 'anti-imperialism', which admittedly was still far removed from a 'Third Path', with its anti-Soviet and pro-Western orientation and hence was hardly in a position to make an impression on the Left. This, however, was the intention of the nationalist revolutionaries as they had already proclaimed, in 1969, the golden age of extra-parliamentary opposition:

> We must use the means of the left to re-channel the restlessness of the left to the right. In the future, right-wing will mean, not reactionary, but progressive; not bourgeois, but socialist-revolutionary; not anti-intellectual, but conscious inclusion of rationality in politics; not state nationalism, but modern European nationalism.[53]

While the nationalist revolutionaries succeeded initially in extending their influence within the ANR, they inevitably became opposed to the 'bourgeois' and 'reactionary' forces, led by the chairman, Pöhlmann. The conflict ended with the nationalist revolutionaries leaving the party and, in March 1974, forming the Nationalrevolutionäre Aufbauorganisation (NRAO). However, disputes immediately erupted within the first ever nationwide, purely nationalist-revolutionary organisation regarding

---

52. On the national-revolutionary concept of socialism one NR member said in 1987: 'The NR [have] never supported the general abolition of private ownership of the means of production, but we do support socialism which is essentially co-operative and which also leaves room for private small-scale production (crafts, etc.) and in which only the major and key industries become state property. Co-operatives, however, are likewise 'private owners' of the means of production, because a co-operative, by its very definition, represents a voluntary merger of private individuals,' (*Studien von Zeitfragen*, 1987, no. 4, p. 12).
53. Margret Feit, *Die 'Neue Rechte' in der Bundesrepublik. Organisation – Ideologie – Strategie*, Frankfurt/New York, 1987, quotation p. 43.

the party programme (mainly concerning the concept of socialism), which led to a split. The right wing founded the Solidaristische Volksbewegung (SVB) on 24 August, while the left wing followed one week later with the Sache des Volkes/Nationalrevolutionäre Aufbauorganisation (SdV/NRAO). While the latter saw themselves as 'nationalist socialists', the members of the SVB described themselves as 'system changers within the framework of the constitution'. They rejected the label 'socialism' for tactical reasons, in order not to shock their target group. These were mainly conservative forces within the ecology movement. Towards the end of the 1970s, the SVB participated in the formation of Green Lists. In particular, they achieved considerable influence in the Hamburg Grüne Liste Umweltschutz (GLU), which was founded to compete with the left-wing 'Bunte Liste'. In the federal party, *Die Grünen* (The Greens), members of the SVB who were involved were initially on the extreme right wing, but left the party together with other conservative groups in 1981 and turned to small ecology parties, but these failed to achieve success in competition with the Greens.

The Sache des Volkes (SdV) saw itself as emphatically radical, conspiratorial/centralist and elitist, and was concerned to copy the cadre structure of the Maoist parties, which had emerged from extra-parliamentary opposition. In addition to the ecology movement, it appealed mainly to the Maoist[54] New Left, as well as to young people from the catchment area of the Old Right, particularly certain circles of the NPD's Junge Nationaldemokraten (JN) who were programmatically oriented towards the socialist nationalist revolutionaries. In 1975, for example, JN members congregated in the Nationalrevolutionärer Bund (NRB), which soon merged with the SdV.

In spite of their left-wing rhetoric, nationalism formed the central theme of the nationalist revolutionaries, who described themselves as socialist:

> The portrayal of events in the German divided states shows that Germany is a colony. Particularly in West Germany, much is made of

---

54. In this offshoot of the APO anti-Soviet and national-communist influences were dominant, in which certain connections to the left-wing Nationalrevolutionäre were to be found.

decolonialisation of the whole world, but they will not accept that they themselves are a colony . . .

The nationalist revolutionaries are in favour of a national, social, ecological, cultural and democratic revolution. It is not by chance that the national element is paramount. All other changes are pointless if our people do not possess any independence and self-determination. This is why Germany in particular must be liberated by nationalism![55]

In November 1979, the SdV split. A group centred on the magazine *Laser*, which had emerged eighteen months previously, condemned the inadequate criticism of capitalism, the anti-Soviet orientation and the centralistic structure of the SdV. A further group, which included JN members, centred on the magazine *Wir selbst*, with the main aim of infiltrating the ecology movement. Since *Wir selbst* and *Laser* could not come to an agreement, in April 1980 the *Laser* group formed the Nationalrevolutionärer Koordinationsausschuß (NRKA), which also included some former members of the Maoist parties. *Laser* merged with the new NRKA magazine *Aufbruch*. In the ensuing period, there was renewed *rapprochement* between the remainder of the SdV and the SVB – since 1980 they have called themselves the Bund Deutscher Solidaristen (BDS).

The small group of NRKA supporters co-operated with *Die Grünen* and the peace movement, where they were quickly persecuted, excluded or expelled as Fascists. Due to what was seen as their Marxist and pro-Soviet views, they were accused by their critics in the nationalist-revolutionary camp of being orthodox Bolsheviks. In order to avoid imminent isolation, the NRKA was disbanded in May 1987 and was replaced by the Politische Offensive (PO). By avoiding the description 'nationalist-revolutionary', it aimed to give its work a broader basis. However, because of this, and the fact that the party aimed to open up towards the left, disputes erupted again in 1987/8. Hence one critic of the left-wing course wrote:

> The current excessive adaptation to our opponents is already showing clear masochistic tendencies. I for one can no longer see why I should kick an NPD man in the behind who holds out his hand in

55. *Neue Zeit*, 1977, no. 4.

friendship but lick the boots of a member of the DKP [German Communist Party] or *Grünen* who is continually attacking me!

Since, overall, the left and the new social movements have proved to be largely immune to nationalist revolutionary ideas, it is possible that a move to the right, or rather a shift of target group, will occur among the few remaining nationalist revolutionaries. There is increasing evidence that they recognise the middle-class/conservative camp as a target group, particularly those groups and journals that support neo-conservative change around the CDU/CSU, including the Republikaner.

Whether or not this change will be successful remains to be seen. In any case the strategic calculation – with regard to the history of New Nationalism – is justified: if one disregards the particular post-war conditions, then the task of the New Right, who have always been insignificant numerically, has been to develop concepts and provoke discussions. New Nationalism was never suited to be a mass movement or a successful electoral party. It was too intellectual and unrealistic for this. Its function was to supply ideas and prepare the ideological ground for Old Nationalism, and it represented the innovative potential within West German right-wing extremism.

Violence and Terrorism

Since the mid-1970s, increasing militant tendencies have become apparent in the forefront of the right-wing extremist parties, which soon escalated to terrorist excesses. It was mainly – but not exclusively – a youth phenomenon and at the same time a renaissance of national socialism.

The causes of radicalisation lay first in the changing political climate since the beginning of the social-liberal coalition. The parliamentary and extra-parliamentary opposition's brusque political style *vis-à-vis* the federal government, which was previously unknown in West Germany, particularly regarding the treaties with Eastern bloc countries, literally encouraged violent action, which provoked secret joy among conservatives.

Second, left-wing terrorism emerged as extra-parliamentary opposition declined. Since 1970, groups like the 'Rote-Armee-Fraktion' (Red Army Faction), the 'Bewegung 2. Juni' (2 June movement)[56] and the 'Revolutionäre Zellen' (Revolutionary Cells) led an 'underground struggle' against the system, committing murders, bank hold-ups, kidnaps and bomb attacks, injuring and killing people in the process. In 1974, for example, the Berlin Supreme Court President, Günther von Drenckmann, was killed. In 1975, terrorists kidnapped the Berlin *Land* Chairman of the CDU, Peter Lorenz, and obtained the release of prisoners as ransom. In 1977, at the peak of their development, the Chief Federal Prosecutor, Siegfried Buback, and the chairman of the Board of Directors of the Dresdner Bank, Jürgen Ponto, were murdered. Shortly afterwards, Hanns Martin Schleyer, the president of the Federal Association of West German Employers' Associations, was kidnapped, costing his driver and several members of the police escort their lives. When the federal government failed to agree to the blackmail demands of the political gangster, Schleyer was executed.

The growth in right-wing violence occurred against the backdrop of increasing German right-wing extremist crimes (see Figure 4.6): it rose from 136 (in 1974) to 2,475 (in 1982). Extensive arms finds also characterised this period. Here are a few examples:

1979[57] 7 kg explosives.
          121 hand grenades.
          13 automatic firearms.
          44 rifles.
          118 hand guns.
          24 other firearms.
          144 cutting and stabbing weapons.
          10,000 rounds of ammunition.

1980   4 kg explosives.
          134 hand grenades and explosive devices.
          10 automatic firearms.

56. On 2 June 1967 a student, Benno Ohnesorg, was shot dead by a police-officer, Karl-Heinz Kurras, during a demonstration against the Shah of Iran.
57. In 1979 the television series *Holocaust* was shown in West Germany portraying the fate of the Jews under national socialism in graphic detail. The programme temporarily upset the way in which the Germans were coming to terms with the past in the form of repressing and glossing over national socialism. This triggered off particularly violent neo-Nazi activity.

Figure 4.6 Recorded crimes committed by German right-wing extremists, 1974–87

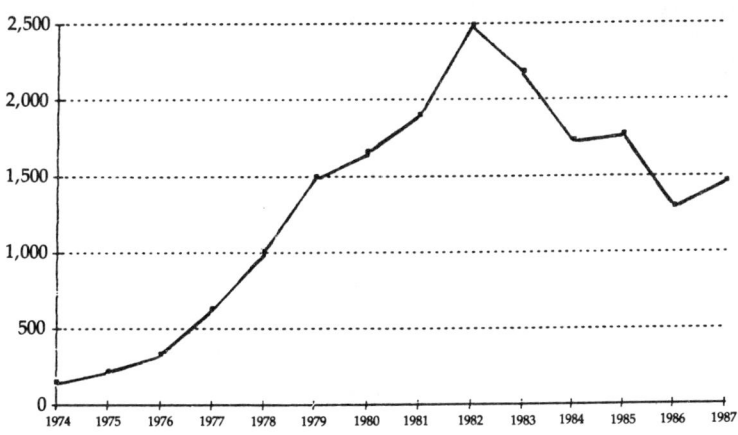

Source: Federal Ministry for the Interior

      55 rifles.
      51 hand guns.
      85 other firearms.
      315 cutting and stabbing weapons.
      21,000 rounds of ammunition.
      2,500 rounds of practice, explosive and tear gas ammunition.

In 1980 the following acts of violence (resulting in a total of seventeen deaths) were recorded:

– 6 bomb attacks.

– 2 murders.

– 15 arson attacks.

– 2 hold-ups.

– 27 cases of bodily harm.

– 61 cases of malicious damage to property.

In 1981 the police raided the arms cache of the forester Heinz

Lembke, who had fled from East Germany and then became active in various right-wing extremist organisations (including the NPD). In thirty-three underground stores he had collected an explosive arsenal:

- 156 kg explosives.
- 230 explosive devices.
- 50 bazookas.
- 258 hand grenades.
- 13,520 rounds of ammunition.
- 15 firearms, some of which were automatic.
- large quantities of chemical substances.

Lembke was arrested and committed suicide while in custody.

The sociological analysis of convicted right-wing extremist criminals in the period from 1977 to 1985 produced the following picture: 39 per cent were aged between 14 and 20, a further 32 per cent between 21 and 30. Nineteen per cent were unskilled labourers, 20 per cent skilled workers or craftsmen and a further 20 trainees.[58] Obviously, young people from the lower classes with below-average vocational training form the social basis of right-wing violence. This reflects the generation change within West German right-wing extremism. While the generation of post-war right-wing extremism had a fixation with the state, and preferred activities that were inherent in the system and (in their view) legal, the younger generation rejected the system to a much greater degree, were more prepared to take risks, and were more fanatic and activist. They sought credible models and supported an idealistic image of national socialism, which in their view comprised uncompromising hostility to the system, the willingness to fight unconditionally, complete brotherhood, unwavering devotion to the people, and heroic devotion to the Reich. Adolf Hitler, who for long had been revered uncritically, did not receive an appropriate acknowledgement until later. In

---

58. These and the previous statistics are taken from the Report on the Defence of the Constitution by the Federal Ministry for the Interior.

1982, the two right-wing terrorists, Odfried Hepp and Walther Kexel, published a statement under the title 'Departure from Hitlerism'. Since then, the number of voices describing Hitler as a betrayer of national socialism (because he, according to them, 'had turned the party into a capitalist, bureaucratic, bourgeois organisation'), has swelled. Instead of this many (but not all) neo-Nazis relate to the 'socialist' left within the NSDAP, led by the Strasser brothers in the tradition of the SA and its leader Ernst Röhm.[59]

The recruitment field for neo-Nazi organisations are, on the one hand, fringe groups of youth protest, particularly football supporters and skinheads (see the following section) and, on the other, right-wing extremist youth organisations, which represent an important halfway-house for neo-Nazi perpetrators of violence. These comprise primarily the Junge Nationaldemokraten (JN), the Wiking Jugend (WJ) and, to a lesser extent, the Bund Heimattreuer Jugend (BHJ).

From 1968, the aggregate development of the youth organisations showed another upturn following the preceding downfall during the mid-1960s, and this lasted until 1978. This upturn was decisively influenced by the JN, but the WJ and BHJ also regained a certain significance as non-party organisations. Since approximately 1973, nationalist revolutionary and neo-Nazi tendencies had been gaining in significance within the JN. In 1974 the organisation did distance itself formally from pro-Nazi circles, but this did not alter their widespread sympathies for the 'armed struggle'. (Former) JN members were becoming increasingly involved in illegal acts and acts of violence. In 1980, weapons, bombs and ammunition were found in the possession of the Junge Nationaldemokraten, in 1983 regional organisations in Bavaria had to be disbanded because they had co-operated with neo-Nazis, and in 1984 an 'organisational state of emergency' was declared on the entire *Land* association in North Rhine-Westphalia for the same reason. At the same time, there was no majority in favour of an incompatibility resolution for the JN with the largely neo-Nazi WJ. This was only possible in 1985,

---

59. Gregor Strasser and Röhm were murdered in 1934 under orders from Hitler. Dr Otto Strasser fled abroad in 1933, returned from exile in Canada to Germany in 1955 and founded an unsuccessful right-wing extremist splinter party (Deutsch-Soziale Union). He died in 1974.

Figure 4.7 Develpment of the membership of extreme right-wing youth organisations, 1959–87

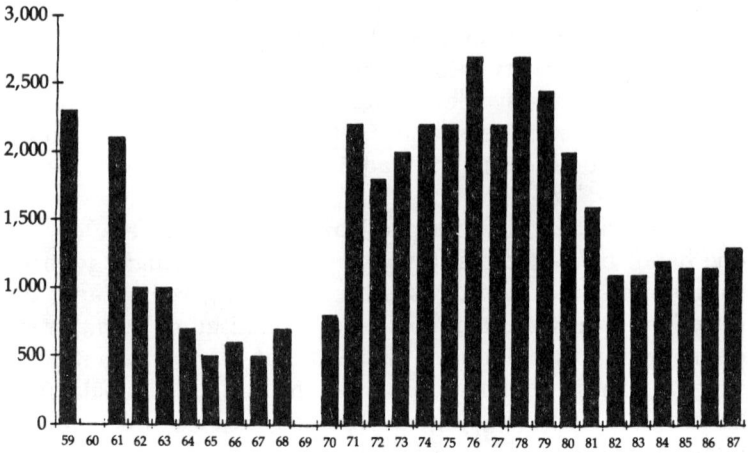

Source: Federal Ministry for the Interior

once the association had been consolidated and the militant influence had been repressed.

In the course of the 1970s, a division of principles characterized the two non-party youth organisations. While the BHJ increasingly gained the appearance of a national scouts' organisation and reduced its right-wing indoctrination of the young people, in the WJ, militarist neo-Nazi forces gained control. Attempts after 1980 to free the BHJ from the odium of right-wing extremism plunged the organisation into internal factional disputes. Following frequent changes in the office of federal leader, their work came to an almost complete standstill in the mid-1980s.

From the end of the 1970s, the WJ came under the influence of neo-Nazi followers, and of Michael Kühnen (see below p. 181ff). Paramilitary field exercises, fights and assaults were an everyday practice for the organisation, which had some 400 young members and which consciously followed the tradition of the Hitler Youth. In 1982 the Berlin authorities disbanded the Deutsche Arbeiter-Jugend (DAJ), which consisted mainly of WJ supporters, because it had conducted paramilitary field exercises, horded weapons and organised brutal attacks. In January 1985, co-operation with the (banned) Aktionsfront Nationaler Sozialisten (ANS), led by Michael Kühnen, adopted a new organisational form following the founding of the Volkstreue Außerparlamentarische Opposition (VAPO). However, within the WJ opposition to close co-operation with neo-Nazis soon emerged. Opposition centred on Rudi Wittig, who in 1987 stood unsuccessfully against the long-time leader Wolfgang Nahrath in the re-elections for a national leadership, and in September of that year Wittig left the organisation, taking his supporters with him. The remainder of the WJ continues to co-operate closely with neo-Nazis.

The neo-Nazi Network[60]

The formation of organised neo-Nazism began in the mid-1970s. Although after 1979 the response of government authorities was increasingly to ban and enforce legal measures, since then the membership figures have not declined noticeably. In 1987 (following the 1979 peak resulting from the screening of the television series *Holocaust*) there was another peak (see Figure 4.8) which was probably connected to Rudolf Hess's suicide. (He had been condemned to life imprisonment in the Nuremberg war trials and had been incarcerated since then in Berlin-Spandau.) Since Hess was one of the few Nazis to serve his full sentence, unable to benefit from the extensive amnesties in the 1950s, he represented a martyr figure for both Old and New Nazis. His supporters claimed that Hess had been murdered by the Allies ('Revenge for Rudolf Hess!'), and in 1987 they conducted a large number of spectacular demonstrations and acts of violence.

Overall, organised neo-Nazism was insignificant in quantitative terms, but its few members, generally active in small groups, possessed enormous criminal power. To my knowledge, no one has ever attempted to combine all neo-Nazi groups in a single organisation. The fact that so many organisations existed made it difficult for the government authorities and anti-Fascists to keep track and prosecute them. In addition, a

---

60. The data for this section are taken mainly from the Reports on the Defence of the Constitution by the Federal Ministry for the Interior.

Figure 4.8 Development of the membership of organised neo-Nazis, 1975–87

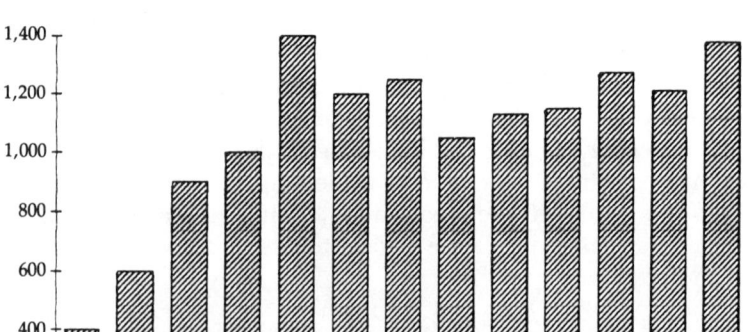

Source: Federal Ministry for the Interior

ban only ever affects one group and not all neo-Nazis.

The beginnings of Neo-Nazi violence can be traced back to 1968, when the NPD had begun to construct its *Ordnerdienst*, which provoked bloody disputes with political opponents in its role as an armed taskforce. Its leader, Klaus Kolley, had shot two demonstrators in 1969, and was sentenced to twelve months' imprisonment in 1974. His seven months in custody awaiting trial were deducted, and the rest of his sentence suspended. Hence the verdict was seen as virtually an incentive for right-wing extremist acts of violence.

Following the disbandment of the *Ordnerdienst* in 1970 by the NPD leadership, an increasing number of illegal armed groups began to form. In the same year, there was a raid on the Europäische Befreiungsfront (EBF), which consisted of members of the NPD and/or its *Ordnerdienst* who had set up an arms cache and, among other things, planned a military campaign against the meeting between Chancellor Brandt and the GDR Prime minister Willi Stoph in Kassel. In 1971, a former NPD member carried out an assassination attempt on the Federal President Gustav Heinemann (SPD), because he supported the federal government's *Ostpolitik*. Likewise, in 1971, a group of NPD members in North Rhine-Westphalia were arrested who were said to have planned armed attacks.

All the groups had some kind of connection with the 'Aktion Widerstand' and had become more radical in relation to the campaign against the treaties with Eastern bloc countries. This was also true of the Nationale Deutsche Befreiungsbewegung (NDBB), which saw itself as a preliminary stage to the formation of a new NSDAP. It comprised mainly NPD and BHJ members and carried out armed attacks. In 1971, the NDBB was raided, but this did not prevent sections of their activists from carrying out further actions later on.

The year 1971 was also very important to the emergence of violent right-wing extremist organisations because at that time the 'Aktion Widerstand', following the retreat of the NPD, began to disband and, as a result, many of the participating groups and organisations went their own way. This also applied to the circle led by Friedhelm Busse. He had joined the NPD in 1966 and had been expelled in 1971 because, together with his supporters – particularly after the 1969 Bundestag elections and particularly in connection with 'Aktion Widerstand' demonstrations – he had attracted publicity by means of riots and brawls. In June 1971, he founded the Partei der Arbeit (PdA) with the subtitle 'Deutsche Sozialisten' and propagated 'popular socialism against capitalist and communist exploitation'. Busse ostentatiously followed the tradition of the left wing of the NSDAP and the Strasser brothers, and moreover made no secret of his sympathies for the left-wing terrorist 'Rote-Armee-Fraktion' (Red Army Faction) which he considered to be a part of the West German nationalist-revolutionary movement.

Consistent with his beliefs, he and his supporters joined the Aktion Neue Rechte (ANR) and took over responsibility for federal executive strategy. Following its disbandment, Busse renamed his organisation the Volkssozialistische Bewegung Deutschlands/Partei der Arbeit (VSBD/PdA) and, following temporary co-operation with like-minded groups, led by Werner Kosbab and Karl Jochheim-Arnim, began to extend his party, which initially was organisationally confined to Bavaria. In 1979, the youth organisation Junge Front (JF) was formed; in 1980 a regional organisation in Hesse; and a further one in Lower Saxony in 1981. In its many, usually illegal and violent, campaigns, the VSBD co-operated closely with other neo-Nazi groups, particularly with the groups led by Schönborn, Christophersen, Kühnen and Curt Müller. In particular, the later Nazi terrorists, Walther Kexel, Frank Schubert, Arnd-Heinz Marx and Kurt Wolfgram, were prominent figures.

Schubert, who had fled from East Germany in 1977, shot and killed a Swiss police officer and a Swiss customs officer and seriously injured two other officials at the Swiss–German border on 24 December 1980. Schubert then committed suicide. Apparently, he had been trying to smuggle weapons and ammunition into the Federal Republic across the Rhine in a rubber dinghy. Two days previously, he had tried in vain with Kexel to call on a Swiss neo-Nazi who was to be a weapons supplier. In October 1980 Schubert was probably involved in a bank raid, when he got away with DM 34,000 (to purchase weapons?).

On 20 October 1981, the Munich police arrested five Nazi terrorists whom they suspected of planning serious crimes. They were armed with submachine guns and threw a hand grenade when they were caught, whereupon the police opened fire, killing two people. These were the VSBD member Wolfgram and the NSDAP/AO activist Klaus-Ludwig Uhl. Both had a previous conviction for a similar offence and had fled to France in 1980/1 to escape prosecution. The five right-wing extremists had previously stayed with the chairman of the VSBD (which now had 120 members) and he was likewise arrested. Large quantities of explosives were found in Busse's garage.

In January 1982, the Federal Minister for the Interior banned the VSBD/PdA and their youth organisation the JF. In 1983, Busse and a few of his accomplices were sentenced, the former to three years and nine months' imprisonment. Meanwhile, Busse's supporters formed a 'Nationale Front – Bund sozialrevolutionärer Nationalisten', which saw itself as the successor to the banned VSBD, and in November 1985 it constituted itself as a party under the name Nationalistische Front (NF). It possessed organisational bases in Munich, Bielefeld, Bremen and Berlin.

Both the VSBD and the NF propagated national socialism à la Strasser, verbally attacked both capitalism and communism, and demanded the unification of Germany and the joining of European nations to form an independent bloc between the two

The Development of Organised Right-wing Extremism

superpowers. Although the VSBD was strongly influenced by nationalist-revolutionary ideology and as such was to be classified as New Nationalism, their alliance partners moved predominantly in the field of Old Nationalism, or more precisely, national socialism or Neo-Nazism. This illustrates how fluid the boundaries are between the Old Right and the New Right.

Old Nationalism also includes those groups centred on the widely admired three 'old masters' of the Nazi scene, Thies Christophersen, Manfred Roeder and Erwin Schönborn, who had long worked closely together in their fight for the vindication of national socialism. Christophersen (born in 1918) had been a committed Nazi in his youth, and in 1944 worked in a satellite labour camp of Auschwitz as a member of the SS. As a result of his experiences, he later claimed, in his capacity as a 'contemporary witness', that in Auschwitz-Birkenau there had not been any mass gassings (see chapter 2). After the war, he claims to have been first a member of the CDU, then the Deutsche Partei (DP) and finally the NPD. In 1971, the Schleswig-Holstein farmer formed the Bürger- und Bauerninitiative (BBI), which still exists today. His publishing company, the Kritik-Verlag, published a number of pro-Nazi works, which were banned at various points in time. In 1980, he moved the publishing company to Denmark and in 1981 he avoided imprisonment by fleeing abroad, where he continued his agitatory and publishing activities as vigorously as ever. In 1983 he was finally arrested at the German–Belgian border and forced to serve his nine-month sentence. In 1984 he was released, but immediately came into conflict with the authorities again. In 1987, he absconded to Denmark, again to avoid imprisonment.

Since 1972, Christophersen had been working with the lawyer Manfred Roeder, who published the 'Auschwitz lie' in 1973. Roeder (born in 1929), was initially also a member of the CDU (from 1965), but he left in 1970 and in 1971 founded the Deutsche Bürgerinitiative (DBI). Politically, he initially fought against pornography, but soon turned to the 'fight for the Reich'. In 1975, he was able to purchase for DM 170,000, apparently from donations, a large estate (a 15-room hotel with 32 hectares of land) which he christened the 'Reichshof' and developed into a meeting point and education centre for his 'movement'.

Roeders fight was initially conducted more or less 'legally', or at least within the framework of those infringements of the law that are usual for right-wing extremists, without employing terrorist methods. For he initially saw himself as a successor to Hitler and Dönitz, as follows:

Since January 1975 he had been in correspondence with the former *Reichspräsident* Karl Dönitz, whom Hitler had named as his successor before committing suicide in April 1945. Dönitz was, in Roeder's opinion, still the legal head of the German state, since he had been prevented by the allies from carrying out his office by illegal means. The Reich government, he believed, had never resigned, never been discharged, never disbanded itself and also had never been dismissed by the German people. On 8 May 1945, only the army had capitulated. And since a valid peace treaty had never been signed with Germany (only a ceasefire), the German Reich, so he believed, still existed in its 1945 borders with Dönitz at its head. Consequently, the occupation and division of the empire were also invalid. He, Dönitz, had to declare whether he intended to continue to accept the office or whether he wished to renounce it. The retired Grand Admiral, having written to the lawyer in February, saying that he would leave it to his discretion to 'draw the legal conclusions', now declared unequivocally that he did not consider himself to be *Reichspräsident* of the German Reich. From this, Roeder concluded with incredible logic that as the Reich and the nation were now without a leader and had become incapable of action, and Dönitz did not wish to accept the responsibility of authorising anyone else, 'it is now a question of a new, original takeover of representation of the Reich. This is an elementary process. . . . The people's right to life bestows legitimacy on this process'.

Roeder summoned a 'Reich assembly' (Reichstag) to Flensburg for 23 May 1975, because thirty years previously the last German Reich government had been arrested in Flensburg following an 'unprecedented bandit raid' by the British and Americans. According to Roeder, those authorised to take part in such a Reich assembly were only those who actively supported the Reich, and since it was not possible for a free public gathering to take place in an occupied country, the first new convening of the Reichstag had to be an emergency assembly. This then took place as planned. In a barn decorated with the

Reich colours (black, white and red), Roeder and his likeminded cronies founded the 'Freiheitsbewegung Deutsches Reich', which elected Roeder as its speaker. Three years later, on 23 May 1978, it took over representation of the German Reich and Roeder was promoted to 'Reich Administrator'.

To those readers unacquainted with West German right-wing extremism, this may sound insane, but it soon became deadly serious. In 1978, Roeder went underground in order to avoid imprisonment (in connection with the Reichstag in Flensburg).

In 1979, Roeder, whom the police were pursuing with moderate diligence, managed to found the Deutsche Aktionsgruppen (DA) unhindered, because the 'legal' path had been exhausted and the fight must now 'be continued at a different level with even greater determination'. 'We will either win or perish.'

From February to August 1980, the DA carried out a total of seven bomb, explosive and arson attacks, primarily on the homes of immigrants and those seeking political asylum. Two people were killed and eight injured, some gravely. In September 1980, Roeder was arrested, and in 1982 sentences were passed against the leading DA terrorists: Raimund Hörnle and Sibylle Vorderbrügge each received life imprisonment for murder, Roeder and Dr Heinz Colditz received thirteen and six years' imprisonment, for being the ringleader and for membership of a terrorist organisation respectively. While in custody, Roeder continued to produce circulars for his supporters, some of whom his wife Gertraud entertained at social gatherings at the 'Reichshof'.

Erwin Schönborn, the third member of this group of former Nazis, is one of the most subversive activists within West German right-wing extremism. At the end of 1950, he moved from the East to West Berlin and began his career as the founder of many new organisations. In 1955 he was temporarily a member of the Deutsche Reichspartei (DRP); in 1956 he joined the Deutsche Gemeinschaft (DG), which he left, however, in 1957. In 1959 he was the co-founder of the Freie Sozialistische Volkspartei (FSVP); and in 1961 of the Freie Sozialisten Deutschlands (FSD). In 1967 he founded the 'Frankfurter Kreis deutscher Soldaten' (Frankfort Circle of German Soldiers), which fought against the apparent humiliation of German soldiers, cooperating closely with Christophersen and Roeder. Schönborn, who had been sentenced many times, transformed his Frankfurter Kreis into the Kampfbund Deutscher Soldaten (KDS) in 1975, and increasingly devoted himself to agitation against the 'war guilt lie' and the 'Auschwitz lie'. In 1977, he achieved considerable publicity with a leaflet offering a reward of DM 10,000 for any 'indisputably proved "gassing" in a "gas chamber" in a German concentration camp'. Of minor importance is the fact that, in 1979, the old man initiated a *Nationalsozialistischer Schülerbund*.

One important area of activity for neo-Nazis is *Wehrsport* (war games). During the mid-1970s, various *Wehrsportgruppen* (war games groups) were formed. They were based on the model created by Karl Heinz Hoffmann, founded in 1973, and banned in January 1980. During raids in Bavaria, Baden-Württemberg and Hesse, the police found twenty lorry-loads of steel helmets, gas masks, bayonets, camouflage battledress, uniforms, pistols, ammunition, hand grenades and propaganda material. It also confiscated twenty-five lorries and cross-country vehicles, a 12-ton armoured personnel carrier in need of considerable repair, an armoured tracked vehicle, military motorcycles, rubber dinghies, personnel carriers, a two-centimetre anti-aircraft gun, etc. Hoffmann's paramilitary *Wehrsportgruppe* (WSG) had 400 members and has had its headquarters in castle Ermreuth since 1978.

Hoffmann's group did not only carry out field exercises (hand-to-hand fighting, camouflage, forced marches, survival training) and military manoeuvres, in order to practise for the day 'when the police can no longer cope single-handed with the left'. It also protected property, policed right-wing events and attacked those of its enemies. Its particularly brutal action using tear gas, clubs, steel bars, iron shot, etc., distinguished it from other groups.

Hoffmann recruited his fighters 'against the red flood' from almost all neo-Nazi groups, from the Wiking Jugend (WJ) to the Roeder–Schönborn–Christophersen Connection to the Volkssozialisten. Walther Kexel and Arnd-Heinz Marx were functionaries of the Hesse WSG branch, Odfried Hepp played a leading role in the WSG combat group in the Black Forest, Udo Albrecht founded a WSG in the Ruhr region, and the editor of the *Deutsche National-Zeitung* and head of the DVU, Dr Gerhard Frey, paid a DM 8,000 fine for Hoffmann.

Figure 4.9 Leaflet issued by Erwin Schönborn in 1977

Kampfbund Deutscher Soldaten

10.000.- DM
Belohnung

zahlen wir für jede einwandfrei nachgewiesene "VERGASUNG" in einer "GAS - KAMMER" eines deutschen KZ's. Wir akzeptieren keine KZ - Zeugen aus Polen, Israel oder den USA, die, wie in den NS - Prozessen, MEINEIDE geschworen haben, ohne dafür belangt werden zu können.

Wir benötigen:
NAME, VORNAME, WOHNORT, GEBURTSTAG, GEBURTSORT, WO VERHAFTET, IN WELCHES KZ EINGELIEFERT UND IN WELCHEM KZ "VERGAST".

Verantwortlich: ERWIN SCHÖNBORN
(KDS) 1. Vorsitzender
6000 Frankfurt 56

Nine months after the banning of the WSG-Hoffmann, in September 1980, the right-wing terrorist Gundolf Köhler carried out a bomb attack at the Munich Oktoberfest, killing thirteen people and injuring 211 others. Köhler was also killed in the attack. Although he had good contacts with the Hoffmann group and had temporarily participated in their training, the attack was portrayed as the single-handed deed of a loner. Hoffmann was once again a free man. Together with the Palestinian resistance organisation 'Fatah', in 1980/1 he founded a paramilitary group in the Lebanon consisting primarily of WSG members for the armed struggle in West Germany. On 19 December 1980, shortly before 7 o'clock in the evening, the Jewish publisher and former chairman of the Israeli religious community in Nuremberg/Erlangen, Shlomo Levin, and his partner, Frieda Poeschke, were machine-gunned to death. The WSG member Uwe Behrendt was a suspect for the crime and died later in Lebanon of unknown causes. In June 1981, Hoffmann and his partner Franziska Birkmann, among others, were arrested on suspicion of their part in the double murder.

In 1982 a terrorist group, led by the former member of the Volkssozialisten, Walther Kexel, who had joined the WSG in Lebanon, and Odfried Hepp, carried out three murder attacks on members of the US army in Hesse, five bank hold-ups and possibly other crimes. In March 1985, five members of the group were sentenced to considerable terms in prison. Kexel received fourteen years' imprisonment, but avoided serving the sentence by committing suicide in prison. Hepp, who had disappeared, had in the meantime joined the 'Palestine Liberation Front' and was operating under orders from them, primarily in France and southern Europe. In April 1985 he was arrested in Paris for illegal arms procurements in the course of official investigations and after a sentence (of two years' imprisonment) was extradited to West Germany, in January 1987. In October 1987 he received ten and a half years' imprisonment for attempted murder, membership of a terrorist organisation, participation in a bomb attack and four bank raids.

One year previously, in June 1986, sentences had been passed on Hoffmann and some of his Lebanon comrades. Hoffmann received nine years and six months' imprisonment for counterfeiting, wrongful imprisonment, grievous bodily harm and offences against the Law on Arms and Explosives. He was cleared of the main charge of taking part in the murder of Levin and Poeschke. The court could find no proof that Hoffmann had ordered his deputy Behrendt to murder them; he could have done this without being ordered to do so by his boss. (The state prosecutor had demanded life imprisonment for Hoffmann.) Frau Birkmann received six months' imprisonment for not reporting a planned crime, which was cancelled out by her period in custody awaiting trial.

Finally, we shall consider one neo-Nazi who for a long time was considered to be a symbolic figure of the right-wing terrorist scene and who stage-managed his political activities largely with public appeal. He regularly invited the press to his planned events and even demanded 'entrance fees' from the journalists, who it seems often paid up. We are talking about the former Bundeswehr Lieutenant Michael Kühnen, who in 1969/70 was first involved in the NPD and the JN, then the ANR, then gave a brief guest performance in a Maoist party, then in the Aktionsgemeinschaft Vierle Partei (AVP) and finally in Roeder's DBI. In 1975, in Hamburg, the 'Freizeitverein Hansa' (Leisure group in Hamburg) was founded, whose circle of supporters was identical to that of the 'NSDAP *Gau* Hamburg'.[61] Kühnen brought together the members of the Freizeitverein to become a powerful combat force, which appeared in public under various names. In 1978, it consisted of some seventy-five young people, mainly from the Hamburg JN but partly from the WJ as well.

In November 1977, Kühnen, then aged 22, who openly declared his support for national socialism more than any other individual, founded the Aktionsfront Nationaler Sozialisten (ANS), which intended standing for the *Land* elections in Hamburg the following year. Schönborn promised to fill the list of candidates, which initially only consisted of Kühnen, Christian Worch and Tibor Schwarz, with representative personalities. The ANS 'battle programme' (see Appendix 7) concentrated on three demands: lifting the ban on the NSDAP, halting the building of atomic power stations and fighting against communism. The ANS withdrew its candidacy shortly before the election for two main reasons: on the one hand, it had failed to enlist

---

61. *Gau*: a Nazi term for an administrative district.

the required number of signatures; and on the other, in February 1978, a number of ANS members had been arrested for terrorist attacks. They had stolen weapons, ammunition and money in raids on a Bundeswehr barracks, an ammunition depot, a NATO military training area, Cologne businessmen and a Hamburg bank. Among those arrested were Uwe Rohwer, the leader of the Nordmark *Gau* of the WJ, who was also active in the NPD and the 'Stahlhelm'. His 'Wiking-Hof' in the north of Schleswig-Holstein was a military training centre for neo-Nazis from various organisations.

Kühnen was not arrested until the beginning of August. By then, he had been arrested nineteen times by the police for illegal flyposting of Nazi literature, marching in SS-type uniform, etc., but had subsequently been released on each occasion.

The ANS trial took place in 1979 in Bückeburg:

On 29 August 1979 the 'Nürnberger Nachrichten' described the atmosphere of the Bückeburg trial as a 'mirror-image of neo-Nazism'. This included the 'appearances of old and new Nazis, who often arrived in black uniforms and greeted the accused with a Hitler salute' and 'almost everyone who had any standing and reputation in the right-wing radical scene' entered the witness box. These ranged from paramilitary sportsmen to fairly mature SA stormtroopers, from members of the 'Gesellschaft für biologische Anthropologie und Eugenik' to the re-founder of the NSDAP, Gary Lauck, to swastika scrawlers, bomb builders and bomb-planters.[62]

Kühnen used the dock extremely shrewdly and successfully to disseminate his Nazi ideology. The press reported this detail, thus contributing considerably to the dissemination of ANS aims. The leading judge did little to check Kühnen and allowed the accused's lawyers a great deal of leeway to play down Nazi slogans. The leaflets that had been posted by the Kühnen group bearing the slogan 'Don't buy from Jews', for example, were publicly justified as a supposedly general call for a boycott. A lawyer (a member of the NPD) was even allowed to slander the chairman of the SPD and former Chancellor, Willy Brandt, saying that he had committed treason and was a spy.

---

62. Rudolf Schneider, *Die SS ist ihr Vorbild. Neonazistische Kampfgruppen und Aktionskreise in der Bundesrepublik*, Frankfurt, 1981, p. 66.

The Development of Organised Right-wing Extremism

On 23 August 1979, the US Nazi Gerald (Gary) Rex Lauck made his spectacular entrance. The court had even promised him 'safe conduct' because of the current preliminary proceedings against him, even though he had managed the NSDAP-AO (Auslands- und Aufbauorganistion) in West Germany from Lincoln (Nebraska) and had provided the Nazis with considerable amounts of propaganda material, especially posters, leaflets and stickers. Lauck has some thirty-five bases in West Germany, although the identity of the individuals involved is unknown. He apparently wishes to create the impression that his followers are the elite, the hardcore of West German neo-Nazis. Kühnen is also said to be, or have been, a member of the NSDAP-AO. At the Bückeburg court, Lauck, of all people, was a witness to the non-violence of the NSDAP-AO, which he then attested, although many direct and indirect indications in his own publications confirm the contrary.

The verdicts were pronounced on 13 September 1979. Kühnen's comrades-in-arms received sentences of between four and eleven years. Kühnen himself received a sentence of four years for incitement, inciting racial hatred, glorifying violence, etc. He was cleared of the accusation of being the ringleader of a terrorist organisation. No ban was issued against the ANS.

While Kühnen was serving his sentence, ANS activities declined dramatically, but his supporters were not completely inactive. At the beginning of 1981, Edgar Geiss distributed leaflets at Dönitz's funeral, in the presence of prominent right-wing extremists and leading representatives of established middle-class society. In May 1981, Friedhelm Enk and Michael Frühauf killed a comrade from their own ranks: Johannes Bügner had been accused of homosexuality and betrayal of the ANS. The 'underworld killing' brought both perpetrators life sentences.

At the end of 1982, Kühnen was released and regrouped his supporters. In mid-January he merged his old ANS group in Hamburg with other groups in Fulda and Frankfurt to become the ANS/NA (Nationale Aktivisten). Former members and supporters of the VSBD and the WSG-Hoffmann were involved. Thomas Brehl, Jürgen Mosler, Christian Worch and Arnd-Heinz Marx (who was later expelled) were given important positions. At the end of 1983, the organisation comprised some 270

Figure 4.10 An example of the propaganda material issued by Gary Rex Lauck

militant young people, who attempted to persuade groups of skinheads, rockers and football supporters prepared to use violence to work with them.

In June 1983 the Aktion Ausländerrückführung – Volksbewegung gegen Überfremdung und Umweltzerstörung (AAR) emerged as the parliamentary wing of the movement. The political party, led by Brehl, was launched during a 'Führer assembly' in the grounds of the house of the Nazi activist Curt Müller, a market-gardener in Mainz. Müller, his wife Ursula and his son Harald, had begun their Nazi career in 1969 with the NPD and the 'Aktion Widerstand', and soon formed bases in various regions of Rhineland-Palatinate. They distributed material from the NSDAP-AO and committed many offences. Müller had several previous convictions. At the end of January 1983, he organised a celebration on his estate for the fiftieth anniversary of Hitler's seizure of power, in which some 100 neo-Nazis took part. The AAR, which had been founded with his support, participated in the Landtag elections in Hesse in September 1983, where they achieved a negligible 890 votes only. The party was probably founded less with the intention of mobilising voters than of capitalising on the so-called 'party privilege': political parties in West Germany may only be banned on the basis of a verdict from the Federal Constitutional Court, while associations can be disbanded without a court verdict by the Federal and *Land* Ministers for the Interior.

Under intensive pressure from the anti-Fascist public, at the beginning of December 1983 the Federal Minister of the Interior disbanded both the ANS/NA and the AAR. The latter was not recognised as an independent party but was classified as a subordinate organisation of the ANS/NA. One month previously, Kühnen had been condemned to eight months' imprisonment in Brunswick. Since the sentence was suspended, he was immediately released, and allowed to pay off his fine of DM 1,200 in twelve monthly instalments.

In mid-April 1984, a trial opened against a mere eight ANS members. The main accused was Arnd-Heinz Marx, who was put behind bars for two years and three months. Proceedings against Kühnen and six other neo-Nazis were conducted separately, so that the leader of the ANS was able to observe the events from the spectators' gallery. He managed to avoid his own trial by fleeing abroad. The French authorities deported him in October, and 'his' trial was able to begin in 1984 – his co-defendant was again Marx. Both men were greeted by their supporters in the courtroom before the trial began with applause and cries of 'Sieg Heil!'. In January 1985 the court sentenced Kühnen to three years and four months' and Marx to two years and six months' imprisonment.

Since the ban on the ANS/NA and the AAR, Kühnen's supporters have sought to join other organisations with the aim of gaining control of them. The objects of their infiltration are the HNG and the FAP.

The Hilfsorganisation für politische Gefangene und deren Angehörige (HNG) was formed in 1979 to support incarcerated neo-Nazis, but soon developed into a control instrument for neo-Nazi groups. The 1984 Report on the Defence of the Constitution classified them as the neo-Nazi organisation with the greatest number of members. At that time, in February 1984, the co-founder and chairman of the HNG, Henry Beier, was replaced by the former ANS activist[63] Christa Goerth, and Christian Worch was appointed editor of the HNG newspaper, *Nachrichten der HNG*. The Kühnen group's influence grew so rapidly that the HNG was soon suspected of being a successor organisation to the banned ANS/NA, especially as Kühnen had the particular privilege of being in charge of the 300 supporters (1988) of the HNG.

Following the ban on the ANS/NA, infiltration of the Freiheitliche Deutsche Arbeiterpartei (FAP), founded in 1978, began. The initiator and only activist of this party, which initially was confined to the Stuttgart area and numbered 196 members, was Martin Pape, who tended to operate at the fringe of the rightwing extremist camp with his pronounced bourgeois views. From 1968 to 1978 his small group of supporters had gone under the name 'Sozial-Liberale Deutsche Partei', which in particular promoted Pape's candidacy as their only candidate in the 1969 and 1976 Bundestag elections, the 1972 Baden-Württemberg

---

63. Neo-Nazi groups consist mainly of boys or men. Girls and women are the exceptions. In April 1983 the ANS founded a 'Mädelbund' ('Girls' League'), and in December 1984 a 'Deutsche Frauenfront' ('German Women's Front') was founded in Hamburg from supporters of Kühnen, in which Ursula Müller and Ursula Worch, wife of Christian Worch, held leading offices.

The Development of Organised Right-wing Extremism

Land parliament elections and the 1974 Stuttgart *Bürgermeister* (mayor) elections. In 1984, ANS activists began to found local and regional associations outside of Pape's catchment area. In 1987, the party had over seven *Land* associations with a total of 500 members (their own figures), with the group in North Rhine-Westphalia particularly active. This is where Jürgen Mosler, the former shop steward in the Rhine-Westphalia *Gau* area and later opponent of Kühnen, operated.

The FAP held their first national party conference in June 1986 in Stuttgart, where they passed a 'programme of action' which – apparently for tactical reasons and in view of future election campaigns – avoided open support of national socialism, thus becoming too 'harmless' for many ANS supporters. By participating in elections the FAP was actually pursuing propagandist aims. The results (see Table 4.10) were hardly worth mentioning; often the party was not even able to gather together enough signatures to take part in the election (for example, in Hesse and Schleswig-Holstein in 1987).

Pape was concerned to repress neo-Nazi influence within the FAP to a certain extent. True, they had helped him to become a nationwide organisation with considerable publicity. But he was always aware of the possibility that his party could be banned, because its members were repeatedly involved in violence and terrorism. In 1986/7 there were numerous arson attacks, assaults, injuries, damage to property and propaganda offences, even within Pape's sphere of influence: the FAP candidate for the 1984 Baden-Württemberg Landtag elections, Markus Mössle (former member of the NPD), was condemned to a total of over sixteen years' imprisonment in 1985 and 1987 for various bank raids. Mössle had joined the neo-Nazi group, led by Ernst Tag, immediately after the 1984 election, which, following Kühnen's arrest, attempted to win his supporters for itself, especially as the two groups entered into a dispute. (The attempt failed, by and large.) Tag polemicised so strongly against the incarcerated Kühnen (whom he accused of being a homosexual) that Kühnen's friends threw him out of the HNG. Tag now manages a 'national socialist centre' in Rhineland-Palatinate to educate and train his supporters, which he re-named 'Rudolf Hess Haus' in 1987 following Hess's suicide.

Among Kühnen's 500 supporters, who have called themselves

Politics Against Democracy

'Die Bewegung' ('The Movement') since 1986, violent disputes erupted to elect a successor which were expressed in the form of verbal attacks against homosexuality and the necessary qualification of leadership forces in the neo-Nazi scene. Kühnen's opponents, led by the organisational leader Jürgen Mosler and his deputy Volker Heidel, denounced homosexuality in Nazi circles with reference to their former leader, describing it as a 'destructive, sick abnormality'. 'Gays will be excluded from the Movement,' they threatened. In this context the editor of *Nachrichten der HNG* and Kühnen supporter, Worch, was replaced by the Mosler supporter, Heidel. Kühnen and his deputy Brehl, on the other hand, justified homosexuality and did everything possible to regain their leadership position. At the end of 1988 it was still uncertain which faction would win.

In total, the dynamism of Nazi terrorism may have been considerably reduced by government and statutory measures against groups led by Busse, Roeder, Hoffmann and Kühnen. It is still uncertain what will happen once the leaders of the neo-Nazi scene are released. I suspect that the phase of violence and terrorism is coming to an end because (as in the area of left-wing terrorism) the opinion, based on personal experience, is asserting itself that in Germany, political aims cannot be realised by means of underground resistance.

There is as yet no academic comparison of state reactions to left-wing and right-wing terrorism. Individual studies,[64] however, support the theory that the police and the judiciary expend considerably less energy in pursuing and sentencing right-wing terrorism than is the case for left-wing terrorism. There are numerous examples of the way in which right-wing terrorism is glossed over, ascribed to individuals and isolated from its right-wing extremist political background.

Protest Behaviour

The increase in violence and terrorism since the mid-1970s went hand in hand with a different phenomenon, which is difficult to understand from an academic point of view, and which is

---

64. Cf., for example, Hermann Vinke (ed.), *Mit zweierlei Maß. Die deutsche Reaktion auf den Terror von rechts. Eine Dokumentation*, Reinbek, 1981.

The Development of Organised Right-wing Extremism

virtually impossible to quantify, but of whose existence the inhabitants of large cities and industrial conurbations, in particular, are continually reminded. We are talking about pro-Nazi protest action: youths painting swastikas, SS runes, Nazi slogans and sayings on walls and school blackboards, chanting nationalist, anti-Semitic and racist slogans and telling so-called Jewish and Turkish jokes, festooning their clothes, school bags or motorbikes with militaristic and Nazi symbols and wearing uniform-like clothing (black leather, army belts, army boots, parachute boots, *Bundeswehr* shirts and trousers). They frequently carry out violent attacks on minorities (teachers, immigrants, participants in anti-Fascist meetings, 'hippies', 'tramps', 'left-wingers'), disrupt meetings or just cause trouble. They sometimes join gangs or motorbike clubs, form football supporter clubs or develop their own style of protest (e.g. rockers, skinheads).

This behaviour is not usually based on a political identification with national socialism. It is the expression of a widespread dissatisfaction, particularly among urban youth, who want to shock and provoke their social milieu and vent their frustrations in aggressive behaviour, abusive language, a militant appearance and acts of violence.

Pro-Nazi protest behaviour came and went like the tide. The statistics for offenders in the Reports on the Protection of the Constitution (which have been published since 1962) show that the extent of neo-Nazi and anti-Semitic, 'crowd psychology-induced' incidents carried out by young vandals fluctuates. In connection with one large anti-Semitic wave of graffiti in 1960 (in which many Jewish cemeteries were desecrated) a total of 1,083 offenders were recorded, and this was only the tip of the iceberg: 46 per cent of recorded incidents – according to the Department for the Defence of the Constitution – were 'carried out by apolitical hooligans or were drug-induced offences' (later also termed 'mindless crimes'). In the following year, 26 per cent of the incidents recorded gave the following motives: a craving for sensationalism and admiration, an aimless, aggressive urge among vandalising hooligans to do something, immature impulses and psychological disturbances.

In the late 1970s, a new wave of pro-Nazi protest activities erupted, which initially engulfed the schools and youth clubs,

189

Table 4.10 FAP election, results, 1980–89

Elections	Year	Number of votes	%	Seats
European Parliament	1989	19,151	0.1	–
Bundestag	1987	403	0.0	–
Land Parliaments				
Baden-Württemberg	1980	69	0.0	–
	1984	338	0.0	–
	1988	54	0.0	–
Bremen	1987	256	0.0	–
Hamburg	1986	713	0.1	–
North Rhine-Westphalia	1985	929	0.0	–

followed a short time later by football fans, punks, motorbikers, rockers and skinheads. In 1979 the 'Nazi renaissance' in schools reached its peak. In Berlin almost all types of school were affected.[65] For example, at a commercial college, pupils were asked to write English sentences in the future tense. One youth wrote, 'Next year I'll smoke a *Jude* in my pipe.' (He did not know the English word for 'Jew'.) During the art lesson pupils in a comprehensive school sang 'The nights in Auschwitz are long'. The walls of a secondary school in Wedding were sprayed with Nazi and racist slogans by unknown culprits. At a secondary school in the same area, a female Jewish teacher was terrorised. The pupils painted the Star of David on the blackboard, put swastikas made of matchsticks on the desk and pronounced 'USA' as 'Jew SA' in the English lesson. At a technical college in Tiergarten, Fascist graffiti was a common sight. In addition to SS runes, it also included the following sentences: 'Erik Dorf[66] lives on!', 'Give us a second Auschwitz!', 'Kill the Turks!', 'Only dead Turks make good firewood!', 'Long live the NPD!', 'Bring back Adolf Hitler!'. Two pupils at a grammar school in Schöneberg

65. Richard Stöss, 'Pronazistisches Protestverhalten in der Schule. Ursachen und Ausmaß', in *Extremismus und Schule, Schriftenreihe der Bundeszentrale für politische Bildung*, no. 212, Bonn, 1984, pp. 171ff.; Stöss, 'Pronazistisches Protestverhalten unter Jugendlichen. Schüler – Fußballfans – Punks – Skinheads – Nazi-Rocker', in Alphons Silbermann and Julius H. Schoeps (eds), *Antisemitismus nach dem Holocaust*, Cologne, 1986, pp. 163ff.
66. Nazi character from the television series *Holocaust*.

The Development of Organised Right-wing Extremism

used anti-Semitic slogans ('The only thing that Jews have in common with human beings is their bone structure'), greeted one another with 'Heil Hitler' or 'Heil Deutschland', and drew up extermination lists. One teacher at a comprehensive school in Tempelhof found scrawled across the blackboard: 'There is nothing more beautiful on earth than when Jews are gassed', 'Gas [name of the teacher] the Jewish pig!'. 'You old Jewish cow' is said to have been a common insult there.

This list could easily be extended if one were to include youth clubs, where the pro-Nazi protest was obviously expressed after school, training centres and the workplace. Extensive instructional and educational policy measures by teachers and social workers caused the protest to fade away at the beginning of the 1980s or to be transferred to other areas, mainly football stadia, where Fascist-inspired brawls, usually among drunken fans, increased. Berlin football supporters unashamedly named their group 'Zyklon B'.[67] In 1982 the brutality and militancy reached proportions previously unknown in Germany. One member of a supporters' club even died during a bloody brawl. Supporters of the opposing team, whose clubhouse was said to have been decorated with swastikas and pictures of Hitler, were suspected of killing him.

Since approximately 1981, anti-Fascist punks[68] and skinheads have been involved in violent street brawls. The targets of the skins' attack are squatters, Turks, Jews and 'hippies'. 'Hunting down the foreigners' is one of their favourite hobbies, and in 1985 two young Turks were killed as a result. And since 'Germany belongs to the Germans' and 'Forcigners out!' are favourite skinhead slogans, foreigners are also the preferred target-groups of right-wing extremist, particularly neo-Nazi, organisations. In this context, one should also mention Kühnen's supporters in the ANS and FAP, as well as the NF in North Rhine-Westphalia and Berlin. However, the NPD did not remain on the sidelines: in Hamburg, connections were discovered with the HLA, and in April 1984, 100 skins actually formed a protection group for the NPD *Land* party conference in

---

67. Gas used by the Nazis to murder Jews in the concentration camps.
68. The campaigns 'Rock against Racism' and 'Punks against Fascism' were also reflected in West Germany.

191

North Rhine-Westphalia. In Baden-Württemberg the motorbike club 'MC National', with some 100 members, is largely dominated by NPD members. The circle, led by Michael Kühnen, devoted particular attention to skinheads, right-wing rockers and football supporters. The leader of the neo-Nazi fanclub 'Borussenfront', Siegfried Borchardt (known as 'SS-Siggi'), was the main FAP candidate for the 1985 Landtag elections in North Rhine-Westphalia and later became the *Land* chairman of the FAP. He is considered to be a brutal thug and has many previous convictions.

Attempts by neo-Nazi organisations to recruit their successors from the field of pro-Nazi youth protest had, and still has, only moderate success, mainly among skinheads, because pro-Nazi protest behaviour has little in common with organisational commitment, regular party work or programmatic identification. The young people can be used temporarily to protect meeting rooms, and for fights and disturbances, but generally will not allow a specific organisation to make demands on them in the long term. They are also afraid of the risk of long prison sentences. Their brutality should not be trivialised and it is not my intention to claim that they are merely apolitical hooligans. They are unsuited to regular opposition activity, but many of them are happy to allow themselves to be used for the aims and means of right-wing extremism.

Outlook: Further Electoral Success?

In the mid-1980s, right-wing extremism's third wave of organised party success commenced in West Germany, and it has probably still not reached its peak. The upwards trend was indicated in the 1984 European elections when the NPD with 0.8 per cent (just under 200,000 votes) was able to chalk up a relatively good result. In 1986, the chairmen of the NPD and Deutsche Volksunion (DVU), Mußgnug and Frey, agreed that the two organisations should work together, producing further electoral success. At the 1987 Bundestag elections, the NPD mobilised over 225,000 voters (0.6 per cent), and in the same year right-wing extremists were able to win a parliamentary seat at *Land* level for the first time since 1968: in Bremen the DVU

The Development of Organised Right-wing Extremism

managed to overcome the restrictive clause. In 1988 the Baden-Württemberg NPD achieved 2.1 per cent of the vote, and in Schleswig-Holstein, 1.2 per cent. In 1989 the Nationaldemokraten in Hesse entered several local government parliaments, in Frankfurt, for example, it has seven members.

However, the real breakthrough was achieved not by the old-established right-wing extremist organisations but by the Republikaner, founded in 1983, who were not considered, officially, to be right-wing extremist. In 1989, they easily overcame the 5 per cent hurdle twice: in Berlin they won eleven seats, and in the European Parliament six seats with over 2 million votes.

Co-operation between the NPD and DVU

The Munich publisher, Dr Gerhard Frey, is one of the most influential and strongest financial representatives of right-wing extremism in West Germany. He controls a printing and publishing conglomerate, which, in addition to records, tapes, medals and trips to South Africa, supplies the three right-wing extremist weekly journals with the greatest circulation: namely, *Deutsche National-Zeitung* (DNZ), *Deutscher Anzeiger* (DA), and *Deutsche Wochen-Zeitung* (DWZ).

The total weekly circulation of the three journals, which in some cases are identical in their content, is some 110,000 copies according to the Office for the Defence of the Constitution. (Frey himself claims 600,000.) The flagship of the Frey press is the DNZ, the largest of the three, a rabble-rousing gutter-press paper which produces countless variations on the theme of questioning Germany's sole guilt for the Second World War and the holocaust, polemicising against the 'victors' (over Hitler's Germany), discriminating against foreigners, and, more recently, strongly criticising the Federal president, Richard von Weizsäcker (CDU), for his balanced evaluation of national socialism (see chapter 2). The same technique is used each time: in giant headlines, statements of fact are suggested, which are either pure polemics or are formulated as questions, promising revelations which do not appear at all in the text. Here are a few examples from the DA and DNZ:[69]

69. All examples are taken from the Reports on the Defence of the Constitution from the Federal Ministry for the Interior of 1985, 1986 and 1987.

193

- Who was responsible for the Second World War – Documents Exonerate Germany – Will Hitler be Reassessed?
- Who forced Hitler into War?
- Hitler's Guilt – Fact and Fiction.
- Was Hess's Sentence Valid?
- Rudolf Hess: The End of a Tragedy – What Happened in Spandau.
- The Plan to Exterminate the Germans – Secret Documents Found.
- Raped, Shot, Killed – the Unatoned Murders of the Victors.
- How Weizsäcker is Burdening the Germans – What is the Federal President's Intention?

Frey's organisational involvement began with the campaign against the 1970/1 social-liberal federal government's *Ostpolitik*. When the decline of the 'Aktion Widerstand' was foreseeable, in January 1971, he founded the DVU as a neutral middle–right alliance against 'anti-constitutional treaties with the East' and as a gathering-place for the declining NPD. Frey encouraged this process by working closely with the ANR chairman, Pöhlmann, although the ANR, which was classified more as a New Nationalist party in terms of its party manifesto, had little in common with Frey's Old Right. In 1972 he created the *Freiheitlicher Rat* as a leadership committee to prepare for a 'March on Bonn', which took place in April of that year with some 5,000 participants. Until 1973 Pöhlman belonged to the Freiheitlicher Rat as a representative of the ANR, as did the Stahlhelm until 1976 and the Wiking Jugend (WJ) and the Jugendbund Adler (JBA) until the end of the 1970s.

In 1979/80, Frey restructured his supporters. In place of the co-ordinating council, organisations gained prominence in the DVU aimed at specific target groups, with membership in one of these organisations automatically conferring membership of the DVU. The following action groups currently exist:

1. Volksbewegung für Generalamnestie [People's Movement for General Amnesty].

The Development of Organised Right-wing Extremism

Figure 4.11 Development of DVU membership, 1971–87 (including subsidiary organisations and Liste D)

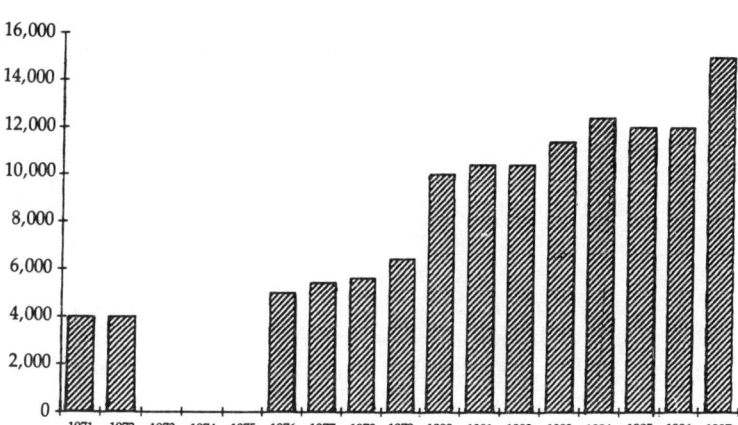

Source: Federal Ministry for the Interior

2. Initiative für Ausländerbegrenzung [Initiative to Limit Foreign Immigration].
3. Aktion deutsche Einheit [Action Group for German Unity].
4. Aktion deutsches Radio and Fernsehen [Action Group for German Radio and Television].
5. Ehrenbund Rudel – Gemeinschaft zum Schutz der Frontsoldaten[70] [Rudel League – Society to Protect Front-Line Soldiers].
6. Schutzbund für Volk und Kultur [Protection League for People and Culture].

Neither these supporting organisations nor the DVU represent actual associations where the members are continually

---

70. Hans-Ulrich Rudel (1916–82) was and still is considered in right-wing extremist circles to be the absolute personification of the brave German soldier. He received the highest military honours and enjoys a legendary reputation. As the pilot in a dive-bomber, he is said to have destroyed 519 Russian tanks in 2,530 attacks. In the 1950s he became involved in the DRP and was a popular guest at all right-wing extremist events. In the 1970s and 1980s he was a publicity magnet, particularly for the business-minded Frey, who used him as a speaker.

195

involved in internal decision-making and political activity in the sociological sense. Basically, they are associations to support the interests of their mentor, both financially and ideologically. Membership is granted in exchange for a low contribution (DM 3 for the action groups and DM 5 for the DVU) and in each case obliges the member to accept a list of insipid (even by right-wing extremist standards) political goals. The members are also obliged to subscribe to the Frey press (at a monthly rate of DM 8.35!) and to participate in the few central 'major meetings' organised by the owner of the group of companies. Therefore, the official membership figures (see Figure 4.11) – 12,000 in 1987; Frey himself claims 16,000 – can only be compared to a very limited extent with the corresponding figures for political parties such as the NPD. Nevertheless, the DVU has been the largest right-wing extremist organisation in West Germany since 1980 (see Figure 4.12).

The DVU is a non-party organisation, and as such, does not participate in elections. Until 1986, Frey rejected all speculations that he intended to convert the DVU into a party. In November, he began to call in his papers for the foundation of an electoral list (which he termed the 'Deutsche Liste', which later became the 'Deutsche Volkliste'). On 5/6 March 1987, the political party 'Deutsche Volksunion – Liste D (DVU)' was eventually founded. It exists independently alongside the non-party DVU and currently has over 2,500 members according to official statistics (Frey claims 6,000). The monthly membership subscription is DM 3. Both DVUs are led by Dr Gerhard Frey himself.

The founding of the Liste D (D standing for Deutschland) and the businessman Frey's entry into party politics was brought about primarily by the fact that there had been no deep political change in government in Bonn, the fact upon which right-wing extremist parties in West Germany base their hopes of a new upswing.

On 1 October 1982, the social-liberal era had come to an end. The Chancellor of the SPD–FDP coalition, Helmut Schmidt, was overthrown by a vote of no confidence. The Bundestag elected the former leader of the opposition, Helmut Kohl (CDU), as his successor, who has been the head of government in a CDU/CSU–FDP coalition since then. The change in power, which the

The Development of Organised Right-wing Extremism

Figure 4.12 A comparison of the development of membership in the NPD and the DVU

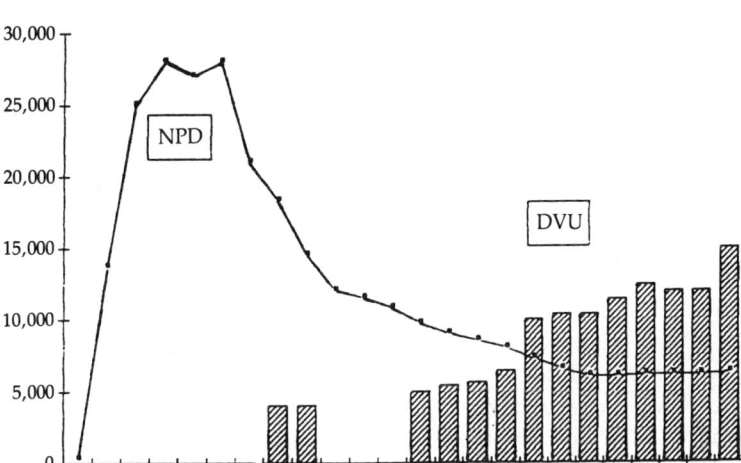

Source: Federal Ministry for the Interior

CDU/CSU had been striving for since 1969, was hence not the result of an electoral decision by the West German people. Rather, the FDP had changed its coalition policy, because its political differences with social democracy, which had been growing since the end of the 1970s (particularly over matters of economic and social policy), had recently begun to appear insurmountable. The Liberals demanded a neo-Liberal turning back ('*Wende*') in economic policy in view of the severe economic crisis, and in particular, demanded swingeing cuts in the social welfare area. This was unacceptable to the SPD. Previous social welfare cuts had already brought the party into headlong conflict with the trade unions, with the effect that loyal voters among the union-oriented SPD were turning away from the SPD in large numbers. On the other side, the Greens were making inroads into the SPD's electorate. Since 1978 the 'parliamentary arm' of the ecology and peace movement had been experiencing a meteoric rise. In 1979, the Greens entered a *Land* parliament for the first time, and since 1983 they have also been represented in the Bundestag.

With regard to electoral success, the SPD had come to the end of the road in 1982, but the FDP also faced considerable problems resulting from the success of the Greens: in 1984 they were only represented in four (out of eleven) *Land* parliaments and had slipped to fourth place in the party stakes, behind the Greens. They hoped to reconsolidate their electoral basis by changing their coalition policy orientation (which has since occurred).

What did not happen, according to right-wing conservative circles, is what the CDU/CSU had supposedly or actually promised during their campaign against the social-liberal coalition: a fundamental intellectual and moral change towards a consistent conservative policy. These circles were stepping up their calls for such a change, which would entail the following: a diminution of the influence of the state and bureaucracy, renewal of the family, overcoming the socialist-nihilistic 'cultural revolution', which had apparently been caused by the social-liberal era, the re-establishment of traditions and historically-proven values and virtues, and finally, the recreation of the German national consciousness.

The dissatisfaction of right-wing conservative circles with CDU/CSU policy was partly reflected in their electoral results (see Table 4.7). When the CSU chairman Strauß negotiated a loan of some thousand million Deutschmarks to the GDR, causing great controversy among his followers, the CSU Bundestag members, Franz Handlos and Ekkehard Voigt, as well as the former Bavarian television editor, Franz Schönhuber,[71] founded the party Die Republikaner (REP) in November 1983 which achieved 3 per cent of the vote in the 1986 Bavarian *Land* parliament elections. This result signalled a possible nationwide restriction of the CDU/CSU's capacity to integrate the right, which was to be spectacularly confirmed in the Berlin elections and the European Parliament elections.

Dr Frey also gambled on the dissatisfaction of right-wing conservative forces with CDU/CSU policies when he launched his DVU – Liste D. He now had in his possession important preconditions for electoral success – a party, considerable financial backing, a group of press companies and a large number of

---

71. Schönhuber, who was very popular in Bavaria, lost his post because he had published an apologetic book of memoirs in 1981 under the title *Ich war dabei* (I was there [in the Waffen SS]).

The Development of Organised Right-wing Extremism

supporters. But because he lacked a functioning organisation capable of conducting election campaigns, he formed an alliance with the NPD, which many right-wing extremists hoped would achieve the long hoped-for revival of nationalist opposition.

At the time of the founding of the NPD, the Frey press had polemicised against the new party and the architect of the organisation, von Thadden, who then adamantly rejected co-operation with Frey. At the 1968 Baden-Württemberg *Land* parliament elections the NPD (the deputy *Land* chairman was the current NPD leader, Mußgnug) and Frey achieved a certain degree of co-operation. In the DNZ, Frey called on his readers to vote for the NPD and also declared his support for Mußgnug as a new *Land* chairman (which he then in fact became). The friendship was too extreme for Thadden: Mußgnug received a harsh rebuke for thanking Frey in a letter for the favour and expressing the hope that the hostility was now over forever.

In 1971, Frey gave his support to the NPD offshoot, the ANR, and made no secret of his satisfaction over the downfall of the NPD. In 1972, contacts between the Federal chairman Mußgnug and representatives of the *Freiheitlicher Rat* were temporarily renewed with the aim of promoting unification in the nationalist camp. The NPD executive disapproved of Mußgnug's activity, whereupon Frey called on his supporters to vote for the CDU/CSU in the forthcoming Bundestag elections.

In 1975, Frey and Mußgnug attempted a new reconciliation: The former campaigned for the NPD during the Bremen elections and even became a member. In exchange, the latter promised to propose the DVU leader for the office of deputy party chairman at the coming NPD party conference and to hand over responsibility to him for editing the NPD mouthpiece. The party then faced another crucial test, and in indignation von Thadden even returned his party card. The party basis then thwarted Mußgnug's plans: Frey failed to be elected his deputy and had to be satisfied with a position on the executive. He accepted this initially, but resigned in summer 1976 and left the NPD shortly afterwards (probably in 1979).

The current phase of co-operation began in 1986: at the Bavarian Landtag elections, Frey again backed the NPD in his newspapers, as was the case in the 1987 Bundestag elections. Since the NPD received over 0.5 per cent of the vote in this election (actually 0.6 per cent), they were able to enjoy government reimbursement of election campaign costs to the tune of DM 1.3 million, which consolidated them financially. Shortly after the founding of the DVU – Liste D, involving leading NPD functionaries, the leadership bodies of the NPD and DVU agreed that they would support one another in elections while continuing to respect the independence of both organisations. The NPD was to stand in 1987 in Rhineland-Palatinate and in 1988 in Baden-Württemberg, and the DVU – Liste D in Bremen in 1987.

The elections to the Bremen parliament were a test-run for the Frey party, which conducted an extremely lavish propaganda campaign from their Munich headquarters without staging a single public event. With DM 2 million, they had greater financial means available than the CDU and SPD were able to spend together. Hence the DVU candidate, Hans Altermann, gained a seat in the parliament, and two further DVU candidates won seats in the town council of Bremerhaven. (In addition, the REP achieved 1.2 per cent of the vote.)

Following this satisfactory result, the election pact between the two parties was amended: the Schleswig-Holstein election (in 1988) and the 1990 Bundestag elections remained the prerogative of the NPD, while the DVU stood for the 1989 European elections. This agreement again led to violent disputes within the NPD. Mußgnug seems to have made a few mistakes, but in any case offended a considerable proportion of the functionaries. In addition, the European elections are particularly lucrative. With comparatively little organisational and financial effort, a party can achieve a sizeable election campaign reimbursement, and this particularly benefits minor parties, which – at least in West Germany – generally achieve better results in the European elections than in federal elections.

Critics of the co-operation with Frey accuse him of being business-minded and exclusively oriented towards profit, and of not placing nationalist concerns and certainly not party politics in the forefront. It is feared that the NPD could be 'swallowed up' by the DVU, or even that Frey is determined (as before) to weaken or split the NPD. In this context, there is a constant rumour that Frey is actually working for the CDU/CSU, which would be the sole beneficiary of any disputes in the nationalist camp and must currently do everything possible to thwart a competing party which could represent a permanent threat to their unstable majority.

However, advocates of a unified right-wing party based their hopes for a nationalist opposition comeback on the apparently lamentable state of the CDU/CSU, especially as further integrative weaknesses were forecast following the death of the CSU chairman, Franz Josef Strauß (FJS), at the beginning of October 1988. Hence the editor of the right-wing extremist paper *Nation Europa*, Peter Dehoust (NPD), wrote:[72]

> FJS represented a considerable right-wing voting potential for the CDU/CSU. His function was to 'integrate the right' into the Bonn party cartel. Without him, the CDU/CSU will have a crippled right wing. This could be the hour of the uprising of an authentic rightwing party, if those concerned are united.

The exhortation to unity did not only apply to Frey and Mußgnug but also to a third man, the chairman of the Republikaner, Franz Schönhuber. The Republikaner were also preparing for their participation in the European elections, and at the time many feared that two parties from the nationalist right competing with one another would inevitably lead to both of them failing the 5 per cent clause. In retrospect, we know that this pessimism was unfounded. At the European elections in June 1989, both parties together received 2,453,550 votes (8.7 per cent). However, it was not the DVU, supported by the NPD, that profited from the considerable trends towards disintegration at the right wing of the party system. They had to be content with roughly half a million votes (1.6 per cent).[73] The Republikaner were the main beneficiaries.

The Republikaner

The Republikaner, as mentioned above, were founded in November 1983 by the two former CSU Bundestag members,

---

72. *Nation Europa*, vol. 38 (1988), no. 10, p. 3.
73. The DVU achieved above-average results in Bremen (3.2 per cent), Baden-Württemberg (2.4 per cent) and Hesse (2.3 per cent). In their Bavarian homeland Frey's party achieved only 1 per cent.

Franz Handlos and Ekkehard Voigt, and the former television journalist, Franz Schönhuber. The impetus came from the widespread dissatisfaction with the CDU/CSU, particularly regarding the 'change', which had failed to materialise.

If one is to believe the Republikaner, politically their party can be classified between the CDU/CSU and the right-wing extremist parties, but is nevertheless 'clearly right of centre', as Schönhuber emphasises. It is therefore very opportune for them that officially, they are described not as right-wing extremist (which would be unconstitutional), but as right-wing radical, hence belonging to the democratic spectrum. In paragraph 3 of their statute, they formally distance themselves from both right and left:

> No one may become a member of the party DIE REPUBLIKANER who belongs to or supports an unconstitutional organisation or a left-wing or right-wing extremist group.

For tactical reasons, the Republikaner had to be careful that they did not become tainted as neo-Fascists and deter potential voters from the CDU/CSU camp. They avoided attributes such as 'German' or 'Nationalist' in their party name. In general parlance, they prefer the description 'patriotic'. Moreover, the name 'Die Republikaner' does not suggest any association to 'party' or 'Union', and certainly not to any historically tarnished or tainted examples. Instead, they have created the image of something new and original. In fact, the most important REP demands coincide largely with those of the NPD and DVU.

The Republikaner's current party manifesto focuses on the demand for 'national self-determination and intellectual/moral renewal'. The opening passage of their political programme, 'The Position of the Divided Nation and the German people', could just as easily have come from the repertoire of the right-wing extremist parties in terms of its content and style. It says, among other things:

> The economically and socially favourable position experienced by the West Germans in comparison with other countries is deceptive, and conceals the fact that all over Germany, intellectual and political culture is increasingly being neglected, customs are not respected and the desire to recreate national unity is disappearing. Due to the

The Development of Organised Right-wing Extremism

conflicting re-education of Germans in the two states, alienation is growing. It is increasing due to the current government policy in West Germany. . . . In contrast to their stated goals when they were in opposition, the CDU/CSU–Liberal government has neither shown any signs of an 'intellectual/moral change' nor has it taken effective measures to protect the people . . .

The worst failure, because it has a long-term effect on all areas of life, has been in the area of the socialisation and education of young people. They have fallen into a moral crisis, combined with an increasing loss of ethical values.

The CDU/CSU government continues to fixate the German past on twelve years of national socialist rule. It has done nothing to instigate the de-criminalisation of German culture, history and the German people. The war propaganda of the victorious powers has entered our history books, and their exaggerations and falsehoods have to be largely believed by our youth, since there is still no possibility of an objective description of history in its entirety.

Reunification of Germany is described as the primary goal of the party. It presupposes the continued existence of the German Reich and insists on a 'peace treaty with the victorious powers as those responsible for Germany as a whole'. Neutralist undertones, not far removed from the NPD, are continued in the following sentence:

Our paramount aim is the reunification of Germany as a whole and must be granted priority over West Germany remaining in NATO. For this reason, membership in the alliance must not necessarily represent an insurmountable hindrance on the road to unity.

In their European election manifesto ('Yes to Europe, No to this EC'), the Republikaner underline the statement that a one-sided Western integration of West Germany makes reunification impossible and demand 'Germany must come first!'. This formulation is also to be found in the DVU, who conducted their European election campaign under the slogan: 'First Germany, then Europe!'.

With regard to the political order of West Germany, the Republikaner support the concept of an authoritarian state with the intention of strengthening the state as a factor of control, and view the organisations and institutions of political decision-making with mistrust and aim to reduce their influence. Viewed against the entire context of statements made in the party programme, the demand that reasons of state and common weal should take priority over reasons of party and group interests can only be understood as a gradual elimination of democracy. The party continually swears its allegiance to partnership, community and public spirit, and individual or group interests are classified as tendentially harmful.

In socio-political terms, the Republikaner consider themselves to be the advocate of the (German) 'man in the street' who is concerned with 'social peace'. The reform of social order for which they strive is to be achieved, they claim, by means of a 'change in consciousness', and 'the feeling of all working people living together and working together' must be created. The party supports the promotion and safeguarding of private wealth, mainly from government intervention, while fighting against the 'formation of economic power blocs'. In the old right-wing extremist tradition, the Republikaner sing the praises of free enterprise and distrust the socialist interests of workers. The unions are obliged to conform to the state and the common weal (as the Republikaner understand it); the right to free collective bargaining is to be abolished. Anti-democratic tendencies are also visible in the section of the party programme regarding their policy on the media. There they bluntly threaten to abolish the freedom of the press.

We have already mentioned the fact that the Republikaner gloss over national socialism and to a large extent also make excuses for it. The exoneration of Hitler and the trivialisation of Nazi crimes represent a central motif of all of Schönhuber's utterances. The chairman, naturally, does not waste his breath on the victims of the Nazi regime. Schönhuber's indirect, subliminal anti-Semitism must be evaluated as particularly perfidious, because he does not directly deny the holocaust but represents it as a question that is apparently still unexplained:

> Were there six, four, two million or even 'only' three hundred thousand dead Jews? Who shot whom where and when first? Such questions must definitely be posed by the historians and answered to the best of their knowledge and conscience.

To sum up: the Republikaner gloss over Nazi crimes and the

The Development of Organised Right-wing Extremism

Table 4.11 Republikaner election results, 1986–89

Elections	Year	Number of votes	%	Seats
European Parliament	1989	2,008,629	7.1	6
Land Parliaments				
Bavaria	1986	342,995	3.0	—
Bremen	1987	4,623	1.2	—
Baden-Württemberg	1988	46,904	1.0	—
Schleswig-Holstein	1988	8,673	0.6	—
Berlin (West)	1989	90,222	7.5	11

holocaust, relativise Germany's war guilt, incite anti-Semitism, racism and racial hatred, and intend to restrict the influence of parties and associations, destroy the right to free collective bargaining and abolish the freedom of the press. In terms of their party manifesto and propaganda, there is no doubt that they are a right-wing extremist party.

The fact that the Republikaner are not generally recognised as such by the public may be one reason for their considerable electoral success. The party, which has some 14,000 members and which is given a great deal of attention by the mass media, is more successful than its rivals in covering the ideological spectrum from right-wing conservatism to right-wing extremism, especially as they are even viewed by sections of the CDU/CSU as a possible coalition partner and hence made acceptable to the voters of the CDU/CSU.

The Republikaner, currently under Schönhuber's unchallenged leadership – Handlos and Voigt have since left the party – are expected to have further electoral success by opinion researchers, although in terms of their membership and voters they remain predominantly a southern German party. It is true that REP functionaries are devoting all their efforts to extend the organisation to middle and norther Länder. They are aided in this by the DM 16 million they will receive in election campaign reimbursements from their European election results.

205

5

Causes and Countermeasures

Keeping Quiet During the Nazi Era

When the Nazis took away the Communists,
I kept quiet;
I wasn't a Communist.
When they locked up the Social Democrats,
I kept quiet;
I wasn't a Social Democrat.
When they removed the Catholics,
I didn't protest;
I wasn't a Catholic.
When they came for me,
There was no one left
To protest.

Martin Niemöller[1]

At first glance it may be surprising that I have chosen to portray the causes of right-wing extremism and the measures directed against it in one chapter. They might appear to be two different topic areas, the former being more analytical and the latter of a more normative (action-oriented) nature. True, this procedure is not common. Nevertheless, in my opinion, there is an internal correlation between the two areas, which must be expressed in their portrayal. The analysis of right-wing extremism, its manifestations and causes, can ultimately only serve the purpose of destroying its conditions for existing. In my opinion, the fight against anti-democratic attitudes and behaviour can only be appropriately conducted if the causes are known.

The words of Martin Niemöller, which will be the leitmotif of this chapter, remind us that we must fight the beginnings, and for this reason is a favourite quotation in anti-Fascist speeches and writings. Based on a broad analysis of causes, in this

---

1. Former president of the Evangelical Church of Hesse and Nassau, incarcerated in a concentration camp from 1938 to 1945.

Causes and Countermeasures

chapter I shall warn against an historically fixed concept of anti-Fascism which is too narrow and one-sided. The popular chant 'Nazis out!' is utterly inadequate. Niemöller's 'Keeping quiet during the Nazi era' teaches us that only by actively supporting democracy can we effectively combat right-wing extremism in the long term.

Klaus Hartung's mordant commentary in the *Tageszeitung* of 8 July 1989 is also thought-provoking:

> Now, with the Republikaner *Land* party conference in Berlin, we are reminded of the fight against the danger from the right. An antifascist cartel of signatures is being mobilised. The order of the day is: 'Fight the beginnings'. . . . As a collective Cassandra for the danger from the right we show, of course, that we have understood the lessons of 1933. Enthusiastic excesses, however, leave an aftertaste. It is doubtful whether the fight against the danger from the right can be related to an understanding of the history of national socialism. . . . I also consider attempts to fight the national socialist movement of that time with the 'Republikaner' of today and to attempt to save the Weimar Republic in retrospect sinister. . . . Is it not true that there is a powerful need among the left for a right-wing danger?

The Causes of Right-wing Extremism in West Germany

This section will not attempt to develop a theory of right-wing extremism. I shall also avoid a corresponding overview of literature. I am solely concerned with summarising the causes previously named or hinted at, to systematise them and – as far as possible – to embellish them with additional factors and considerations.

Right-wing extremism was defined at the beginning of this book as the totality of attitudes and behaviour which are directed at abolishing or permanently restricting democratic rights, structures and processes. Hence right-wing extremism needs to be explained simultaneously both as a social and a political mass phenomenon.

This phenomenon has both an *individual* component and a component relating to *society as a whole*. Initially, it is individuals who develop right-wing extremist views, act in a right-wing extremist way and in some cases co-operate with other individuals in order to gain further supporters and realise common goals.

The organisational and political success of this type of co-operation, however, does not depend solely on the number of individuals concerned and their willingness to act, but also on the overall social conditions. These either encourage or discourage the spread of anti-democratic views, the extent to which the individual is prepared to adopt corresponding modes of behaviour, and the way in which individual activities are condensed to collective action.

The individual causes of right-wing extremism and those relating to society as a whole hence form a uniform correlation of effects. Nevertheless, one must distinguish conceptually between the two groups of factors, both for analytical purposes and for the development of countermeasures, which is of paramount importance.

Individual Factors

The expression of anti-democratic attitudes can be traced back mainly to an authoritarian, prejudiced character formation. This results from shortcomings and mistakes made during early childhood socialisation, from which the following personality characteristics can result:

- lack of self-confidence and assuredness.
- blind obedience to authority; identification with power and strength.
- a need for hero and anti-hero role-models, for leaders, classification and subordination, community and security.
- a tendency towards hierarchies.
- thinking in black and white terms.
- hatred of everything that is weak or unfamiliar.
- conventionalism, conformism and inflexibility.
- inability to cope with conflict.

Causes and Countermeasures

The psychology of the (mainly youth) right-wing extremism is increasingly being explained in terms of social change within modern industrial societies and the tendencies towards individualisation associated with this. Following the loss of significance of social milieux, which formerly facilitated the formation of a collective identity, today people have to rely on themselves. They have to cope alone with ambivalence, conflicts and contradictory constellations, and hence have to withstand greater pressures when developing the ability to act autonomously. Individualisation reduces the resistance to right-wing extremist manifestations and tendencies, and the lack of social relationships can lead young people in particular to search for 'surrogate collective identities',[2] in which they hope to find strength, protection or security.

Socialisation within the family, then, plays an important part in the development of anti-democratic opinions. It is true that the decisive vulnerable point takes place in early childhood, but this is also reinforced by specific styles of socialisation and may also be inherited. Furthermore, extra-familial socialisation forces (such as kindergarten, school, university, military service, work) and role-models (friends, teachers) are capable of either promoting or preventing the development of the autonomous personality with a strong ego. Finally, the significance of reading material and the mass media, particularly television, must not be underestimated in the dissemination of right-wing extremism.

The formation of anti-democratic attitudes occurs in the course of constant interaction between the individual and the environment, and is also dependent on coincidences. In the course of development, dissatisfaction with one's situation in life, internal distance and, later, profound alienation from the existing social conditions develop. Coping with dissatisfaction and alienation, and individual strategies for solving this, are characterised in (potential) right-wing extremists by authoritarian characteristics. Surrogate worlds are sought, symbols, people or groups who promise strength, power, inviolability, perfection, safety, security and community, and who facilitate identification and goals.

2. Wilhelm Heitmeyer, *Rechtsextremistische Orientierungen bei Jugendlichen*, Weinheim and Munich, 1987, p. 101.

The transition from right-wing extremist attitudes to right-wing extremist activity (regardless of whether this is protest behaviour or purposeful political behaviour) does not occur abruptly but rather is fluid and incremental. This also applies to the change from individual to collective action. The following stages can be distinguished:[3]

- procuring information: interest in the programmes and ideologies of right-wing extremist groups, taking out subscriptions to and reading appropriate journals, taking part in (election) events as a mere observer.

- individual and covert activities without directly declaring support for right-wing extremism: telling anti-Semitic or racist 'jokes', drawing swastikas, sticking up leaflets, making small donations to right-wing extremist organisations, subscribing to right-wing extremist journals, voting for a right-wing extremist party.

- individual activities with an open declaration of support for right-wing extremism: wearing uniform-like clothes with Nazi symbols, publicly declaring anti-democratic viewpoints, justifying or formalising national socialism, baiting immigrants, Jews, etc.

- collective non-violent activities: participating in organised events (distributing propaganda material, demonstrations, military exercises), joining a group (Nazi-rockers, skinheads), membership of an organisation or party, accepting offices in organisations or parties.

- collective acts of violence: physical attacks on people, disrupting meetings, fights with political opponents, raids on hostels and businesses belonging to foreigners, bank hold-ups, arson attacks, murder.

The development from holding anti-democratic attitudes to carrying out right-wing extremist terrorist activities must be seen as a process, in the course of which the individual has to

---

3. The examples given here are only intended to illustrate a point, and by no means represent a comprehensive list of right-wing extremist forms of activity.

Causes and Countermeasures

overcome increasingly greater hurdles, particularly individual psychological inhibitions and societal sanctions.

The first important barrier to be overcome is to emerge from anonymity, openly declaring support for a political attitude that clearly deviates from, or even is clearly rejected by, the mainstream of the population. The individual has to accept the disapproval of his social milieu, and sometimes put up with being mocked. In any event, he cannot generally hope for understanding let alone recognition, and hence there is the probability that he will seek a new network of social contacts in order to be closer to people with anti-democratic views (unless he is already in this type of milieu). The next barrier he faces is participating in organised action against the status quo. He now faces the threat of social rejection and vocational disadvantage. The person's communication is restricted to the right-wing extremist camp. The final hurdle comes in violent action. The consequences are social isolation, going underground, prosecution by the police and the judiciary, and finally imprisonment.

To overcome these hurdles not only requires great courage and a willingness to take risks, but also involves an overwhelming need for admiration and destructiveness, plus blind rage, enormous helplessness and a permanent lack of perspective. The more pronounced these characteristics are in a person, the greater their willingness to use violence.

One central problem, which has still not been solved satisfactorily from an academic point of view, is the question of which actual conditions cause attitudes to develop into (collective) behaviour. This question is very important in relation to West German right-wing extremism because it involves a broad potential for anti-democratic views, but usually with relatively low organisational activity. A mechanical causal connection between the two variables obviously does not exist. Views probably only become concrete practice if specific conditions (intervening variables) are present:

- anti-democratic attitudes condense to mass dissatisfaction with the existing conditions, which are not dealt with individually (e.g. by taking drugs).
- the dissatisfaction concerns important spheres of life for entire

211

social groups, e.g. classes, social strata, minorities or other clearly defined groups.

- the causes for the dissatisfaction cannot be overcome within the existing democratic structures, in the opinion of those concerned.
- the willingness to bear the social consequences, to take risks and accept sanctions, is considerable, and/or the tolerance of the social environment towards right-wing extremist activities is considered to be large.
- the prospects of success for right-wing extremist actions are not considered to be bad.

The interdependence of individual causes of right-wing extremism and those relating to society as a whole cannot be overlooked. Important links are first, the extent and spread of dissatisfaction, which is generally economically, socially or politically based, and second, the reactions of the immediate or wider social environment, and finally of the public as a whole. The state of political culture, the establishment of democracy and humanitarianism in the consciousness of the population, the rejection of anti-Semitism, racism, authoritarianism and militarism and, finally, the involvement with a free social order are decisive for stemming right-wing extremism. On the other hand, it is encouraged by passivity, ignorance or latent sympathy.

Factors Relating to Society as a Whole

When considering the factors relating to society as a whole, we must distinguish between crises in the economic, social and political sphere, and those more or less constant elements of a political culture, which favour the spread of anti-democratic thought and action.

Economic Crises The significance of economic crises for the success of right-wing extremism is frequently overestimated, but nevertheless should not be overlooked. Favourable conditions for work, production and income are an important requirement for people's personal satisfaction. Permanent shortcomings in any of these necessarily lead to dissatisfaction in those concerned. Hence absolute deprivation (impoverishment as a result of unemployment, poverty, etc.), as well as cyclical economic crises and regional and sectoral structural crises (particularly in agriculture and the bourgeoisie or medium-sized businesses), encourage the spread of right-wing extremism. In many cases it results from the process of economic restructuring: for example, the threat to medium-sized business by major capitalists, the penetration of capitalist forms of production into agriculture and the trades, or the destruction of rural areas by progressive industrialisation and urbanisation.

A further important cause of anti-democratic attitudes and modes of behaviour is relative deprivation. This refers to quantitative or temporal differences in the development of different economic branches or different social groups. In the 1950s, for example, German nationals primarily profited from the economic upturn, while the expellees found it much more difficult to find adequate accommodation and a job. Today, in particular, structural changes in industrial society have caused greater inequality between more traditional and more futuristic sectors of the economy or between those who have gained from modernisation and those who have lost. As a result of the decline in significance of the 'primary sector' (agriculture) and the old 'smokestack industries', specific occupational groups (e.g. farmers, agricultural workers, miners, etc.) are threatened with a loss of social standing and a devaluation of their skills and are suffering from poor future prospects, while the 'sunrise' industries (electronics, the chemical industry, transport) offer their loyal workforce secure jobs and a high degree of vocational qualifications in the long term.

Being affected by crises and gloomy expectations for the future creates a feeling of being disadvantaged and of alienation and isolation; it stimulates prejudice towards outsiders and the weak, and creates the desire for authoritarian concepts: community, security, safety, goals, peace and order. Only a 'strong' political leader who rules the country with an 'iron fist' is entrusted with improving the economic conditions.

Social Crises Of greater significance than economic crises for the success of right-wing extremism are poor general living conditions. This is primarily concerned with housing, neighbourhood relations, social contacts and social care, cultural infrastructures and opportunities for leisure. Studies on youth right-wing extremism show that the inhospitable concrete jungles in the big cities, high-rise flats or rundown areas of towns contribute to social isolation and cultural impoverishment, leading young people to alcoholism and drug abuse and making them susceptible to gambling dens, amusement arcades, fascistic backstreet gangs, rocker groups or football supporters' clubs where they can allow their aggression to run riot. The types of young people who seek this sort of sanctuary are usually those who have a disposition towards authoritarianism, suffer from difficult conditions at home and do not have any friends or people close to them who can offer them help and support to overcome their problems.

Since social crises are largely determined by economic factors, there is generally also a lack of adequate means for public facilities (youth clubs, old people's homes, meeting places, sports centres, etc.) which could improve social conditions. In this way, areas or subcultures emerge that are virtually predestined to produce right-wing extremist youth.

There is also a connection between economic crises and social misery with regard to the problem groups of industrial modernisation. The exhaustion of entire industrial areas, combined with structural change, necessarily leads to the increased mobility of the people afflicted. This means breaking the ties that have developed to the old home, social upheaval and often impoverishment and isolation. The radical changes in the agricultural sector, which are manifested differently in different regions, mean that the rural population is faced with similar problems.

The social basis of right-wing extremism is very broad and multifaceted. In principle, there is no major social group that would be completely immune to it and none that is predestined *per se* towards right-wing extremism. This cannot be said exclusively of the middle class any more than anti-Fascism is confined to the working class. The conditions were not this simple even at the end of the Weimar Republic. Generally, though, it is true that women are somewhat less susceptible than men, and that in particular, close ties to the Church or the unions, as well as higher education, form something of a barrier to anti-democratic influences.

Political Crises Economic and social crises can be compensated for or exacerbated by political action. The global economic crisis at the end of the 1920s proved that even drastic economic crises by no means necessarily led to Fascism. This was the case in some countries but not in others. A decisive factor is the extent to which the political system is capable of producing the necessary degree of control, legitimacy and integration, and whether the political process is based on consensus between the competing social forces regarding the democratic 'rules of play' in politics. The development of Fascism in the Weimar Republic only became possible because such a consensus regarding the constitution did not exist. Authoritarianism, the notion of the authoritarian state and a subservient mentality prevented the democratic constitution from developing its full potential. The global economic crisis was not the cause of the process of decline of the Republic, it merely accelerated it.

In a society with no established democratic tradition, there is a particular danger that individual deficits in the legitimacy of public rule are blamed on the democratic system as a whole, that temporary crises in sub-areas of society lead to the rejection of democracy *per se*. If, for example, the material needs of all classes of society are not fulfilled or only inadequately so, then it is not possible to convey values and political goals with which the people can identify and no adequate balancing of interests can be guaranteed. As a result:

- the acceptance of democratic institutions is reduced.

- the intermediary organisations lose their integrative power and representative capacity.

- cohesiveness among parties and associations breaks down.

- political forces, which propagate opposition to the democratic system, gain in popularity.

In West Germany, political crises are expressed primarily in the party system (including its subsidiary and affiliated organisations), because in our system, the political parties are the means and mediators above all of democratic rule. They have a heavy responsibility to legitimise government action and represent the formative interests and concepts in West German society, which is a party-state democracy. The predominant party type here, which is the catch-all party (*Volkspartei*) embodied by the CDU/CSU and SPD, does tend to neglect the representative function in favour of the legitimising function. The consequence is that the parties are alienated from the people, the people are distrustful of the parties, and the party system faces crises of legitimacy. In particular, at times of social upheaval (as in the 1960s and 1970s, for example), when the fundamental elements of the basic consensus are questioned, the parties consider themselves to be exposed to enormous integrative demands.

If democratic means of social integration, representation and consensus formation fail, ideologies begin to influence the consciousness of those people with a disposition towards authoritarianism, who:

- recognize the strong state as the only principle of order (Reich, Führer, etc.) and demand the primacy of governmental power and political stability over social interests, associations, parties, etc.

- create unity between individuals and the state by placing the individual under an obligation to the (people's) community (*Volksgemeinschaft*) usually by means of violence.

- control social relations by classification, superordination and subordination, by inequality and dependency.

Integrative weaknesses and legitimising deficits within the political system, however, only form the necessary precondition for the success of right-wing extremism. In addition, right-wing extremism must prove itself capable in terms of organisation, personnel and ideology of using political crises for its own ends. In order to mobilise supporters, members and voters, it must:

- create an aura of political competence and credibility.

- present programmatic alternatives and goals with which people can identify.

- demonstrate internal unity and avoid organisational fragmentation.
- include popular and respected people in the leadership body.
- obtain good coverage in the media.

Anti-Democratic Elements in Political Culture

In the section regarding individual causes, I have already mentioned the significance of democratic traditions and convictions as a possible barrier to the spread of right-wing extremism. Hence I shall restrict myself here to a resumé and a few additional comments.

Repressing and Glossing over National Socialism The difficulties and failings of the Germans in coming to terms with their past are also expressed in the way in which they deal with right-wing extremism. One cannot talk of a consistent rejection, instead, it is glossed over and relativised by means of right–left comparisons. The debates, often conducted in public with little sense of responsibility for the uniqueness and unprecedentedness of the national socialist annihilation of the Jews, in particular, are no doubt evaluated by right-wing historical revisionists as a success and as an invitation to intensify their pro-Nazi activities. And how teachers, educators and social workers can openly and actively debate with young people's pro-Fascist views and protest activities, if, for example, the young people can justify their swastika graffiti by referring to established historians who consider it a measure against communism?

The Lack of Democratic Consciousness and the Discrediting of Anti-Fascism West German society is characterised by a basic consensus (which guarantees political stability) regarding major domestic and foreign policy questions. However, there exists a broad potential for anti-democratic attitudes, which is largely contained within the institutional system but which is expressed from time to time in right-wing extremist practice. Characteristic of West Germany's political culture, moreover, are the 'bridges to the right', which are to be found at all levels, and are more or less fluid crossover points between the democratic and the

Table 5.1 The prosecution of war criminals in the eyes of the population (1988)

Question: 'Do you think that war criminals from the Second World War should still be prosecuted and sentenced in 1988?'

	Yes	No	No reply
Total	47	51	2
Manual workers	50	48	2
White-collar employees	54	43	3
Civil servants	55	32	13
Self-employed	45	55	—
Pensioners	29	70	1
Students	56	44	—
Union member			
Yes	60	38	2
No	44	54	2

Source: EMNID-Informationen, 4/1988, p. 11f.

anti-democratic camps. On the level of public opinion there is a 'grey area' of authoritarian but not extremist orientation; in the area of intermediary institutions one speaks of a 'right-wing cartel' when describing the multiple connections between conservative organisations and the nationalist opposition, and also in individual questions of daily politics, for example, the policy towards South Africa, in the treatment of people seeking political asylum or in the way immigrants are dealt with, there is endemic evidence of an appalling lack of humanity and liberality. The similarity between the revisionists and the historians' dispute has already been mentioned.

An important characteristic of political culture is reflected in people's attitudes towards the criminal prosecution of Nazi crimes, war crimes or neo-Nazi activities. I have already shown that the number of people who supported prosecuting Nazi crimes in the 1970s – intensified by the impressions gained from the screening of the television programme *Holocaust* (1979) – has grown. Nevertheless, in 1979 46 per cent of those questioned were of the opinion that one should close the door to the past. In 1988 over half of West Germans voted against the continued prosecution and sentencing of war crimes. In particular, pen-

Causes and Countermeasures

Table 5.2 The criminal prosecution of neo-Nazis in the eyes of the population (1980–85)

Question: 'Should people who openly approve of national socialism and its ideologies and who are actively involved in bringing it about in West Germany be criminally prosecuted – or should they simply not be stopped?'

	Criminal prosecution	Allow to continue	No reply
March 1980	54	44	3
October/November 1980	69	27	3
November 1981	80	18	3
March 1983	70	26	4
December 1983	75	23	2
December 1985	72	28	1

Source: EMNID–Informationen, 9–10/1985, p. 7f.

sioners and the self-employed express above-average rejection of such measures. On the other hand, the majority of manual and non-manual workers, civil servants, students and especially union members support continued judicial prosecution.

Table 5.2 is a striking example of the fact that the degree to which West Germans are concerned about right-wing extremism depends on specific events. In the first half of the 1980s, the public was shocked by outrageous terrorist attacks, arrests, banning orders and trials,[4] and hence the proportion of the population that supported the prosecution of neo-Nazis grew from 54 per cent (in March 1980) to over 80 per cent (in November 1981). However, the figures can also be interpreted in a different way: in spite of the intensive public debate regarding the holocaust in 1980, just under half of West Germans wanted to allow the neo-Nazis to do as they wished, and in the following five years this liberal attitude oscillated between one fifth and one third of those questioned.

Nevertheless, in the 1980s the West Germans underwent a process of sensitisation to neo-Nazism. Yet again, it was proved that consciences can be changed by information, education and

---

4. See the sections above on violence and terrorism, and on neo-Nazis.

discussion. This represents an opportunity for anti-Fascism, although it faces a great deal of hostility in West Germany and has little chance of being recognised as an independent political value and as the norm for education. The term anti-Fascism is generally discredited as a term supposedly invented by the communists, and anti-Fascists are always open to the accusation that they are in fact working for the communists with the aim of diverting attention away from the communist threat. Hence anti-Fascist activities are always subject to restrictions, initiators and initiatives are considered suspect, and anti-Fascist demands are held to reflect a one-side and unbalanced critique of West German society.

In summary, anti-democratic elements in West German political culture encourage the development of individual right-wing extremist views with respect to individual and collective modes of behaviour, to the extreme of right-wing extremism, as a social and political mass phenomenon. However, because the anti-democratic elements named are in no way constitutive of political culture, and because (at least to date) the economic, social and political crises have been contained, in the past, right-wing extremism has never taken on proportions that would threaten the state of West German democracy.

On the Interdependence of the Explanatory Factors

The individual causes of right-wing extremism and those relating to society as a whole form a unified system of interconnected effects; at the same time, the factors relating to society as a whole have an effect on all stages of the development, from possessing an 'authoritarian character' caused by socialisation, to participating in right-wing extremist activities. Specific conditions relating to life-history influence this development in the individual. Just when the qualitative leap from one stage to the next occurs depends on particular conditions, actual experiences and learning processes, and is strongly influenced by conjunctures of events. This development, moreover, does not necessarily occur (that is the reason why countermeasures are so significant). On the contrary, at each stage, the possibility exists for nothing to change, for a change of hearts, or for progression.

Any attempt to formulate 'if . . . then' statements or to con-

Causes and Countermeasures

Figure 5.1 The interrelation between individual causes of right-wing extremism and relating to society as a whole

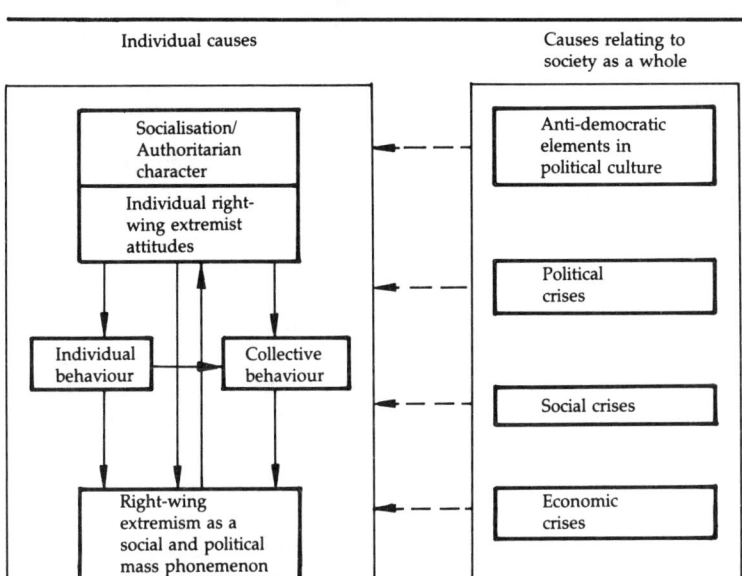

struct simple 'cause/effect models' will fail. Moreover, to date, it has proved impossible to typify with any conviction the career patterns of right-wing extremists. I doubt whether this is possible.

Anti-Fascism – Problems and Perspectives

The term anti-Fascism describes opposition to Fascism. Anti-Fascism is a political term, and is also widely used as a war cry. It has become established as a political term, it has an historical tradition and (in Germany) a history that is simultaneously characterised by serious failures and dire consequences until 1933, by persecution, internment in concentration camps and death, by brave and outstanding deeds and, finally, by stubborn opposition to the way in which national socialism and right-wing extremism were played down after 1945. In my opinion there is no reason to avoid this term as a political norm and as an educational aim, since all the problems of the German past and present are mercilessly reflected in it.

Nevertheless, some critical remarks are necessary with regard to the methods and aims of anti-Fascism. Strictly speaking, the opposite of Fascism is not anti-Fascism but democracy. Anti-Fascism only expresses opposition, not the desired alternative. Many political parties have used the term anti-Fascism and frequently practised methods that are hardly reconcilable with the ideal goal.

Organised Anti-Fascism since 1945[5]

Many writers have expounded the theory that an anti-Fascist consensus existed in the immediate post-war years, which was subsequently destroyed as the East–West conflict worsened and capitalism was restored in the Western zones. I consider this theory to be incorrect. There was no Fascist consensus either before or after 1933; nor can one talk of an anti-Fascist consensus. In my opinion, the survey statistics produced by the US military government and the controversies surrounding de-Nazification and Nazi trials show clear evidence to the contrary.

It is indeed true that in 1945 the major parties, associations and the Churches distanced themselves from national socialism and demanded a new social order. At that time, even the CDU spoke out in support of a 'true Christian socialism'. However, no consensus emerged among opponents of national socialism regarding which lessons were to be learned from the past, how the new order was to be created or how the complete elimination of Nazism and militarism was to be achieved. Even within the left, and particularly within organised anti-Fascism, opinions varied.

In 1945 the resistance fighters, survivors of concentration camps and victims of political persecution joined to form Vereini-

5. There is no satisfactory overall portrayal of anti-Fascism after 1945. The following titles will convey an overview: Thomas Doerry, *Antifaschismus in der Bundesrepublik. Vom antifaschistischen Konsens 1945 bis zur Gegenwart*, Frankfurt, 1980; Max Oppenheimer (ed.), *Antifaschismus. Tradition – Politik – Perspektive. Geschichte und Ziele der VVN – Bund der Antifaschisten*, Frankfurt, 1978; Peter Brandt and Ulrich Schulze-Marmeling (eds), *Antifaschismus – Ein Lesebuch. Deutsche Stimmen gegen Nationalsozialismus und Rechtsextremismus von 1922 bis zur Gegenwart*, Berlin, 1985.

gungen der Verfolgten des Naziregimes (VVN). In March 1947 an umbrella organisation (termed *Rat*) was formed for all four occupation zones, which represented some 300,000 members, most of whom were communists. One year later, the SPD passed a decree declaring membership of the SPD to be incompatible with membership of the VVN and created the Arbeitsgemeinschaft verfolgter Sozialdemokraten (AVS). At the beginning of 1950, a further split occurred, resulting in the formation of the Bund der Verfolgten des Naziregimes (BVN), reducing the VVN to its communist membership core. In the ensuing period, however, the AVS and BVN were unable to continue to develop independent activities alongside the VVN. In the course of the general persecution of communists in the 1950s, VVN members were also excluded from public service, and in 1959 the federal government even applied to the Supreme Administrative Court to ban the VVN. Not least because of considerable protest both at home and abroad, the trial fizzled out in 1962, especially as the president of the court was found to be a former NSDAP and SA member.

The political work of the VVN in the 1950s and 1960s was mainly directed against rearmament, the presence of former Nazis in public service and in the private sector, emergency laws, the NPD and neo-Fascism. In 1971, the VVN added the description 'Bund der Antifaschisten' (BdA) to their name in order to enable opponents of right-wing extremism (particularly young people) to become members who had not themselves been victims of national socialism. This enabled them to increase their supporters to non-communist circles. The Federal Ministry for the Interior currently considers the VVN-BdA to be a communist-influenced organisation and estimates its membership at 14,000 (1987).

The VVN is not the only group to organise anti-Fascist activities. The other main groups involved are the unions and various youth organisations, as well as the SPD, the Evangelical Church, and sections of the FDP. Although CDU members also participate from time to time in individual actions, the attitude of the CDU/CSU as a whole ranges from scepticism to outright rejection of such intentions.

Politics Against Democracy

Should we Ignore it? Ban it? Discuss it? Explain it? Or Conquer it?

For some ten years intensive discussions have been conducted in West Germany regarding the methods and aims of dealing with right-wing extremism. The traditional demands of the opponents to and victims of national socialism – which are directed at peace, democracy and anti-Fascism – no longer do justice to the problem today. They are:

- compensation and pensions for all victims of national socialism.
- prosecution and punishment of Nazi criminals.
- banning or disbanding Nazi and right-wing extremist organisations.
- prohibiting all right-wing extremist activities.
- disseminating the history of anti-Fascist resistance and honouring its legacy.

Current discussions focus on five problems, which I shall now briefly introduce and discuss. Such discussions, which are conducted with great seriousness, aim to find new solutions.

Is 'Grandpa's Fascism' Dead? Anti-Fascists are always open to the accusation that they view the conditions in West Germany through 'Weimar-tinted glasses' and continually refer to the dangers of Fascism, which in reality do not exist, because historical developments do not repeat themselves. The actual threat to our democracy, it is claimed, lies in the dismantling of democratic fundamental rights, combined with tendencies towards an 'atomic state', a 'police state' or a 'security state'. All our energies must be directed against this, it is claimed.

I consider this argument correct in principle and likewise do not see the possibility of national socialism in its historical form arising again. Viewed in this way, 'Grandpa's Fascism' is indeed dead, and those who do not wish to believe it really are imprisoned by Weimar thinking. However, one cannot conclude from this that the fight against right-wing extremism is irrelev-

Causes and Countermeasures

ant. The opposite is true: even if right-wing extremism does not represent the *main* danger to West German democracy, it must not be neglected as one danger among others and must form an integral part of attempts aimed at establishing and consolidating democratic structures and processes.

Is Right-wing Extremism's Status Increased by Anti-Fascist Activities? Critics maintain that right-wing extremism is inappropriately afforded enhanced status by spectacular counter-demonstrations. Small-scale events with only a few participants only achieved coverage in the media because of the mass protests and hence achieved attention which they barely deserved. Hence the anti-Fascists, it is claimed, achieved precisely the opposite of what they were actually striving for: they helped individual right-wing extremist organisations to achieve a large amount of publicity (which they would never have been able to achieve on their own) and hence possibly in some cases even attracted new supporters and members.

This argument is not to be rejected without a second thought. In fact, the relationship between effort and effect should be carefully weighed in order to prevent the feared effect from occurring. This objection is frequently raised by people who in principle support a radical reduction of anti-Fascist activity. The reply to this is that they are confusing cause and effect. For Fascism and right-wing extremism are not products of anti-Fascism, but the result of an extraordinarily complex mixture of individual factors, and factors relating to society as a whole, the most important of which were described in the previous section. Knowledge of individual right-wing extremist procedures gleaned from the media only plays a marginal role, if any.

What can be Gained from Anti-Fascist Violence? Since the beginning of the 1980s, the extent to which anti-Fascist groups and initiatives are prepared to employ violence has grown. As a reaction to increasing violence from the right, practised largely by youth groups, militant anti-Fascism is gaining influence, with the aim of conquering its political enemies in street brawls or intimidating and demoralising neo-Nazis by means of deliberate attacks on people and objects. Cars are set alight or blown up, arson attacks are carried out on flats and meeting rooms, indeed whole houses are 'burnt off'. Militant 'antifas', as they are known, draw up dossiers with photographs and car number plates of leading neo-Nazis who are on their 'hit-lists'.

The role of anti-Fascism can only be to sensitise the public to threats to democracy, to convince them of its own aims and to gain more co-fighters. In a democracy, one must pay meticulous attention to the legality of one's actions. The methods practised by neo-Fascists must not become the methods practised by anti-Fascists! The variety of instruments of non-violent protest is currently so large, imaginative and effective on the public that in this way – as experience has shown – even large meetings and marches can be prevented or avoided. In view of the numerous attacks by neo-Nazis on anti-Fascist meetings, events and demonstrations, adequate protection is urgently needed, but the organisers must restrict themselves solely to preventing attacks.

In view of the analysis of causes, in my opinion, it can be stated definitively that violence is not a suitable means of restricting, preventing or even conquering right-wing extremism as a social and political mass phenomenon in an open battle. Violence usually breeds counter-violence, strengthens the ranks of the opposition and increases their fanaticism.

What is the Significance of Bans and Sanctions? Clearly directed against the aims and methods of the traditional victims' associations, it is frequently claimed that bans on parties and organisations are highly problematic in terms of democratic theory and are just as ineffective as other administrative sanctions in overcoming the real causes of right-wing extremism. Anti-Fascism must not restrict itself to the fight against organised right-wing extremism, because this would only be to work against its symptoms. The main starting point should be the motives, problems and structures that favour the spread of right-wing extremism.

Such arguments are primarily voiced by teachers, educators, psychologists, social workers and youth sociologists, who come face-to-face with everyday right-wing extremism in the course of their work (mainly from young people) and are forced to develop concrete countermeasures to them. They relate to one thread of a complicated network of causes, the significance of which for anti-Fascism has indeed been completely underesti-

Causes and Countermeasures

mated for some time: the individual psychological causes of anti-democratic attitudes and modes of behaviour, as well as those that are caused by socialisation. In particular, such people who are not yet firmly bound to the organised network of right-wing extremism can undergo learning processes and change their orientation, e.g. as the result of educational measures or youth work projects. Stigmatising and excluding them would most probably have the consequence that they would slip further into the right-wing camp.

In reaction to the pro-Nazi protest wave in schools and youth clubs, which began at the end of the 1970s, new teaching methods and project models have been developed which combine explanation and involvement, whereby the people involved develop activities themselves, and in doing so base them on their own interests and needs, and relate them to personal experience.[6] Here are some examples:

- interviews and discussions with witnesses, particularly from their own families and neighbourhood.

- local history projects: the history of the school, the area, etc., during the Nazi period.

- anti-Fascist town tours to historical places associated with both national socialism and the resistance.

- planning and staging exhibitions or theatrical productions.

- visiting memorials and former concentration camps.

Experience with these types of project has been largely positive, and many of the concepts have now become common practice in schools and youth clubs. However, confronting organised right-wing extremism does not become irrelevant as a result of this. As we have seen, it also has its roots in problem areas over which youth work, both in and out of school, has little or no influence.

6. *Wider das Vergessen. Antifaschistische Erziehung in der Schule. Erfahrungen – Projekte – Anregungen*, published by Gewerkschaft Erziehung und Wissenschaft, Berlin, Frankfurt, 1981; Benno Hafeneger, Gerhard Paul and Bernhard Schoßig (eds), *Dem Faschismus das Wasser abgraben. Zur Auseinandersetzung mit dem Rechtsradikalismus*, Munich, 1981.

This leads us back to the question of bans and sanctions. The only point of banning an organisation is to make it more difficult for people who are already organised to be effective. It is mainly a question of setting organisational thresholds for vulnerable people as high as possible. Since joining an illegal organisation requires a high degree of conviction and willingness to take risks, many people, particularly young people involved in pro-Nazi protest behaviour, would probably be severely deterred by a ban. For this reason, banning right-wing extremist clubs and associations in particular cases would seem to me to be a perfectly reasonable means in the fight against neo-Fascism. This also applies to the full utilisation of judicial, administrative and police measures, which, however, must satisfy particularly strict criteria applying to a state under the rule of law. Punishments and sanctions do not overcome the causes of right-wing extremism, but arguably they do make it more difficult for right-wing extremists to exist and, when successful, considerably restrict their freedom of movement and opportunities for growth.

Bans on parties, on the other hand, are extremely questionable from the point of view of democratic theory, and in all cases must only be considered as a last resort. In a party state democracy they represent a very serious intervention in the formation of the political will, which is characterised by the principle of the people's sovereignty.

Is the Fixation of Anti-Fascist Education with the Past Still Current? Finally, I would like to raise a problem which I have identified as a central theme: if it is true that there is no danger of a revival of historical national socialism, and if the list of causes stated in the previous section is an accurate depiction of reality, then one will not achieve much on the basis of improved and more intensive education regarding national socialism alone. This is because the conditions for success of right-wing extremism are rooted predominantly in the current societal conditions. This does not mean that the burdens of the past, traditions and tendencies should be completely obliterated. I am only concerned with putting those factors that have emerged from the present and those that are determined by history into perspective.

The anti-Fascist imperative can be reduced to the following

Causes and Countermeasures

common denominators: countermeasures must be aimed at both the subjectivity of those in danger and those affected as well as at the overall social conditions. This creates the necessity to expand historical knowledge, communicate democratic norms and practise social behaviour, as well as to overcome the antidemocratic elements that exist in West German political culture and to create acceptable economic and social opportunities, as well as a political order with which people can identify and which is capable of integration.

In order to educate youth in anti-Fascism, therefore, we face the task of creating the foundations for a common democratic culture, by introducing everyday democratic forms of interaction and patterns of behaviour.[7]

Countermeasures aimed at youth should focus on learning and working experiences, as well as on group behaviour and attitudes towards parents, teachers, employers, etc. By learning and through work, young people are directly reproducing their lives. They must learn actively to discuss and come to terms with their environment, productively solve existing conflicts and resist the attempt to delegate responsibility for their own lives to the supposed all-powerful authority.

Hence it is particularly important to create initiatives and projects that provide opportunities for collective action and qualifications, creating a feeling of solidarity, and facilitating self-organisation and self-help.

---

7. Peter Dudek (ed.), *Hakenkreuz und Judenwitz. Antifaschistische Jugendarbeit in der Schule*, Bensheim, 1980, p. 126.

6
Summary of the Theories Outlined in this Analysis

1. The term right-wing extremism refers to all attitudes and behaviour patterns that are directed towards the abolition or permanent restriction of democratic rights, structures and processes. In short, right-wing extremism, in my opinion, implies anti-democratic thought and behaviour.

2. West German organised right-wing extremism focuses its efforts on the 'national question', that is, the re-establishment of national unity and strength in the form of the (Greater) German Reich. Justifying and glossing over the Nazi past is an integral part of this. Nationalism is a categorical imperative at the head of the right-wing extremist hierarchy of values, and it has no respect for elementary rights, which are essential to dignified human life, such as freedom, equality and social justice.

3. It is true that, since 1945, sympathy for national socialism has manifestly declined. However, in West Germany today, a broad potential for right-wing extremist attitudes exists: pro-Nazi, anti-Semitic and xenophobic tendencies are to be found in 20–40 per cent of the population. The proportion of West Germans with an intransigent right-wing extremist view of the world is currently put at around 15 per cent.

4. The existence of this enormous potential for right-wing extremist views can only be understood against the background of German history. There has never been a widespread and intensive critical analysis of the Nazi past, and the common way of overcoming the past is to repress it, gloss over it or ignore it. Hence, even today, national socialism still exercises a considerable influence over the political culture of West Germany. It was impossible for a new,

Summary of the Theories

democratically founded, national identity to develop under these conditions in West Germany.

5. After 1945 the opportunity to purge the German people of the middle and higher leadership groups of the Nazi regime was wasted – to a certain extent deliberately. In 95 per cent of cases, de-Nazification (whose approach was wrong from the outset) only unearthed 'hangers-on', people who were subsequently exonerated and people who were not involved. After the founding of the Federal Republic of Germany, de-Nazification came to an abrupt halt, and its results – apart from a few exceptions – were annulled. The judicial prosecution by German courts of Nazi crimes was also very hesitant. By 1985, the West German judicial authorities had tracked down and sentenced 172 murderers for the Nazis' mass murder of millions.

6. Hence after 1945, many people in all areas of society retained their positions, this destroying any hope of a fundamentally new orientation in West German politics. Even the top positions in politics, administration, associations and publishing were not dominated by critics or opponents of national socialism, but by people who had been neutral or ambivalent towards German Fascism.

7. Fears which were originally thoroughly justified of a strong, organised post-war right-wing extremism have not proved to be well founded, in spite of apparently optimal social conditions after 1945 for the success of anti-democratic efforts. The integrative capacity of the *bürgerblock* parties, which influenced West German policies until 1966, grew surprisingly quickly, and organised right-wing extremism initially lost a large proportion of its social basis. In view of the economic prosperity and tendencies towards concentration within the party system, facilitated by basic consensus (regarding the important questions of domestic and foreign policy), the political and programmatic alternatives offered by the right-wing extremist parties and organisations soon found little response among the people. West German citizens concentrated their energy on reconstruction, growth, prosperity and consumerism, and were less concerned with the new structure of society.

8. In spite of the considerable dissemination of anti-democratic views, to date, organised right-wing extremism has remained more or less within modest limits in terms of membership numbers. According to official figures, the highest number, in the mid 1950s, was just under 80,000 members. In 1987, the Federal Ministry for the Interior registered 25,000 organised right-wing extremists. When one considers the considerable membership gains experienced by the Deutsche Volksunion and the Republikaner, by mid-1989 this number may have doubled to around 50,000.

9. The development of organised right-wing extremism occurred in two major stages, with 1965 representing the turning point.

10. Post-war right-wing extremism initially profited to a certain extent from the far-reaching economic, social and political post-war problems. At the first Bundestag elections, the licensed right-wing extremist parties achieved 1.4 million votes. A further 1.1 million voters plumped for candidates or groups that could be classified as anti-democratic. The right-wing extremist parties, however, have not succeeded in obtaining long-term commitment from this potential, which in total comprised around 11 per cent of the electorate. By the 1953 Bundestag elections *bürgerblock*'s integration, led by the CDU/CSU, began to prove successful. By 1961, the right-wing extremist electorate had shrunk to 0.9 per cent of the total electorate.

11. The decline of post-war right-wing extremism, however, was not caused purely by external factors. It failed to present any attractive and realistic alternative to the policies of the *bürgerblock*. Moreover, their credibility and competence were restricted by a high degree of organisational fragmentation and permanent conflict between the leaders of the small parties.

12. With the 'end of the post-war era', the phase of New Right-Wing Extremism began. The decline of the *bürgerblock*, the formation of a Grand Coalition from the CDU/CSU and SPD, and the first major economic crisis favoured the rise of the Nationaldemokratische Partei Deutschlands, which en-

Summary of the Theories

tered seven *Land* parliaments between 1966 and 1968, and only just failed to enter the Bundestag in 1969 with 1.4 million votes.

13. With the formation of the social-liberal coalition in 1969, the CDU/CSU completed a clear swing to the right and formed a solid conservative opposition. Confrontation and polarisation in the political system dried up the NPD's electoral base, a party that was also falling apart from within. The raw political climate, however, encouraged the emergence of a violent youth right-wing extremism outside of the parliamentary field. After 1977/8, this escalated to neo-Nazi terrorism; however, by the mid-1980s, it had been weakened organisationally by the police and judicial measures and had become politically disillusioned.

14. In the mid-1980s the third wave of successful organised right-wing extremism began, and has probably not yet reached its peak. Comparatively good election results were achieved by the NPD–DVU alliance, and in 1987 they even achieved a parliamentary seat, again at *Land* level (in Bremen), for the first time since 1968. However, it was not the old-established right-wing extremist organisations that achieved the actual breakthrough, but the Republikaner, founded in 1983, who officially were not considered to be right-wing extremist. They immediately and easily overcame the 5 per cent hurdle in 1989: in Berlin they gained eleven seats and in the European elections over 2 million votes (six seats). Never in West German history has such a good result been achieved at federal level by a right-wing extremist party.

15. The Republikaner, who currently have some 14,000 members, are predominantly a southern German party in terms of the origins of their members and voters. In terms of their party programme and propaganda, they gloss over the Nazi crimes and the holocaust, relativise Germany's war guilt, and incite anti-Semitism, racism and racial hatred. They want to restrict the influence of parties and associations, destroy the right to free collective bargaining and abolish the freedom of the press. The Republikaner are a right-wing

extremist party directed against the free democratic basic order of the Federal Republic of Germany.

16. The Republikaner succeeded in outstripping the NPD/DVU alliance in elections, mainly because they are not seen as a neo-Fascist party by the vast majority of the population, because, ideologically, they cover the area from right-wing conservatism to right-wing extremism, and because they have received a great deal of publicity from the media. In addition – and in contrast to the NPD and the DVU – they are not officially considered to be right-wing extremist. As a result of this, possible inhibition thresholds are lowered among the electorate, and membership of the party (e.g. by people employed in public service) is not countered with any form of sanctions. In many cases, the Republikaner are not even excluded from the democratic spectrum, but are rendered quite acceptable as potential coalition partners.

17. Regarding the causes of right-wing extremism, one must distinguish between individual factors and those relating to society as a whole. Individual factors focus on the 'authoritarian character' and other mistakes made during socialisation, which encourage the emergence of anti-democratic attitudes. Additional factors are dissatisfaction with one's personal situation in life and alienation from the existing economic, social and political conditions. In this situation, surrogate worlds are often sought (in the form of people, groups, symbols), which promise power, strength, security and protection and facilitate identification and orientation.

18. The causes of right-wing extremism relating to society as a whole include crises in the economy (e.g. unemployment, poverty, structural disadvantages of individual economic sectors or social strata), the social field (e.g. unsatisfactory living conditions and accommodation, a decaying infrastructure, and lack of leisure opportunities or neighbourly relations) and the political field (e.g. a low degree of acceptance of the democratic institutions, lack of capacity for integration or loss of ties in intermediary organisations). Furthermore, the spread of right-wing extremism is favoured by anti-democratic elements in political culture:

Summary of the Theories

repressing and playing down national socialism, a lack of democratic consciousness and discrediting anti-Fascism.

19. The individual causes of right-wing extremism and those relating to society form a uniform pattern of effects: the factors relating to society as a whole have an equal effect on all stages of development, from the development of an 'authoritarian character' to right-wing extremist activities. The specific conditions under which this development occurs vary from one individual to another. Exactly when the qualitative leap from one level to the next occurs depends on special circumstances, actual experiences and learning processes, and is strongly characterised by conjunctures of events.

20. The success of organised right-wing extremism does not only depend on the effects of the individual conditions and those relating to society as a whole (described above). Right-wing extremism must for its part be capable of using political crises for its own ends by creating an aura of political competence and credibility, presenting attractive programmatic alternatives and goals with which people can identify, avoiding organisational fragmentation and giving prominence to popular personalities.

21. The very complex conditions for success for right-wing extremism are rooted largely in the current conditions in West Germany. I would warn against a concept of anti-Fascism that is too narrow, one-sided and historically fixed. Countermeasures should equally be directed at the subjectivity of those in danger and those concerned, as well as at the overall social conditions. This creates the need both to extend historical knowledge, convey democratic norms and practise social behaviour, and overcome the anti-democratic elements in political culture and create acceptable socio-economic opportunities and create political conditions with the ability to integrate and with which people can identify.

22. When confronting right-wing extremism, the main concern is to protect youth from anti-democratic forces in order to prevent right-wing extremists from recruiting its next generation of supporters. Countermeasures aimed at youth

subjectivity should focus on their experiences of learning and at work, as well as their behaviour in groups and towards people who are close to them. By learning and through work, young people are directly reproducing their lives. They must learn actively to confront their environment, to resolve existing conflicts in a productive manner and to resist the temptation to abdicate responsibility for their own lives to a supposed all-powerful authority. Hence particular importance is attached to those initiatives and projects that provide young people with the opportunities for direct collective action and qualifications, in a spirit of solidarity, and that facilitate self-organisation and self-help.

Appendix: Selected Documents

Document 1: Wahlprogramm der Deutschen Reichspartei zur Bundestagswahl 1953

Deutsche Reichs-Partei (DRP)

Unser politisches Ziel ist:
1. Politik der Unabhängigkeit, Souveränität und Gleichberechtigung zur Wahrung der Lebensinteressen unserer Nation und des Friedens der Welt.
2. Wiederherstellung der Reichseinheit und Gleichheit aller Reichsbürger vor dem Gesetz.
3. Festigung einer rechtsstaatlichen, freiheitlichen Demokratie, getragen vom Vertrauen des deutschen Volkes und gestützt auf eine Auswahl der tüchtigsten Kräfte.
4. Überwindung aller trennenden Gegensätze innerhalb unseres Volkes durch den Geist echter Volksgemeinschaft und die Sicherung des sozialen Friedens.
5. Einigung der europäischen Völker auf Grund der Gemeinsamkeit ihrer Geschichte und Kultur.

1. Wir fordern
   das „Reich" als inneren Bestandteil Europas.
   Wir wollen das ganze Reich im ganzen Europa.
2. Wir fordern
   die Einheit des Deutschen Reiches in seinen geschichtlichen Grenzen.
3. Wir bedauern,
   daß es einer Betonung der Reichseigenschaft des Saargebietes bedarf. Die Saar ist deutsch!
4. Wir anerkennen
   die völkische Gemeinsamkeit der europäischen Nationen. Sie kann nicht genug verdichtet werden. Beibehaltung der nationalen Eigenart der europäischen Völker ist Voraussetzung für ihr friedliches und geordnetes Zusammenleben.
5. Wir streben an,
   daß die Blocks der Großmächte die friedliche Sicherheit des zen-

Appendix

tral-europäischen Raumes durch gegenseitige Garantien gewährleisten. Darin sehen wir die beste Art der Sicherung des Friedens in Europa.

6. Wir wollen
für Westdeutschland die Freiheit der eigenen Entschließung durch das Volk für jetzt und die Zukunft. Wir lehnen eine zwingende Bindung an den Westen für Westdeutschland und das ganze Deutschland ebenso ab wie eine zwingende Bindung Ostdeutschlands und des ganzen Deutschlands an den Osten.
Wir wollen
das Selbstbestimmungsrecht einer wirklichen Souveränität zunächst für Westdeutschland, später für das vereinte ganze Deutschland.
Die Regierung hat dem deutschen Volk im voraus versprochen, daß die beabsichtigten kommenden Westverträge uns volle Souveränität bringen würden. Das Versprechen ist nicht gehalten worden.
Der Generalvertrag ist ein Zwangs-Ketten-Vertrag, aufgebaut auf Unwahrheit. Hierin soll Versailles wiederholt werden. Die Folgen schrecken.
Wir lehnen diese Verträge ab.

7. Wir wollen
unter der Voraussetzung voller staatlicher Souveränität, daß das deutsche Volk bewaffnet sei.
Auch die Westdeutsche Bundesrepublik soll bewaffnet sein.

8. Wir fordern
die Freihelt der Entschließung, wirtschaftliche wie wehrpolitische Verträge, Nicht-Angriffs-Pakte oder Bündnisse zu schließen in gleichem Grade freier Selbstbestimmung, wie sie etwa das Königreich Schweden, die Republik der Schweiz oder Spanien beanspruchen.

9. Wir lassen wissen,
daß bei einem Konflikt zwischen den großen Mächten des Westens und des Ostens die Deutschen unter keinen Umständen auf Seiten des Angreifers stehen werden.
Deutsche Waffen werden nur zur Verteidigung des eigenen Raumes gegen einen Angreifer, von welcher Seite er auch kommen mag, da sein.

10. Wir anerkennen
das Bonner Grundgesetz als rechtliche gültige Verfassungsgrundlage der Westdeutschen Bundesrepublik. Es ist aus Krieg und Besatzung entstanden und auch nach unserer Ansicht revisionsbedürftig.

11. Wir fordern
eine neue Ordnung eines Rechtsstaates.

Appendix

Durch Heranziehen und Einschmelzen aller positiv wirkenden Kräfte sowohl der Kaiserzeit, als der 1. Republik, der Zeit des Nationalsozialismus, wie auch der Zwischenzeit der Bundesrepublik und der sogenannten Deutschen Demokratischen Republik soll die Vergangenheit überwunden und ein neuer Weg in die Zukunft beschritten werden.

12. Wir fordern
Sauberkeit in Regierung, Verwaltung und Rechtsprechung.
Der hemmungslose Kampf der Parteien um die Macht ist Gift im Volkskörper und verhindert Sauberkeit im öffentlichen Leben. Das Gift ist zu beseitigen!

13. Wir fordern,
daß Rechtsprechung, Justizverwaltung und Polizei bewußt und vollständig aus dem Parteiengetriebe herausgelöst werden.
Die geistige, rechtliche und personelle Korruption hat Formen angenommen, die für das Empfinden der noch gesunden Teile des Volkes unerträglich sind.

14. Wir fordern
eine Stärkung der Stelle des Staatsoberhauptes, wie auch die Wiederholung von Volksbegehren und Volksentscheid gegen die totalitären Neigungen einer jeweiligen Mehrheit.

15. Oberster Souverän ist das Volk!
Das Wahlrecht ist so zu ändern, daß unverfälscht und ungehemmt das ganze Volk spricht.
Dieser Grundsatz ist der einzige gültige demokratische. Er darf durch Zweckmäßigkeiten niemals verfälscht werden.
Parteien, die ein Wahlrecht suchen nach den Interessen einer Koalition oder ihrer eigenen Macht, werden abgelehnt.

16. Wir wünschen,
daß die Kontrolle des öffentlichen Lebens beim Staatsoberhaupt und bei der Gesamtheit des ganzen Volkes liege.
Hierbei sollen Persönlichkeiten von Leistung und Anerkennung, die Berufsverbände ebenso wie die Vertreter der Gewerkschaften durch Gesetz ihren Platz angemesserer Wirksamkeit zur Mitverantwortung erhalten.

17. Wir fordern
als Grundlage des Wirtschaftslebens Anerkennung von Eigentum, Unternehmer-Verantwortung und-Risiko, Wertung des Marktes als regelnde Ordnung, Rückschrauben staatlicher Eingriffe.
Das freie Spiel der Kräfte jedoch muß dort gezügelt werden, wo es das Wohl der Allgemeinheit erfordert oder der Schutz der Schwachen gegenüber dem Stärkeren.
Die Grade, Formen und Mittel verstraffender Eingriffe werden als wandelbar nach Raum, Zeit, Fachgebiet und Gegenstand anerkannt.

Appendix

Je stärker die Spannung, um so strenger kann eine Verstraffung sich als notwendig erweisen.

Zugespitzt einseitiges Verdienst- und Machtstreben, Überwältigung der Kleinen durch die Großen, Mangelzeiten und Mangelwaren, die Forderung gleichmäßiger Versorgung aller mit dem Notwendigen ergeben die Pflichten zu ordnenden Eingriffen.

Kampfparolen wie: Hie Freie Wirtschaft, Hie Planwirtschaft werden als überholt erachtet.

18. Dem wirtschaftlich Schwachen gehört die Hilfe der Gemeinschaft.

Sie soll in erster Linie in einer Eingliederung in den Arbeitsprozeß der Nation bestehen.

Die lebenspendende Arbeit ist das Ziel der Wohlfahrt.

Mitbestimmung, Mittragen der Verantwortung im Betriebe gehört zur Arbeit selbst. Sie gehört den Betriebsangehörigen als ein Teil des Arbeitsbegriffes.

19. Wir wissen,

daß das deutsche Volk – insbesondere auch nach der endlich erreichten und so lange ersehnten Wiedervereinigung – ein armes Volk sein wird. Die Hilfe, die der Osten braucht, muß ihm von den Deutschen des Westens kommen.

Damit wird dem deutschen Volke auferlegt sein, in Bescheidenheit zu leben.

So wird und soll der Wert der Familie und der Kinderzucht sich neu beleben. Das häusliche Glück der Menschen soll wieder höher stehen als der Gelderwerb.

Den Kindern soll alle Arbeit gelten!

20. Wir fordern,

gleiche Chancen für den Beginn der beruflichen Lebensbahn jedes Deutschen. Abstammung, Eltern, Partei, Konfession, Besitz dürfen keine Rolle spielen.

Schulausbildung und Arbeitsplatz werden dem jungen Menschen gewährleistet. Darüber hinaus wird als Maßstab für Aufstieg und Verdienst allein die Tüchtigkeit in der Leistung nach meßbaren Werten wie nach der Anständigkeit der Gesinnung gelten.

21. Wir wollen,

daß jedweder konfessioneller Streit sich auf Religion und Kirche beschränkt. Im politischen Leben darf er nicht in Erscheinung treten.

22. Wir wissen,

daß die Geschichte dem deutschen Volke Leiden und Lasten auferlegt hat, die unwägbar sind. Wir wollen, daß eine Frage nach der geschichtlichen Schuld der Geschichte überlassen bleibe. Sie zu beantworten ist weder Sache der Lebenden unter den Deutschen noch in anderen Ländern.

Appendix

Es ist eine Frage übernationalen Geschehens. Wir lehnen auch jede Art von Selbstbeschuldigung der Deutschen ab. Niemals in der Geschichte war ein Mann oder ein Volk allein schuld. Sicher erscheint aber, daß Schuld am Kriege diejenigen sind, die keinen Frieden zu schaffen verstehen. Deshalb heißt es nicht zurückschauen, sondern schöpferisch zu zeugen für eine Zeit, nunmehr eine Zeit wirklichen Friedens.

Helft alle mit! Kommt zu uns! Es gibt noch mehr als nur die Wahl zwischen Rot und Schwarz!
Mit Hans Grimm, Dr. Werner Naumann, H. H. Scheffer, Ulrich Rudel, Adolf v. Thadden, Prof. v. Grünberg, General Andrae für die Vertretung des nationalen Deutschlands im neuen Bundestag.

Source: Dudek and Jaschke, *Rechtsextremismus*, vol. 2, p. 38f.

Appendix

Document 2: Außenpolitisches Zehn-Punkte-Programm der Deutschen Gemeinschaft (1954)

1. Erringung und Bewahrung der absoluten, uneingeschränkten Souveränität auf allen Gebieten, grundsätzliches Verbot jeder Art von Abtretung von Hoheitsrechten.
2. Anerkennung jeder fremden Regierung, die de facto die Gewalt in einem souveränen Staat verkörpert, ohne Rücksicht darauf, wie sie zur Macht gekommen ist und welche Ziele sie verfolgt, und Enthaltung jeglicher Kritik an innenpolitischen Einrichtungen anderer Staaten.
3. Verhinderung jeder Agententätigkeit von Emigrantengruppen auf deutschem Boden.
4. Verbot jeglicher Unterstützung materieller oder moralischer Art für politische Gruppen im Ausland durch deutsche Staatsangehörige und entsprechendes Verbot der Annahme ausländischer Unterstützung für politische Gruppen innerhalb Deutschlands, soweit beides nicht in normalen Regierungsverträgen zwischen den betroffenen Staaten ausdrücklich gestattet ist.
5. Ersatz der öffentlichen internationalen Konferenzen mit ihren Propagandareden zum Fenster hinaus durch die klassische Kabinettsdiplomatie.
6. Kündigung der Teilnahme an allen kollektiven und multilateralen Vereinbarungen oder internationalen Behörden mit Ausnahme von Abmachungen humanitären Charakters (IRK, Haager Landkriegsordnung, Genfer Konvention usw.); an ihre Stelle haben zweiseitige kündbare Verträge von Regierung zu Regierung zu treten.
7. Staatliche Lenkung des Außenhandels zur Vermeidung einseitiger wirtschaftlicher Abhängigkeit und zur ökonomischen Untermauerung der Beziehungen zu politischen und militärischen Partnerstaaten.
8. Befreiung der Verhältnisse zu anderen Staaten von jeder Rücksichtnahme auf rassische, sprachliche, kulturelle, religiöse, ideologische, gesellschaftliche oder sonstige innere Strukturgegebenheiten der Partner sowie von Rache- oder Haßgefühlen und Erbfeindlegenden.
9. Verurteilung jeder Form von nationaler Fremdherrschaft, wie Unterdrückung von nationalen Minderheiten, Rassendiskriminierung, Kolonialismus, Imperialismus oder Besatzungsregime; Abbruch der diplomatischen Beziehungen zu offensichtlichen Marionettenregierungen.
10. Revision der Grenzziehung von 1945 auf friedlichem Wege bei definitivem Verzicht auf jede „Landnahme" über den naturgegebenen historischen und geographischen Siedlungsraum unseres Volkes hinaus.

(Verabschiedet auf dem Münchener Parteitag, 14./15.8.1954)

Appendix

Document 3: Nationaldemokratisches Manifest (1978)

Fremde Gewalt lastet auf dem geteilten Deutschland im geteilten Europa. Die politischen Systeme der Gegenwart zerstören die Demokratie. Sie sind als Handlanger der weltbeherrschenden Mächte unfähig, die Freiheit der Völker zu erkämpfen.

Aus dieser Erkenntnis stellen wir fest:

1. Die NATIONALDEMOKRATIE ist die Verwirklichung der Einheit von Volk und Nation in freier Selbstbestimmung aufgrund des geltenden Völkerrechts.
2. Die NATIONALDEMOKRATISCHE LEBENSORDNUNG ist der Garant für die Freiheit des Menschen in der Gemeinschaft seines freien Volkes. NATIONALDEMOKRATIE bedeutet: Freie Menschen in einem freien Land.
3. Die NATIONALDEMOKRATISCHE WELTANSCHAUUNG beruht auf modernen naturwissenschaftlichen Erkenntnissen und auf den unverzichtbaren Überlieferungen deutscher und europäischer Geistesgeschichte und Kultur. Sie garantiert die Erhaltung der natürlichen Lebensbedingungen für Mensch, Volk und Umwelt.
4. Das WESEN DER NATIONALDEMOKRATIE beruht auf dem Respekt und der Achtung vor der natürlichen Ungleichheit der Menschen. Gleich sind die Menschen nur vor dem Gesetz und in der Unantastbarkeit ihrer Würde.
5. Die NATIONALDEMOKRATISCHE GEMEINSCHAFTSORDNUNG ist eine Ordnung umfassender sozialer Gerechtigkeit. Oberste Richtschnur ist das Wohl der Volksgemeinschaft auf rechtsstaatlicher Grundlage. Das heißt: Verpflichtung und Verantwortung des Einzelnen für die Gemeinschaft und der Gemeinschaft für jeden Einzelnen.
6. Die NATIONALDEMOKRATISCHE WIRTSCHAFTSORDNUNG beruht auf dem Primat der Politik, ausgerichtet an den Notwendigkeiten und Bedürfnissen einer vernünftigen Volkswirtschaft.
7. Die NATIONALDEMOKRATIE ist die EINZIGE ALTERNATIVE zum Machtanspruch der internationalistischen Ideologien und Systeme.
8. NATIONALDEMOKRATIE ist die wahre Verwirklichung einer SOUVERÄNEN VOLKSHERRSCHAFT, die auf der Unantastbarkeit der, auch im Grundgesetz verankerten, freiheitlichen Grundordnung beruht.
9. Die NATIONALDEMOKRATISCHE POLITIK ist Friedenspolitik, da sie die Freiheit und Unabhängigkeit aller Völker, sowie die absolute Nichteinmischung in die inneren Angelegenheiten

Appendix

anderer Staaten, als unumstößlichen Grundsatz proklamiert.
10. Die NPD ist der Zusammenschluß der Nationaldemokraten in Deutschland. Ihr höchstes Ziel ist die Neuvereinigung zu einem DEUTSCHEN REICH.

Appendix

Document 4: 24 Thesen zum Nationalismus (1977)

[Junge Nationaldemokraten]

Der Dritte Weg

1. Nationalismus ist das Streben nach Unabhängigkeit, Freiheit, Selbstbestimmung und Einheit aller Völker.
2. Der Nationalismus bekämpft jedes Fremdherrschaftsstreben (Imperialismus), gleichgültig, ob es militärische, wirtschaftliche, politische oder kulturelle Mittel benutzt.
3. Nationalismus ist eine internationale Notwendigkeit im Interesse aller unterdrückten, gespaltenen, ausgebeuteten und geknechteten Völker. Der gemeinsame Gegner der Völker ist der Imperialismus jedweder Schattierung.
4. Der Nationalismus erkennt das von den Wissenschaften erschlossene neue Menschenbild an und wird fortgestaltend neue Erkenntnisse in seine programmatische Aussage einbeziehen.
5. Der Nationalismus bekämpft Liberalismus und Marxismus, weil beide Ideologien wissenschaftsfeindlich und nicht lebensrichtig sind. Der Nationalismus bekämpft deshalb auch die Erscheinungsformen von Liberalismus und Marxismus: den Kapitalismus und den Kommunismus.
6. Nationalismus läßt sich nicht mißbrauchen im Scheinkampf des kapitalistischen mit dem kommunistischen System. Hier gibt es kein kleineres Übel, für das sich Nationalisten entscheiden könnten. Beide Systeme sind das große Übel in zwei verschiedenen Ausformungen.
7. Da der Imperialismus der Großmächte und der multinationalen Konzerne sich der verschiedensten Mittel (Kriege, wirtschaftliche Ausbeutung, Umerziehung, Konzentrationslager ...) bedient, müssen auch die Mittel des nationalistischen Befreiungskampfes weltweit verschieden sein.
8. Die Nationalisten Westdeutschlands richten sich in ihrem Kampf nach dem Wortlaut des Grundgesetzes. Das GG darf von den Herrschenden nicht länger mißbraucht und entfremdet werden, sondern muß – notfalls gegen sie – verwirklicht und durchgesetzt werden.
9. Der Nationalismus erfaßt alle Gebiete der Politik. Hierbei sind Innen- und Gesellschaftspolitik genauso wichtig wie die Außenpolitik.
10. Das wissenschaftliche Menschenbild widerlegt die Grundthese der Liberalisten und Marxisten: die angebliche »Gleichheit« aller Men-

schen. Diese Falschthese ist die Voraussetzung für die Manipulierung und Entmündigung der Menschen.
11. Der Nationalismus erstrebt den Dritten Weg jenseits von Liberalismsus/Kapitalismus und Marxismus/Kommunismus. Dieser Dritte Weg ist etwas grundsätzlich Neues auf wissenschaftlicher Grundlage.
12. Der Nationalismus erstrebt soziale Gerechtigkeit und Nationale Solidarität. Nationale Solidarität ist kein Zustand gesellschaftlicher Friedhofsruhe, sondern ein Ziel, um das immer gerungen werden muß.
13. Der Nationalismus wendet sich gegen Ausbeutung, Unterdrückung und Entmündigung der Menschen. Er bekämpft den Klassenkampf von »oben« und von »unten«.
14. Der Nationalismus erkennt die Taktik des Imperialismus, die Völker von ihrem Befreiungskampf dadurch abzulenken, daß ihnen der Scheingegensatz »Kapitalismus gegen Kommunismus« vorgegaukelt wird. Dieser Scheingegensatz soll die Völker davon abhalten, ihre wirklichen Interessen zu erkennen.
15. Der Nationalismus erkennt, daß nicht die Völker sich Feinde sind, sondern daß der gemeinsame Feind der Völker die gemeinsamen Unterdrücker sind.
16. Der Nationalismus trennt nicht die Völker, wie es Liberalisten und Marxisten behaupten. Vielmehr verbindet der Nationalismus die Völker im gemeinsamen Kampf gegen liberalistische und marxistische Imperialisten.
17. Wer vorgibt, Nationalist zu sein, andere Völker aber spaltet, unterdrückt, knechtet oder ausbeutet, ist ein Imperialist. Der moderne Nationalismus ist der stärkste Feind des Imperialismus: Nationalismus ist antiimperialistischer Kampf.
18. Wer glaubt, Nationalist zu sein, und gleichzeitig andere Völker bekämpft, leistet Handlangerdienste für die Imperialisten.
19. Der Nationalismus bekämpft alle diejenigen, die mit Imperialisten aus Ost und West »Verständigung«, »Frieden«, »Versöhnung« usw. anstreben. Denn es sind gerade die Imperialisten, die der Verständigung und Versöhnung der Völker im Wege stehen.
20. Nationalismus heißt nicht, andere Völker in ihren Rechten zu beschneiden, sondern das gerade Gegenteil: die Solidarität der Völker gegen den gemeinsamen Feind voranzutreiben.
21. Die Hauptträger des heutigen Imperialismus sind die UdSSR und die USA.
22. Der Nationalismus bekämpft die multinationalen Konzerne, die aufgrund ihrer Profitinteressen weltweit bestrebt sind, die Völker auszubeuten, zu unterdrücken, zu entmündigen. Die Multis sind, entweder direkt oder über den Umweg der von ihnen beeinflußten

Appendix

Regierung, wesentliche Träger des modernen Imperialismus.
23. Aus nationalistischer Sicht löst sich der scheinbare Gegensatz zwischen Kapitalismus und Kommunismus auf: Der Sowjetkommunismus ist ein großer Konzern (und das Moskauer Politbüro dessen Vorstand) – deshalb auch der Begriff »Staatskapitalismus« –, während es in den westlichen Staaten mehrere Großkonzerne gibt. Es wird weltweit um Marktanteile gestritten, dieser Zustand wird als »Entspannung«, »Detente« oder »friedliche Koexistenz« bezeichnet. Dieser Kampf um Marktanteile wird auf dem Rücken der Völker ausgetragen, deren Freiheit, Selbstbestimmung und Unabhängigkeit hierdurch zunehmend eingeengt werden.
24. Der europäische Nationalismus erstrebt ein gemeinsames Europa der Völker, um ihre Freiheit, Einheit, Unabhängigkeit und Selbstbestimmung gemeinsam gegen die Großmächte, falsche Ideologien, die Multis und kleinbürgerlichen Chauvinismus durchzusetzen.

Source: Meyer and Rabe, *Unsere Stunde die wird kommen*, pp. 232ff.

Appendix

Document 5: Ausländische Arbeiter in Deutschland (1979) [NPD leaflet]

Die NPD stellt fest:

- Deutschland ist kein Einwanderungsland!
- Den etwa 1. Millionen Arbeitslosen und Kurzarbeitern (unter ihnen ungefähr 100,000 Jugendliche) stehen in Westdeutschland immer noch rund zwei Millionen ausländische Arbeiter gegenüber.
- Zwar geht die Zahl ausländischer Arbeiter zurück. Dennoch nimmt die Zahl der ausländischen Wohnbevölkerung ständig zu. Die Gründe dafür liegen in der Geburtenfreudigkeit und im Familiennachzug, der vor allem eine Auswirkung der SPD/FDP-Kindergeldgesetzgebung darstellt.

Die NPD verlangt:

- Rückwanderung der Gastarbeiter!
Keine Eingliederung (Integration). Ausländer bleiben mit allen Rechten und Pflichten (Wahlrecht, Wehrpflicht) Staatsbürger ihrer Heimatländer.
- Beschränkung der Verweildauer nach dem Rotationsprinzip, da sie nur Arbeitspartner auf Zeit sind.
- Zuzugsverbot in Ballungsräume, die 10% ausländische Wohnbevölkerung erreicht haben.
- Einstellen des Familiennachzugs.
- Schrittweiser und systematischer Abbau der ausländischen Arbeitskräfte; einweisen von Deutschen in frei werdende Arbeitsplätze.

Die NPD verlangt weiter:

- Deutsche Arbeitsplätze für deutsche Arbeitnehmer!
- Ausgliederung der Ausländer aus der deutschen Arbeitslosen- und Rentenversicherung; keine Umschulung auf unsere Kosten. Verlassen des Landes nach einer Arbeitslosenzeit von zwei Monaten.
- Aufheben oder Einschränken der freien Arbeitsplatzwahl für Angehörige anderer EG-Staaten; keine Freizügigkeit für Arbeitskräfte aus Ländern, die der EG nur angeschlossen sind (z. B. Griechenland, Türkei u. a.).
- Beibehaltung des Anwerbestopps auch bei einer Konjunkturbelebung; im Bedarfsfall steuerfreie Überstunden für Deutsche!
- Kindergeld nur für Deutsche! Keine deutsche Steuerprämie, um die Zeugungs- und Geburtenfreudigkeit der Gastarbeiter-Exportländer noch mehr anzuregen, die jetzt schon ihren Arbeitskräfteüberschuß

Appendix

nicht verkraften können.
- Deutsche Mithilfe bei der Verbesserung der Infrastruktur und industriellen Entwicklung der ,,Gastarbeiter-Importländer": Maschinen zu den Menschen, statt Menschen zu den Maschinen! Deutsche Arbeitsplätze für deutsche Arbeitnehmer!

Appendix

Document 6: Aktion Neue Rechte

Grundsatzerklärung (1972)

Neue Kräfte stehen in Europa auf. Im Ostblock fordern die unterdrückten Völker Freiheit. In Westeuropa wird um ein echtes Selbstbestimmungsrecht gerungen. Im geteilten Deutschland wächst die Protestbewegung gegen die Selbstaufgabe der in Jahrhunderten gewachsenen deutschen Nation. Überwindung der nationalen Zerrissenheit bedeutet zugleich Neugestaltung der sozialen Ordnung. Die ANR ist der Zusammenschluß der politischen Kräfte in Deutschland, die die Durchsetzung dieser Ziele als ihre unabdingbare Pflicht erkannt haben.

Die Grundsätze der ANR sind:

1. Das 20. Jahrhundert, das technische Zeitalter, stellt uns vor Aufgaben völlig neuer Art. Altkommunisten und Neomarxisten sind nicht in der Lage, die gesellschaftspolitischen Probleme zu lösen. Die bürgerlichen Konservativen beschränken sich auf oberflächliche Reaktion. Die wissenschaftlich technische Revolution erfordert daher eine Bewegung neuen Typs: den Europäischen Sozialismus.

2. Die Menschen in Europa wollen eine Neue Ordnung persönlicher Freiheit, menschlicher Solidarität, sozialer Gerechtigkeit und nationaler Selbstbestimmung.
Dies kann nur durch die moderne Bewegung des Europäischen Sozialismus verwirklicht werden.

3. Der Europäische Sozialismus ist antimarxistisch. Er ist der Überwinder des Marxismus. Er bekämpft den lebensfeindlichen Kommunismus, der die Menschen knechtet und die Völker versklavt.
Der Europäische Sozialismus beruht auf dem natürlichen Wesen des Menschen und ist daher lebensrichtig.
Europäischer Sozialismus heißt Primat der Politik über das Kapital. Das bedeutet Absage an den Kapitalismus als Herrschaft des Kapitals über die Politik. Europäischer Sozialismus ist die Voraussetzung dafür, daß der in freien Wahlen geäußerte Volkswille tatsächlich in politische Entscheidungen umgesetzt werden kann.

4. Europäischer Sozialismus bedeutet: eine neue Wertschätzung der Arbeit. Arbeit geht vor Kapital. Europäischer Sozialismus ist – im Gegensatz zum bürokratischen Kommunismus – Solidarität der Menschen in der Gemeinschaft und das Recht der Selbstorganisation der Arbeitenden.

Appendix

Die Wirtschaft dient dem Volk. Das Eigentum an Produktionsmitteln anonymer Großkonzerne ist nicht unantastbar. Die Konzentrationsprozesse zugunsten der internationalen Hochfinanz müssen unterbunden werden.
Private, genossenschaftliche und staatliche Initiative müssen nebeneinander bestehen und miteinander den Fortschritt der Nation fördern.
Diese Forderung ist revolutionär in einer Zeit, in der die Städte vergiftet und von Autolawinen verstopft, die Gewässer verseucht, die Landschaft in Müllhalden verwandelt und unkontrolliert zersiedelt, Millionen von Menschen als Fremdarbeiter entwurzelt und vom internationalen Kapital hin- und hergeschoben, Milliardenbeträge durch Bodenspekulation dem Volk entzogen werden.
Nur unter den Perspektiven des Europäischen Sozialismus und mit modernsten technologischen Mitteln läßt sich die Umweltkatastrophe der nahen Zukunft abwenden: Gemeinschaftsinteresse muß vor Einzelinteressen gehen.

5. Die neue Europäische Sozialordnung hat das Ziel, die Leistungsgemeinschaft zu schaffen. Leistungsgemeinschaft bedeutet, daß der soziale Rang des einzelnen allein von seiner persönlichen Qualifikation, vom Wert seiner Leistung abhängen soll.
   – Gleichheit der Chancen für alle, die durch eine moderne Bildungspolitik zu sichern ist,
   – soziale Mobilität, Aufstieg für den Tüchtigen,
   – wirtschaftliche Freiheit für den einzelnen, Sicherung der unternehmerischen Initiative, ohne die dynamische Wirtschaft nicht möglich ist.
   Europäischer Sozialismus ist Solidarität. Solidarität insbesondere mit den wirtschaftlich Schwachen, die – entgegen ihrer Bedeutung für die Nation – im gegenwärtigen System benachteiligt werden: mit Lehrlingen, Bauern, Frauen, Alten.

6. Solidarität in der Gemeinschaft der Schaffenden – das ist zugleich der moderne Nationalismus. Der Marxismus begegnet dem Nationalismus mit Feindschaft, die bürgerlich-liberale Mitte mit opportunistischer Ablehnung, die bürgerlich-konsevative Rechte mit Unverständnis. Der Nationalismus ist überall in der Welt die Grundströmung unserer Zeit. Nationalismus ist politischer Fortschritt!

7. Moderner Nationalismus ist antiimperialistisch.
   Moderner Nationalismus in Deutschland ist Befreiungspolitik. Gegen die Nutznießer von 1945, gegen die Spalter und Bürokraten setzen wir die Politik der Neuvereinigung Deutschlands. Neuverei-

Appendix

nigung Deutschlands bedeutet Kampf gegen den status quo, Kampf gegen die Kleinstaaterei und die Zementierung irrsinniger Grenzen. Das System von Jalta, das System des Mauermords, der territorialen Zerstückelung und der Fremdherrschaft muß verschwinden zusammen mit allen, die es heute zu rechtfertigen versuchen.
Die Lösung der nationalen Frage in Deutschland ist nicht zu trennen vom Kampf gegen den Sowjetimperialismus. Der Kapitulationspolitik der Verträge von Moskau und Warschau setzen wir die Solidarität aller unterdrückten Völker entgegen. Die Aufstände in Mitteldeutschland 1953, Polen und Ungarn 1956, Tschechoslowakei 1968, Danzig 1970, die permanente Unruhe im Baltikum, in der Ukraine, in Kroatien sind Ausdruck ein- und derselben Kraft: Befreiungsnationalismus der europäischen Völker. Wir erklären uns solidarisch.

8. Moderner Nationalismus kennt also keinen verengten Horizont, sondern eine Öffnung nach vorn: Unser Ziel ist die Nation Europa als politische Einheit. Grundlage des modernen Europa können nicht die verknöcherten Kleinstaatensysteme mit ihren Egoismen und Grenzen sein, nicht das bürgerliche Europa der Bankiers und Ausschüsse. Das Europa des Europäischen Sozialismus ist das Europa der Völker. Die Nation Europa als Großmacht in gleichberechtigtem Bündnis mit den USA ist der einzige Schutz gegen den Imperialismus der aggressiven, friedensfeindlichen Sowjetunion. Nur der Wirtschaftsgroßraum Europa hat die Chance, die wissenschaftliche – technische Revolution mit allen ihren Folgen zu bewältigen.

9. Europäischer Sozialismus und Befreiungsnationalismus lassen sich nur verwirklichen auf der Basis einer freiheitlichen Demokratie. Darum erfordert ihre Durchsetzung den Kampf gegen alle Umerzieher, gegen alle Konzepte einer Erziehungsdiktatur, gegen die rote Vorherrschaft in Massenmedien und Gewerkschaftsbürokratie. Nicht minder gilt der Kampf all denen, die ihre wirtschaftliche Macht zur Verbiegung und Manipulation des Volkswillens einsetzen.

10. **Die notwendigen Veränderungen können nur durch den Aufbruch neuer politischer Kräfte erzwungen werden. Die Jugend Europas wird sich mit kommunistischer Tyrannei und bürgerlich-reaktionärer Erstarrung nicht abfinden.**

Appendix

Document 7: Aktionsfront Nationaler Sozialisten, Kampfprogramm für die Hamburger Bürgerschaftswahl, 1978

AKTIONSFRONT NATIONALER SOZIALISTEN
ANS

Wir fordern:
- NS – Verbot aufheben
- Baustop für Atomkraftwerke
- Antikommunistischer Kampf

Das Kampfprogramm der ANS für
die Bürgerschaftswahl in Hamburg

ANS
Aktionsfront nationaler Sozialisten

KAMPFPROGRAMM

für die Hamburger Bürgerschaftswahl
1978

Vorbemerkung
Dieses Kampfprogramm gilt als die Grundlage für die politische Arbeit der ANS seit dem 1. Dezember 1977. Es ist außerdem in seinem zweiten Teil identisch mit der Wahlplattform für die Hamburger Bürgerschaftswahl 1978. Ein endgültiges Programm wird erst auf einem Programm-Parteitag der ANS beschlossen, wenn die Bewegung in allen Gauen (Landesverbänden) organisiert ist.

Appendix

Präambel
Die Aktionsfront Nationaler Sozialisten ist der Zusammenschluß deutscher Patrioten für Großdeutschland.
Die ANS fordert auf der Grundlage des Selbstbestimmungsrechtes der Völker den Zusammenschluß aller Deutschen zu einem Großdeutschen Reich.
Die ANS fordert den Ersatz des abgewirtschafteten liberalkapitalistischen Systems durch eine wirkliche Demokratie, d.h. den ständisch organisierten starken Volksstaat.
Die ANS erklärt, in Übereinstimmung mit den geltenden Gesetzen ihre Ziele durchsetzen zu wollen.

Forderungen der ANS
1. *Aufhebung des NS-Verbots*
Die Mitglieder der Aktionsfront Nationaler Sozialisten sind keine Nationalsozialisten im herkömmlichen Sinn. Dennoch fordern wir die Aufhebung des NS-Verbots aus folgenden Gründen:

a) *Das Verbot ist wirkungslos*: Seit Anfang 1971 arbeitet in der Bundesrepublik eine illegale NSDAP, ohne daß dies von den Staatsschutzbehörden verhindert werden kann.

b) *Das Verbot ist ungerecht*: Das Verbot der NSDAP ist unvereinbar mit den Grundlagen einer liberalen Demokratie. Angesichts der freien politischen Tätigkeit von Kommunisten, Maoisten und Anarchisten ist die Fortdauer des NS-Vebots unverständlich.

c) *Das Verbot ist fortdauerndes Besatzungsrecht*: Mehr als dreißig Jahre nach der deutschen Niederlage werden in Deutschland Menschen wegen ihrer politischen Gesinnung verfolgt. Dies geschieht aufgrund von Gesetzen, die die alliierten Sieger uns 1945 aufgezwungen haben. Die Aufhebung des unsinnig gewordenen NS-Verbots wäre ein Zeichen wiedergewonnener Souveränität des westdeutschen Staates. Die Fortdauer ein Beweis des Gegenteils.

d) *Das Verbot verhindert die Lösung gegenwärtiger Probleme*: Innerhalb weniger Jahre beseitigte der Nationalsozialismus die Massenarbeitslosigkeit, stellte den sozialen Frieden wieder her, steigerte die Volkswohlfahrt, einigte alle Deutschen und errang Weltgeltung für das Großdeutsche Reich. Heute sind andere Lösungen erforderlich, die Geschichte wiederholt sich nicht. Mit der Fortdauer des NS-Verbots ist jedoch antideutschen Kräften die Möglichkeit in die Hand gegeben, jede Regung für Deutschlands Wiederaufstieg als Fortführung der NSDAP zu unterdrücken.

Appendix

2. *Baustopp für Atomkraftwerke*
Die westdeutsche Wirtschaft braucht zusätzliche Energiequellen. Die ANS fordert aus diesem Grunde den großzügigen Ausbau einheimischer Kohlekraftwerke. Atomkraft gefährdet die Existenz des deutschen Volkes:

a) *Verteidigungsfähigkeit*: Ein Land, das mit einem Netz von AKWs überzogen ist, kann weder nach innen noch nach außen verteidigt werden. Feindliche Armeen brauchen gar nicht erst zu marschieren, sie brauchen nur mit der Bombardierung der AKWs zu drohen, um eine Kapitulation zu erzwingen. Für Terroristen gilt entsprechendes.

b) *Umweltschutz*: Entgegen den Beteuerungen unverantwortlicher Machthaber ist die Atomtechnologie noch längst nicht ausgereift. Alle entscheidenden Probleme sind ungelöst. Deshalb ist der Ausbau von Kernkraftwerken, die zur Verseuchung unseres Vaterlandes über Generationen hinaus führen kann, ein Verbrechen am Volk.

c) *Abhängigkeit vom Ausland*: Ebenso wie bisher das Erdöl müßte auch das Uran als Grundstoff zum Betrieb von AKWs aus dem Ausland eingeführt werden. Dies macht uns hilflos gegenüber möglichen Erpressungen von außen. Nur der Ausbau von Kohlekraftwerken, die mit heimischen Bodenschätzen betrieben werden können, führt zur deutschen Unabhängigkeit.

3. *Kampf dem Kommunismus*
Liberale haben den Kommunisten aller Schattierungen die Herrschaft über die Straße überlassen. Diese allein sind fast nur noch dort zu sehen. Gegen Andersdenkende üben sie Gesinnungsterror. Vor allem nationale Verbände haben dies jahrelang miterleben müssen.
Die ANS tritt den Kommunisten hier auf ihrem ureigensten Gebiet entgegen. Sie wird die Straße zurückerobern, damit deutsche Bürger wieder durch die Stadt gehen können, ohne ständig vom Anblick langhaariger Politspinner beleidigt zu werden! Die ANS ist das entschlossene Gegengewicht zur Bolschewisierung Deutschlands.

Zur Durchsetzung dieser drei Kernforderungen wird die Aktionsfront Nationaler Sozialisten an der Hamburger Landtagswahl teilnehmen mit dem Ziel, im Parlament als Anwalt der deutschen Patrioten ihre Stimme zu Gehör zu bringen.

Appendix

In der Hamburger Bürgerschaft wird unsere Fraktion folgende Maßnahmen vorschlagen:

1. Der Hamburger Senat wird aufgefordert, im Bundesrat ein Gesetz einzubringen, das die ersatzlose Streichung des Art. 139 GG und des § 86 StGB (Verbot der Fortführung der NSDAP) zum Inhalt hat. Bis dahin werden Polizei, Staatsanwaltschaft und Staatsschutz angewiesen, keine Maßnahmen mehr gegen Mitglieder und Anhänger der vorbotenen NSDAP zu ergreifen. Alle NS-Kämpfer fallen unter eine Amnestie.

2. Der Hamburger Senat wird aufgefordert, im Bundesrat ein Gesetz einzubringen, mit dem ein sofortiger Baustopp für Atomkraftwerke erreicht werden soll. Die ANS ist die einzige Partei in Hamburg, die mit ihrer Forderung nach gleichzeitigem entschiedenen Ausbau von Kohlekraftwerken ein realistisches Konzept für Deutschlands Energiewirtschaft vorzuweisen hat.

3. Der Hamburger Senat wird aufgefordert, im Bundesrat ein Gesetz zum Verbot folgender Gruppierungen vorzulegen: DKP und alle Untergliederungen, KPD, KPD/ML, KBW, KB, GIM und alle Untergliederungen, sowie aller sonstigen politischen Organisationen, die durch Propagierung des Klassenkampfes einen Teil des deutschen Volkes gegen den anderen aufzuhetzen versuchen.

Dieses Kampfprogramm gilt als Grundlage unserer Bewegung bis zum Programmparteitag der ANS sowie als Wahlprogramm für die Hamburger Bürgerschaftswahl.
Deutsche, wacht auf!
     Hamburg, den 1. Dezember 1977
Source: Broder, *Deutschland erwacht*, Cologne, 1978, p. 104

Bibliography

Backes, Uwe and Jesse, Eckhard (1989), *Politischer Extremismus in der Bundesrepublik Deutschland*, vol. I, Literatur, Cologne
Backes, Uwe and Jesse, Eckhard (1985), *Totalitarismus, Extremismus, Terrorismus. Ein Literaturführer und Wegweiser zur Extremismusforschung in der Bundesrepublik Deutschland* (2nd edition), Opladen
Bartsch, Günter (1975), *Revolution von rechts? Ideologie und Organisation der Neuen Rechten*, Freiburg
Benz, Wolfgang (ed.) (1984), *Rechtsextremismus in der Bundesrepublik. Voraussetzungen – Zusammenhänge – Wirkungen*, Frankfurt
Beyme, Klaus von (ed.) (1988), *Right-wing Extremism in Western Europe*, London
Biemann, Georg and Krischka, Joachim (eds) (1986), *Nazis, Skins und alte Kameraden*, Dortmund
Bott, Hermann (1969), *Die Volksfeind-Ideologie. Zur Kritik rechtsradikaler Propaganda*, Stuttgart
Brandt, Peter and Schulze-Marmeling, Ulrich (eds) (1985), *Antifaschismus. Ein Lesebuch. Deutsche Stimmen gegen Nationalsozialismus und Rechtsextremismus von 1922 bis zur Gegenwart*, Berlin
Brüdigam, Heinz (n.d.), *Der Schoß ist fruchtbar noch . . . Neonazistische, militaristische, nationalistische Literatur und Publizistik in der Bundesrepublik*, Frankfurt
Butz, Arthur R. (1977), *Der Jahrhundert-Betrug*, Vlotho
Christophersen, Thies (1975), *Die Auschwitzlüge. Ein Erlebnisbericht, Deutsche Bürger-Initiative*, no. 2 (3rd edition), Mohrkirch
Doerry, Thomas (1980), *Antifaschismus in der Bundesrepublik. Vom antifaschistischen Konsens 1945 bis zur Gegenwart*, Frankfurt
Dohse, Rainer (1974), *Der Dritte Weg. Neutralitätsbestrebungen in Westdeutschland zwischen 1945 und 1955*, Hamburg
Dudek, Peter (ed.) (1980), *Hakenkreuz und Judenwitz. Antifaschistische Jugendarbeit in der Schule*, Bensheim
Dudek, Peter (1985), *Jugendliche Rechtsextremisten. Zwischen Hakenkreuz und Odalsrune 1945 bis heute*, Cologne
Dudek, Peter and Jaschke, Hans-Gerd (1981), *Die Deutsche National-Zeitung. Inhalte – Geschichte – Aktionen*, PDI-Taschenbuch 8, Munich
Dudek, Peter and Jaschke, Hans-Gerd (1981), *Revolte von rechts. Ana-

Bibliography

tomie einer neuen Jugendpresse, Frankfurt and New York

Dudek, Peter and Jaschke, Hans-Gerd (1984), *Entstehung und Entwicklung des Rechtsextremismus in der Bundesrepublik. Zur Tradition einer besonderen politischen Kultur*, 2 vols, Opladen

Elm, Ludwig (1972), *Hochschule und Neofaschismus*, Berlin (GDR)

European Parliament, Investigating Committee (1985), *'Wiederaufleben des Faschismus und Rassismus in Europa'*: Bericht über die Ergebnisse der Arbeiten, December

Faller, Kurt and Siebold, Heinz (1986), *Neofaschismus. Dulden? Verbieten? Ignorieren? Bekämpfen?*, Frankfurt

Feit, Margret (1987), *Die 'Neue Rechte' in der Bundesrepublik. Organisation – Ideologie – Strategie*, Frankfurt and New York

Fink, Willibald (1969), *Die NPD bei der Bayerischen Landtagswahl 1966. Eine ökologische Wahlstudie*, Munich

Frederik, Hans (n.d.), *NPD – Gefahr von rechts?*, Munich-Inning

Friedrich, Jörg (1984), *Die kalte Amnestie. NS-Täter in der Bundesrepublik*, Frankfurt

Fürstenau, Justus (1969), *Entnazifizierung. Ein Kapitel deutscher Nachkriegspolitik*, Neuwied and Berlin

Gewalt von rechts. Beiträge aus Wissenschaft und Publizistik (1982), published by the Department for 'Public Relations Work to Combat Terrorism', in the Ministry of the Interior, Bonn

Hafeneger, Benno, Paul, Gerhard and Schoßig, Bernhard (eds) (1981), *Dem Faschismus das Wasser abgraben. Zur Auseinandersetzung mit dem Rechtsradikalismus*, Munich

Hartmann, Ulrich, Steffen, Hans-Peter and Steffen, Sigrid (1985), *Rechtsextremismus bei Jugendlichen. Anregungen, der wachsenden Gefahr entgegenzuwirken*, Munich

Haug, Wolfgang Fritz (1987), *Vom hilflosen Antifaschismus zur Gnade der späten Geburt*, Berlin

Heitmeyer, Wilhelm (1987), *Rechtsextremistische Orientierungen bei Jugendlichen. Empirische Ergebnisse und Erklärungsmuster einer Untersuchung zur politischen Sozialisation*, Weinheim and Munich

Hellfeld, Matthias von (ed.) (1989), *Dem Haß keine Chance. Der neue rechte Fundamentalismus*, Cologne

Herb, Hartmut, Peters, Jan and Thesen, Mathias (1980), *Der neue Rechtsextremismus – Fakten und Trends*, Lohra-Rodenhausen

Hirsch, Kurt and Sarkowicz, Hans (1989), *Schönhuber. Der Politiker und seine Kreise*, Frankfurt

'Historikerstreit'. Die Dokumentation der Kontroverse um die Einzigartigkeit der nationalsozialistischen Judenvernichtung (1987), Munich

Hoggan, David L. (1966), *Der erzwungene Krieg* (7th edition), Tübingen

Jäger, Siegfried (ed.) (1988), *Rechtsdruck. Die Presse der neuen Rechten*, Berlin and Bonn

Bibliography

Klingemann, Hans-D. and Pappi, Franz U. (1972), *Politischer Radikalismus. Theoretische und methodische Probleme der Radikalismusforschung, dargestellt am Beispiel einer Studie anläßlich der Landtagswahl 1970 in Hessen*, Munich and Vienna

Knütter, Hans-Helmuth (1988), *Hat der Rechtsextremismus in der Bundesrepublik eine Chance?*, Bonn

Kühnl, Reinhard (1974), *Texte zur Faschismusdiskussion 1. Positionen und Kontroversen*, Reinbek

Kühnl, Reinhard (1979), *Faschismustheorien. Texte zur Faschismusdiskussion 2. Ein Leitfaden*, Reinbek

Kühnl, Reinhard, Rilling, Rainer and Sager, Christine (1969), *Die NPD. Struktur, Ideologie und Funktion einer neofaschistischen Partei*, Frankfurt

Leggewie, Claus (1989), *Die Republikaner. Phantombild der Neuen Rechten*, Berlin

Meinhardt, Rolf (ed.) (1984), *Türken raus? oder Verteidigt den sozialen Frieden. Beiträge gegen die Ausländerfeindlichkeit*, Reinbek

Meyer, Alwin and Rabe, Karl-Klaus (1979), *Unsere Stunde, die wird kommen. Rechtsextremismus unter Jugendlichen*, Bornheim-Merten

Mitscherlich, Alexander und Margarete (1967), *Die Unfähigkeit zu trauern. Grundlagen kollektiven Verhaltens*, Munich (new edition, Munich, 1987)

Müller, Ingo (1987), *Furchtbare Juristen. Die unbewältigte Vergangenheit unserer Justiz*, Munich

Niethammer, Lutz (1969), *Angepaßter Faschismus. Politische Praxis der NPD*, Frankfurt

Noelle-Neumann, Elisabeth and Ring, Erp (1984), *Das Extremismus-Potential unter jungen Leuten in der Bundesrepublik Deutschland 1984*, Allensbach

Nolte, Ernst (ed.) (1972), *Theorien über den Faschismus* (3rd edition), Cologne

NPD – Weg, Wille und Ziel, (1967), Hannover

Opitz, Reinhard (1984), *Faschismus und Neofaschismus*, Frankfurt

Oppenheimer, Max (ed.) (1978), *Antifaschismus. Tradition – Politik – Perspektive. Geschichte und Ziele der VVN-Bund der Antifaschisten*, Frankfurt

Panahi, Badi (1980), *Vorurteile. Rassismus, Antisemitismus, Nationalismus . . . in der Bundesrepublik heute. Eine empirische Untersuchung*, Frankfurt

Paul, Gerhard and Schoßig, Bernhard (eds) (1979), *Jugend und Neofaschismus. Provokation oder Identifikation?*, Frankfurt

Pröhuber, Karl-Heinz (1980), *Die nationalrevolutionäre Bewegung in Westdeutschland*, Hamburg

Rabe, Karl-Klaus (ed.) (1980), *Rechtsextreme Jugendliche. Gespräche mit Verführern und Verführten*, Bornheim-Merten

Rajewsky, Christiane and Schmitz, Adelheid (1988), *Nationalsozialismus*

Bibliography

und Neonazismus. Ein Reader für Jugendarbeit und Schule, Düsseldorf

Rassinier, Paul (1979), *Was ist Wahrheit? Die Juden und das Dritte Reich* (5th edition), Leoni

Ratz, Michael (1979), *Die Justiz und die Nazis. Zur Strafverfolgung von Nazismus und Neonazismus seit 1945*, Frankfurt

Rechtsradikalismus im Nachkriegsdeutschland. Studien über die 'Sozialistische Reichspartei' (SRP) (1957), Berlin and Frankfurt

Richards, Fred H. (1967), *Die NPD. Alternative oder Wiederkehr?*, Munich and Vienna

Rückerl, Adalbert (1982), *NS-Verbrechen vor Gericht. Versuch einer Vergangenheitsbewältigung*, Heidelberg

Schneider, Rudolf (1981), *Die SS ist ihr Vorbild. Neonazistische Kampfgruppen und Aktionskreise in der Bundesrepublik*, edited by the leadership of the VVN – Bund der Antifaschisten, Frankfurt

Silbermann, Alphons (1982), *Sind wir Antisemiten? Ausmaß und Wirkung eines sozialen Vorurteils in der Bundesrepublik Deutschland*, Cologne

Smoydzin, Werner (1966), *Hitler lebt. Vom internationalen Faschismus zur Internationale des Hakenkreuzes*, Pfaffenhofen Ilm

Smoydzin, Werner (1967), *NPD – Geschichte und Umwelt einer Partei*, Pfaffenhofen Ilm

Sochatzy, Klaus et al. (1980), *Parole: rechts! Jugend, wohin? Neofaschismus im Schülerurteil. Eine empirische Studie*, Frankfurt

Stäglich, Wilhelm (1979), *Der Auschwitz-Mythos. Legende oder Wirklichkeit. Eine kritische Bestandsaufnahme*, Tübingen

Stöss, Richard (1978), 'Väter und Enkel: Alter und Neuer Nationalismus in der Bundesrepublik', in *Ästhetik und Kommunikation* 32, vol. 9, pp. 35–57

Stöss, Richard (1979), 'Konservative Aspekte der Ökologie- bzw. Alternativbewegung', in *Ästhetik und Kommunikation* 36, vol. 10, pp. 19–28

Stöss, Richard (1980), *Vom Nationalismus zum Umweltschutz. Die Deutsche Gemeinschaft/Aktionsgemeinschaft Unabhängiger Deutscher im Parteiensystem der Bundesrepublik*, Opladen

Stöss, Richard (ed.) (1983/84), *Parteien-Handbuch. Die Parteien der Bundesrepublik Deutschland 1945–1980*, 2 vols, Opladen

Stöss, Richard (1984), 'Pronazistisches Protestverhalten in der Schule. Ursachen und Ausmaß', in *Extremismus und Schule. Daten, Analysen und Arbeitshilfen zum politischen Rechts- und Linksextremismus, Schriftenreihe der Bundeszentrale für politische Bildung*, vol. 212, Bonn, pp. 171–94

Stöss, Richard (1984), 'Die Entwicklung des Rechtsextremismus', in Gert-Joachim Glaeßner, Jürgen Holz and Thomas Schlüter (eds), *Die Bundesrepublik in den siebziger Jahren. Versuch einer Bilanz*, Opladen, pp. 53–70

Bibliography

Stöss, Richard (1986), 'Pronazistisches Protestverhalten unter Jugendlichen. Schüler – Fußballfans – Punks – Skinheads – Nazi-Rocker', in Alphons Silbermann and Julius H. Schoeps (eds), *Antisemitismus nach dem Holocaust. Bestandsaufnahme und Erscheinungsformen in deutschsprachigen Ländern*, Cologne, pp. 163–92

Stöss, Richard (1988), 'The Problem of Right-Wing Extremism in West Germany', in *West- European Politics*, vol. 11, no. 2, pp. 34–46

Stöss, Richard (1990), *Die Republikaner*, Cologne

Tauber, Kurt P. (1967), *Beyond Eagle and Swastika. German Nationalism Since 1945*, 2 vols, Middletown

Tsiakalos, Georgios (1983), *Ausländerfeindlichkeit. Tatsachen und Erklärungsversuche*, Munich

Vinke, Hermann (1981), *Mit zweierlei Maß. Die deutsche Reaktion auf den Terror von rechts. Eine Dokumentation*, Reinbek

Die Volkssozialistische Bewegung Deutschlands – Sammelbecken militanter Rechtsradikaler (1981), PDI-Sonderheft 17, Munich

Weber, Jürgen and Steinbach, Peter (eds) (1984), *Vergangenheitsbewältigung durch Strafverfahren? NS-Prozesse in der Bundesrepublik Deutschland*, Munich

Wider des Vergessen. Antifaschistische Erziehung in der Schule. Erfahrungen, Projekte, Anregungen (1981), Frankfurt

Winter, Franz Florian (1968), *Ich glaubte an die NPD*, Mainz

'Wir sollten wieder einen Führer haben . . .'. Die SINUS-Studie über rechtsextremistische Einstellungen bei den Deutschen (1981), Reinbek

Zaleshoff, Andreas P. (1989), *Der zweite Frühling der NPD*, Hannover

INDEX

Action Community for a Fourth Party (AVP), 154, 181
Action Community of Independent Germans (AUD), 104–7, 135, 158–61
Action Fellowship of Free Germans (TFD), 117, 119
Action Front of National Socialists (ANS), 171, 191
ANS/NA, 183, 185–7
battle programme, 181–2, 253–6
Action Group for German Radio and Television, 195
Action Group for German Unity, 195
Action for a New Right (ANR), 156, 161–2, 173, 194, 199, 250–6
Action Rally (SzT), 85–6
Action Resistance, 152, 161, 173, 185
Action 'Send Foreigners Home' (AAR), 185, 186
Adenauer, Konrad, 80, 88, 121–4, 133, 135, 143, 145
Adenauer government, 89, 91, 98, 139
Ahrensburg, 4
aims, *see* right-wing extremism (definitions)
Albrecht, Udo, 178
All-German Bloc (GB), 121, 124, 130
All-German Party (GDP), 131, 134
Allied Control Council, 58, 64, 66
allies commence de-Nazification, 60–3
Altermann, Hans, 200
Andrae, Alexander, 115
anti-Bolshevism, 24, 25, 26, 27, 117, 127, 145
anti-capitalism, 66, 156
anti-communism, 24, 81–2, 88, 94, 96
anti-democratic attitudes, 15–19, 36, 121, 204, 206, 231–2
development, 208–17
elements (political culture), 217–20, 234–5

glossing over the past, 38–53, 59, 90
protecting youth from, 235–6
anti-Fascism, 17, 59–61, 113, 206–7, 235
anti-communism instead, 81–2
discrediting, 217–20
organised (since 1945), 222–9
problems and perspectives, 221–9
anti-imperialism, 157, 161–5, 245–7
anti-Semitism, 46, 48–50
events (1988 survey), 5, 7, 8, 9
protest behaviour, 188–92, 217
Republicans, 204–5
revisionism, 31–6
Aretz, Emil, 33
armed struggle, 169–74 *passim*
arms finds, 166–8, 172
arms question, 25–6
Asbach, Hans Adolf, 119
Association for a German National Assembly (VDNU), 135
Association of German Soldiers (VdS), 137, 138
Associations of Victims of the Nazi Regime (VVN), 222–3
Atlanticists, 24, 25, 133, 143
Aufbruch, 164
Augsburg, 6
Auschwitz, 29, 33–4, 36, 140, 175, 178, 190
authoritarian conservatism, 19, 27, 85, 104, 113, 133
authoritarian democracy, 94, 95
authoritarianism, 16, 28, 213–16, 218, 220
'automatic arrests', 61, 62

bans (on anti-Fascism), 226–8
basic consensus, 92–9, 142, 216, 217
Basic Law, 67, 93–4, 111
battle programme (of ANS), 181–3, 253–6
Bavarian Party (BP), 85

262

Index

Bayernkurier, 153
Behrendt, Uwe, 180, 181
Beier, Henry, 186
Berlin, 4–5, 7–8, 9–10
Berlin blockade, 67
Berlin Centre for Research into Anti-Semitism, 49
Berlin Document Centre, 9–10
Berliner Morgenpost, 9
Berufsverbot, 64
bi-zone, 66
Birkenau, 33, 34, 175
Birkmann, Franziska, 180, 181
Bloc of Expellees and Victims of Injustice (BHE), 92, 110–11, 118–22 *passim*, 124, 130–4 *passim*
Bolshevism, 24, 25–6, 35, 112, 164
 see also anti-Bolshevism
Boppard, 8
Borchardt, Siegfried, 192
Bormann, Martin, 74
Boßmann, Dieter, 41
bourgeois classes, 95
bourgeois democratic parties, 9, 27–8, 83, 88–9, 98, 100, 110, 149
Brandt, Willy, 144, 150, 151, 172, 182
Brecht, Bertolt, 38
Brehl, Thomas, 183, 185, 188
Bremen Liste, 134, 200
British de-Nazification, 64, 66, 68, 85
British zone, 64, 66, 85
Brown Book, 80
'brown zone', 9
Brühl, Willi, 8
Buback, Siegried, 166
Buchenwald, 60
Bügner, Johannes, 183
Bundestag, 12, 121, 232
 de-Nazification, 67–8, 71, 77, 85
 development of extremism, 101–2, 109, 111, 114, 117–18, 121, 124–6, 128, 130–5, 140, 142–55, 158, 173, 196
 elections (1949), 87–92, 97, 109, 111, 117, 124
 elections (1949–61), 92, 93, 97
 elections (1965–88), 145, 146–7
 statute of limitations, 77–8
bürgerblock
 collapse, 142–4
 development of extremism, 101–3, 110–13, 115–17, 126, 129–32, 145, 153, 158

 integrative role, 88–93, 97–8, 231–2
 New Right, 118–25
Busse, Friedhelm, 173, 174
Butz, Arthur R., 33

capital mobility, 96
capitalism, 15, 69, 88, 95–6, 109, 113, 173, 174
 Third Path, 25, 28, 157, 162
 see also anti-capitalism
Catholic Church, 6
causes and countermeasures, 206, 236
 anti-Fascism
 (problems/perspectives), 221–9
 causes (explanatory factors), 207–21, 234–5
CDU/CSU, 82, 88–9, 92–3, 108, 110, 116, 121, 124, 129–35, 150, 153–5, 165, 196–203, 205, 216, 223, 232
 Grand Coalition, 102, 143, 145, 150, 151, 232
 CDU state, 90, 92, 97, 101, 135–6, 143
Central Council of Jews in Germany, 12
Christian Democratic Union (CDU), 5, 7–8, 11–12, 40, 84–5, 108–12, 119, 145, 152–3, 166, 175, 200, 222
 CDU state, 90, 92, 97, 101, 135–6, 143
 see also CDU/CSU
Christian-Social Union, 84–5, 116, 119, 145, 152, 153, 154–5
 see also CDU/CSU
Christian socialism, 222
Christophersen, Thies, 33, 174, 175, 177
Churchill, W.S., 57
Citizen and Farmer Initiative (BBI), 175
Citizens' Action Group to Stop Foreign Immigration, 158
class struggle, 86
Cold War, 95, 101
Colditz, Dr Heinz, 177
collective guilt theory, 59, 61, 71
combat groups, 152
communism, 14, 15, 59, 91, 125, 144, 173, 174, 181, 223
 Third path, 25, 28, 157, 162
 see also anti-communism;
 Communist Party of Germany (KPD); German Communist

263

Index

Party (DKP)
Communist Party of Germany (KPD), 61, 69, 84, 89, 111, 124
Comradeship Circle of Nationalist Youth Associations (KNJ), 141, 142
concentration camps, 54
  Auschwitz, 29, 33–4, 36, 140, 175, 178, 190
  Birkenau, 33, 34, 175
  Buchenwald, 60
  Großrosen, 76
consensus, 14, 82–3, 215
  basic, 92–9, 142, 216, 217
  constitutional, 93, 96
  popular, 93
Conservatism
  authoritarian, 19, 27, 85, 104, 113, 133
  definitions, 14–15
  see also German Conservative Party (DKP)
Conservative revolution, 115
constitutional consensus, 93, 96
countermeasures, *see* causes and countermeasures
crime, *see* war criminals
cultural revolution, 198
currency reform, 67

de-Nazification, 30, 122–3, 231
  allies commence, 60–3
  anti-communism, 81–2
  failed attempt, 55–60
  German involvement, 64–8
  German views, 70–1
  licensing policy, 83–7
  Nazi criminals, 72–6
  Party dispute and, 68–72
  post-war elites, 79–81
  trials, 76–9
  victims, 136, 139–41
Deckert, G., 8
definitions, *see* right-wing extremism (definitions)
Dehoust, Peter, 201
democracy
  antipathy towards, 15–17, 18
  authoritarian, 94, 95
  definitions, 14
  pluralism, 94, 95
  see also anti-democratic attitudes
democratic bourgeois parties, 9, 27–8, 83, 88–9, 98, 100, 110, 149

democratic consciousness, 217–20
democratic consensus, 14
Democratic Union (DU), 158–9
democratisation policies, 58–9
détente, 133, 135, 144, 145, 159
Deutsche Gemeinschaft, 106
'Deutsche Liste', 8, 196
Deutsche Nachrichten, 105
Deutsche National-Zeitung (DNZ), 4, 106, 178, 193, 199
Deutsche Stimme, 105–6
'Deutsche Volkliste', 196
Deutsche Wochen-Zeitung (DWZ), 4, 193
Deutscher Anzeiger (DA), 193
Dietl, General, 6
displaced persons, 62
Diwald, Hellmut, 34–5
'Doldrum Years', 127–30, 134
Dönitz, Karl, 58, 74, 176, 183
Dorls, Fritz, 109, 110
Drenckmann, Günther, 166
Dudek, 148
Düsseldorf, 5, 6

East-West conflict, 75, 81, 88n, 94, 125, 132, 222
ecology movement, 45, 105, 155, 157, 159–60, 163–4, 197
Economic Council, 66
economic crises, 212–13
'economic miracle', 95, 96
Economic Reconstruction Association (WAV), 85, 86, 87
Edinger, L.J., 80
education, 7–8, 13, 58–9, 203
  anti-Fascist, 228–9
  protest behaviour in schools, 189–91, 227
Eichberg, Henning, 161
Eisenhower, D.D., 57–8
electoral success (outlook), 192–205
elites, post-war, 79–81
EMNID study, 50, 218, 219
Enabling Law (1933), 53
Enk, Friedhelm, 183
Erhard, Ludwig, 143
Etzel, Richard, 141
European-neutralist conception, 24–5
European elections, 102, 146, 201, 205
European Liberation Front (EBF), 172
European People's Movement of

Index

Germany, 86
Evangelical Church, 223
everyday scenes of extremism
  January 1988, 4–5
  February 1988, 6–7
  March 1988, 7–13
Executive Committee, 66
expellees, 83–4, 86–7, 90, 112–13,
  117, 127, 149, 152, 153
BHE, 92, 110–11, 118–22 *passim*,
  124, 130–4 *passim*
Extra-Parliamentary Opposition
Loyal to the People (VAPO), 171

Fascism
  definitions, 14–15, 16
  'Grandpa's', 224–5
  see also anti-Fascism; neo-Fascism
Faßbender, 134
'Fatah', 180
Federal Association of Former
  Internees and Victims of
  De-nazification, 140
Federal Constitutional Court, 111,
  113
Federal Republic of Germany
  Basic law, 67, 93–4, 111
  emergence, 21
  foreign workers (attitudes to), 50
Fragmente, 161
Frank, Hans, 74
Frankfurt, 6
Frankfurt Circle of German Soldiers,
  177
Frankfurt Institute for Social
  Research, 46
Frankfurter Rundschau, 9–11
Free Democratic Party (FDP), 46, 84,
  88–9, 92, 108, 110–11, 119, 121–2,
  124, 130, 143, 152–5, 196–8, 223
Free German Workers Party (FAP),
  5–8, 104, 107, 186–7, 190, 191–2
Free Peoples Party (FVP), 130
Free Socialist People's Party (FSVP),
  177
Free Socialists of Germany (FSD), 177
Freiheitlicher Rat, 194, 199
'Freizeitverein Hansa', 181
French de-Nazification, 64, 66, 68,
  85–6
French zone, 64, 66, 85–6
Frey, G., 4–5, 8, 12, 106, 178, 193–4,
  196, 198–201

Frick, Wilhelm, 74
Friends of Nationalist Youth, 142
Fritsche, Hans, 75
Front National, 11
Frühauf, Michael, 183
Fulda, 4
Funk, Walther, 74

Galinski, Heinz, 12
gas chambers, 31, 33, 178
Gaulle, Charles de, 133, 135
Gaullists, 24, 25, 133, 135, 143, 151
Gebhardt, Werner, 132
Geisel, Alfred, 12
Geiss, Edgar, 183
German Action Groups (DA), 177
German Bloc (DB), 123, 124, 141
German Centre Party (DZP), 85
German Citizen Initiative (DBI), 175
German Communist Party (DKP), 6,
  165
German Community (DG), 91–2, 104,
  106–7, 117–21, 123–30, 134–5, 138,
  140–1, 158, 160–1, 177, 242
German Conservative Party (DKP),
  85–7, 104, 106–8, 109–10
German Democratic Republic
  (emergence), 21
German Freedom Party (DFP), 107,
  132, 135, 158
German involvement
  (de-Nazification), 64–8
German Labour Front, 119
German National Peoples Party
  (DNVP), 85, 106, 108, 134, 138
German Party (DP), 85, 88, 108–11,
  119–22, 124, 130–4, 175
German Peoples Union (DVU), 5, 8,
  103–4, 107, 178, 192, 202–3, 232
  NPD and, 6–7, 11–12, 193–201,
  233–4
German Reconstruction party, 107
German Reich Party (DRP), 237–41
German Research Society, 48
German Rightist Party (DRP), 85–7,
  92, 104–5, 107–11, 113–15, 123–35,
  138, 140–1, 177
German Social Movement, 123, 124
German Social Union, 154
German Union, 153
German Workers Youth, 170
*Gesamtdeutsche
  Unabhängigkeitsbewegung*, 134–6

265

Index

ghetto-dwellers, 50
Gleichschaltung, 16
Globke, Hans, 80
Godesberg change, 134–5
Goerth, Christa, 186
Göring, Hermann, 74
Grand Coalition, 102, 143, 145, 150, 151, 232
Graue Front, 138
Green Lists, 160, 163
Green Party, 6, 12, 105, 154–5, 160, 163, 197–8
Großrosen, 76
Grünen, Die, 106, 160, 163, 164
Gutmann, Wilhelm, 134

Hamburg List to Stop Foreign Immigration (HLA), 146–7, 158, 191
Handlos, Franz, 198, 202, 205
Hannover, 5, 8
Hansen, Karl-Heinz, 10–11
Hartung, Klaus, 207
Harzburg Front, 26–7, 113
Hassebroek, J., 76
Haußleiter, A., 105–6, 115–17, 119–20, 123–4, 130, 134–5, 159–60
Heidel, Volker, 188
Heidelberg, 7
Heinemann, Gustav, 150, 172
Hepp, Odfried, 169, 178, 180
Hess, Otto, 132
Hess, Rudolf, 74, 171, 187
Heuss, Theodor, 53, 55
historical past, 53–82
historical revisionism, 28–36, 140, 217
Hitler, Adolf, 136, 168–9, 176, 185
 Freeman status, 6, 9, 13
 historical revisionism, 29, 31
 repressing the past, 51–2, 55, 58–9, 204
 views on, 39–43, 44
Hitler Youth, 141
Hoffmann, K.H., 178, 180–1
Hoggan, D.L., 31
Holocaust (TV film), 79, 171, 218
Homan, Thomas A., 9
homosexuality, 187, 188
Hörne, Raimund, 177

immigrants, 195
 NPD campaign, 157–8, 248–9
imperialism, anti-, 157, 161–5, 245–7

Independent German Community, 117, 119
individual factors (causal theory), 208–12, 220, 221, 235
industrial society (structural change), 213, 214
INFAS, 49–50
Initiative to Limit Foreign Immigration, 195
integration, 90–1, 95–6, 123, 125–6, 130
 for stability, 98–9
interest party, 118, 119, 121

Jaschke, 148
Jewish World Congress, 31
Jews, *see* anti-Semitism
Jochheim-Arnim, Karl, 173
Jodl, Alfred, 74
journalism, 105–6, 108, 193–4
Junges Forum, 161

Kaltenbrunner, Ernst, 74
Kaufman, T.N., 31
KDS, 178, 179
Keitel, Wilhelm, 74
Kennedy, J.F., 132–3
Kexel, Walther, 169, 174, 178, 180
Kiel List to Reduce Foreign Immigration, 158
Kirkpatrick, Sir Ivone, 122, 123
Kitzelmann, Michael, 6
Klingemann, Hans D., 1
Kohl, Helmut, 155, 196
Köhler, G., 180
Kolley, Klaus, 148, 172
Kosbab, Werner, 173
Kraft, Waldemar, 92, 119, 130
Krause, Justus, 109
Kritik-Verlag (publisher), 175
Kruger, Gerhard, 109, 110
Kühnen, Gegner, 187
Kühnen, M., 170–1, 174, 181–3, 185–8, 191–2
Kuntsmann, Heinrich, 132, 135

Labour Party (PdA), 173, 174
Land, 68, 120–1, 145
 elections, 8, 11–12, 66, 87, 92, 102, 114, 146, 159, 181, 187, 192, 198–9, 205, 233
Landtag, 7, 127
 elections, 91–2, 118–20, 134, 147,

Index

185, 187, 199
Laser, 164
Lauck, G.R., 183
Le Pen, Jean-Marie, 11
League of Anti-Fascists (BdA), 223
League of Former Members of the Armed Forces Entitled to Pensions, 137
League for a Free Germany, 154
League of German Solidarists, 164
League of National Revolutionaries, 163
League of Nations, 19
League of Patriotic Youth (BHJ), 142, 169, 170, 173
League of Victims of the Nazi Regime, 223
left-wing terrorism, 165–6, 173, 188
Lembke, Heinz, 167–8
Levin, Shlomo, 180, 181
Liberation Law, 64, 65, 68, 85
licensing policy, 82, 83–7, 90, 91, 109, 126
Little Germany, 18–19
living conditions, 213–15
London Six Powers Conference, 66–7
Lorenz, Peter, 166
Lummer, Heinrich, 5
Lutz, Oskar, 132, 135

Maoism, 163, 181
Martial Sports Group (WSG), 178–80, 183
Marx, Arnd-Heinz, 174, 178, 183, 185–6
MC National (motorbike club), 192
Meinberg, W., 115, 131, 132
Meissner, Karl, 123–4
Meldorf, 8
middle class, 24–5, 28, 59–60, 69, 96–7, 108–9, 133–4, 144–5, 149, 151–2
militarism, 57–8, 83, 126, 136, 222
liberation law, 64, 65, 68, 85
military government's licensing policy, 83–7
Mitscherlich, M. and A., 51, 97
Morgenthau, Henry, 58
Moscow Three-Powers Declaration, 56–7, 72
Mosler, J., 183, 188
Mössle, Markus, 187
'Movement, The', 187–8
Movement for People's Socialism in Germany (VSBD), 173–5, 183
Müller, Curt, 174, 185
Müller, Sigfried, 8
Munich, 5, 6–7
Mußgnug, Martin, 8, 156, 199, 200, 201
Mutual Aid Association of Former Combat SS Members (HIAG), 138, 139

Nachrichten der HNG, 186, 188
Nahrath, Wolfgang, 171
Nation Europa, 161, 201
National Activists (NA), 183, 185–6
National Democratic Party (NDP), 110
National Democratic Party of Germany (NPD), 1, 8, 92, 109, 134, 136, 173, 175, 181–2, 191, 202, 203, 223
collapse, 150–8
DVU and, 6–7, 11–12, 193–201, 233–4
leaflet, 248–9
manifesto, 243–4
Ordnerdienst, 148, 172
National German Liberation Movement, 173
National Liberal Action, 153
national neutralist conception, 25–6
'National Opposition', 17–22
'National Question', 27–8, 37, 230
conceptions, 22–6
National Opposition and, 17–22
National Revolutionaries, 107
National Revolutionary Coordinating Committee, 164
National Revolutionary Preparatory Organisations, 162–3
National Socialism, 26
historical revisionism, 28–36
influence, 1–3
liberation law, 64, 65, 68, 85
repressing the past, 41–6, 50–1, 53–4, 57–9, 69, 72, 99, 217
views on, 41–4
see also Action Front of National Socialists (ANS); de-Nazification; Nazi past; Nazism; neo-Nazism
National Socialist German Workers Party (NSDAP), 9–11, 40, 54–5, 60–1, 63, 65, 68, 70, 83–4, 109–10,

267

Index

113, 116, 119, 122, 149, 169, 173-4, 181-3, 185, 223
Nationaldemokratische Sammlung, 130-4
nationalism, 21-2, 133-5, 230
anti-imperialism, 157, 161-5, 245-7
see also New Nationalism; Old Nationalism
Nationalist Front, 6, 174, 191
nationalist opposition, 118-24, 201
anachronism of, 125-7
decline of support, 136-42
nationalist rally strategy, 120
NATO, 95-6, 156, 203
Naumann circle, 122-3
Nazi past
continuous presence, 9-13
denial of, 50-3
return of, 53-82
views on National Socialism, 41-4
Nazism
causes and countermeasures, 206-29
pro-Nazi protest, 188-92
victims of, *see* victims of Nazi regime
see also de-Nazification; neo-Nazism; war criminals
neo-Fascism, 27, 101-2, 104, 108, 110, 113, 234
neo-liberalism, 143, 197
neo-Nazism, 102, 103, 104, 157
criminal prosecution, 219
network, 171-88
protest behaviour, 188-92
role of anti-Fascist violence, 225-6
violence and terrorism, 165-71, 233
Neurath, Konstantin von, 74
neutralism, 24-7, 117, 126-7, 129-30, 132, 133, 135
new extremism, 101, 102, 103
New Nationalism, 26-8, 86, 92, 105, 129, 134, 152, 156-7, 175
development, 158-65
formation, 115-18
nationalist opposition, 125-7
support for, 118-25
new right-wing extremism (1966-88)
end of post-war era, 142-4
neo-Nazi network, 171-88
New Nationalism (development), 158-65
NPD (collapse), 150-8
NPD (rise), 144-50

protest behaviour, 188-92
violence and terrorism, 165-71
Niemöller, Martin, 206-7
Niethammer, Lutz, 101
Nolte, Ernst, 35, 45
North Atlantic Alliance, 95-6, 156, 203
'Notgemeinschaft', 87, 117
Nuremberg trials, 42, 72-3, 74-5, 171

Oberländer, Theodor, 119, 130
occupation zones, 23
de-Nazification, 57-64, 66-9, 88-9
formation, 57, 58
licensing policy, 83-7
occupational structure of NPD, 149-50
Old Nationalism, 26-8, 86, 92, 104-5, 116, 129, 163, 165, 175
Nationalist opposition, 125-7
reorganisation, 106-15
support for, 118-25
Opitz, Gerhard, 116
Ordnerdienst, 148, 172
Organisation for the Support of National Political Prisoners, 186, 187-8
organised anti-Fascism, 222-9
organised right-wing extremism, 100, 233
new (1966-88), 142-92
outlook (trends), 192-205
overview of development, 101-6
post-war (1945-65), 106-42
Ostpolitik, 144-5, 150-1, 172, 194

Palestine Liberation Front, 180
Pape, Martin, 186-7
Papen, Franz von, 75
paramilitary field exercises, 170-1
war games, 178-81, 183
Pax Christi, 6
peace movement, 164, 197, 203, 204
Peak Association of the Nationalist Rally (DNS), 124, 125
People's Court, 77, 78
People's Movement for General Amnesty, 194
Peoples Cause, The (SdV), 163-4
pluralist democracy, 94, 95
Poeschke, Frieda, 180, 181
Pöhlmann, Siegfried, 155-6, 162, 194
policies, *see* right-wing extremism

(definitions)
political crises, 215–17
political culture (anti-democratic elements), 217–20, 234–5
political integration (after 1945), 82–99
Political Offensive, 164
Pollock, Friedrich, 48
Ponto, Jürgen, 166
popular consensus, 93
popular socialism, 173
post-war élites, 79–81
post-war era (end), 142–4
post-war right-wing extremism (1945–65) doldrum years, 127–30
Gesamtdeutsche Unabhängigkeitsbewegung, 134–6
Nationaldemokratische Sammlung, 130–4
nationalist opposition, 125–7
New Right, 115–25
Old Nationalists reorganised, 106–15
support organisations, 136–42
press, 105–6, 108, 193–4
Priester, Karl-Heinz, 123
prisoners-of-war, 54
pro-Eastern, national Bolshevist conception, 24, 25, 26
pro-Nazi protest behaviour, 188–92, 217, 227, 228
pro-Western, anti-Bolshevist conception, 24, 25
production relations, 15, 96
Protection of Information Act, 11
Protection League for People and Culture, 195
protest behaviour, 188–92, 217
bans/sanctions, 226–8
psychology of right-wing extremism, 209
purging committees, 61

Raeder, Erich, 74
rapprochement, 135, 164
Rassinier, Paul, 31, 33
Rat, 223
Red Army Faction, 165, 173
Reich assembly, 176–7
Reich Main Security Office, 76
'Reich myth', 114–15
Reich Youth, 141
Reichsblock, 124

'Reichsof', 175, 177
Reichsruf, 105
Reichstag, 176–7
relative deprivation, 213
religious conflict, 18
Remer, Otto E., 109, 110
Republicans (REP), 2, 3, 11–12, 51, 99, 102–3, 165, 193, 198, 200–5, 232–4
research (topics), 36–7
reunification, 24, 25, 91, 94, 110, 116, 121, 126, 129, 133, 135, 156, 203
revisionism, 16, 23
historical, 28–36, 140, 217
Revolutionary Cells, 166
Ribbentrop, J. von, 74
Richelieu, 135
right-wing extremism
causes, *see* causes and countermeasures
definitions, aims and policies, 14–37
everyday scenes, 4–13
German situation (nature of), 1–3
new, *see* new right-wing extremism (1966–88)
organised, *see* organised right-wing extremism
role (in political culture), 38–99
status, 225
summary of theories, 230–6
support organisations, 136–42
right-wing extremism (definitions), 14
antipathy towards democracy, 15–17
historical revisionism, 28–36
National Question, 17–26
nationalism, 26–8
as research topic, 36–7
right-wing extremism (integral role)
anti-democratic attitudes, 38–53
return of the past, 53–82
political integration, 82–99
Ring of German Soldiers Association, 137
Roeder, Gertraud, 177
Roeder, Manfred, 33, 175–7
Röhm, Ernst, 169
Rohwer, Uwe, 182
Roosevelt, F.D., 57, 58
Rosenberg, Alfred, 74
Rößler, Fritz, 108

Index

Rückerl, 65
Rudel League, 195

sanctions (on anti-Fascism), 226–8
Sauckel, Franz, 74
Schacht, Hjalmar, 75
Scheel, Walter, 153
Scheffer, Hans-Heinrich, 115, 135
Schenke, Wolf, 135
Scheuch, E.K., 1
Schirach, Baldur von, 75
Schleyer, H.M., 166
Schlüter, Leonhard, 109
Schmidt, Helmut, 196
Schnoor, Herbert, 5, 6
Schönborn, E., 174, 175, 177–8, 181
Schönhuber, F., 11, 198, 201–2, 204–5
Schramm, Hilde, 2
Schroder, Gerhard, 133
Schubert, Frank, 174
Schukow, Marshall, 58
Schumacher, K., 53, 71, 89
Schütte, Renate, 29–30
Schütz, Waldemar, 132
Schützinger, Jürgen, 8
Schwann, Hermann, 135
Schwarz, Tibor, 181
scientific analysis, 36–7
'2 June Movement', 165–6
Security Squad (SS), 9, 175
    Waffen SS.,8, 11, 54, 136n, 137–9
sentencing chambers, 64–5, 67–8, 71–2, 139
Seyss-Inquart, Arthur, 74
Silbermann, Alphons, 48
Sindelfingen, 8
SINUS study, 44–6, 47–8
skinheads, 5, 8, 169, 185, 190–2
social-liberal coalition, 159, 165, 194–6, 198, 233
    resistance to, 150–8
social class, 86
    NPD membership by, 149–50
    see also middle class; working class
social crises (significance), 213–15
Social Democratic Party (SPD), 4–5, 7, 12–13, 216, 223
    de-Nazification and, 68–72, 82
    Grand Coalition, 102, 143, 145, 150, 151, 232
    organised extremism, 102, 108, 110–11, 120, 134, 142–5, 152–5, 196–7, 200

repressing the past, 40, 46, 84, 88–90, 92, 95, 97
social justice, 15, 99, 230
social market economy, 96
social peace, 204
social policy, 96
social welfare, 197
socialisation (anti-democratic attitudes), 208, 209, 220
socialism, 15, 59–60, 144, 157, 162–3
    de-Nazification and, 69–71, 89, 97
Socialist German Students League, 77
Socialist Reich Party (SRP), 1, 91, 104, 107, 110–14, 120–1, 123, 140
Socialist Unity Party of Germany, 40, 61
society as a whole (causal theory), 212–17, 220, 221, 235
socio-structural characteristics, 46–8
Sokolovski, Marshall, 66
soldiers' organisations, 136–9
Solidaristic Peoples Movement, 163–4
Soviet military courts, 73
Soviet occupation zone, 60–1, 66–7
Special Courts, 78
Speer, Albert, 75
Spiegel crisis, 143
stabilisation (doldrum years), 127–8
Stäglich, Wilhelm, 34
Stahlhelm League of Front-Line soldiers, 138
Stalin, Joseph, 57, 59
Stalinism, 15
statute of limitations, 77–8
Staudinger, Karl, 130
Stoph, Willi, 172
Storm Detachment (SA), 119, 169, 223
Strasser brothers, 173
Strauß, F.J., 154–5, 198, 201
Strecker, R.M., 77
Streicher, Julius, 74
Stuttgart, 7, 8
summary of theories, 230–6
Sündermann, Helmut, 30
support organisations (decline), 136–42

Tag, Ernst, 187
Tageszeitung, 207
Tauroggen Convention (1812), 24

270

Index

territorial development (1871–1957), 22
territorial losses, 19–22
terrorism, *see* violence (and terrorism)
Thadden, Adolf von, 109, 115, 130–4, 145, 151, 152, 155–6
theories outlined (summary), 230–6
Thielen, Friedrich, 134, 145
Third Force, 130–4
Third Front, 24, 28
Third Path, 25, 28, 157, 162
Third Power, 24, 25, 28
Third Reich, 21, 26, 43, 44
Thousand Year Empire, 42
totalitarianism, 14
Travemünde, 7
Treaty of Rapallo, 24
Treaty of Versailles, 19, 30
tri-zone, 66
trials, 29, 30, 231
 Nuremberg, 42, 72–3, 74–5, 171
 results (significance), 72–6
 sentencing, 56–9, 61, 64–5, 67–9
 West German courts, 76–9

Uelzen, 7
Uhl, Klaus-Ludwig, 174
Unabhängigen, Die, 106
unemployment, 155, 157
United Nations, 56, 57
United States
 de-Nazification, 61–4, 66, 68
 military courts, 73
 occupation zone, 85

victims of de-Nazification, 136, 139–41
victims of Nazi regime, 222–3, 224
 bans/sanctions, 226–8
 BHE group, 92, 110–11, 118–22 *passim*, 124, 130–4 *passim*
Viking Youth (WJ), 4, 141–2, 169–71, 178, 181, 182, 194
violence (and terrorism), 45, 102, 103
 anti-Fascist, 225–6
 armed struggle, 169–74 *passim*
 collective acts, 210, 211
 combat groups, 152
 left-wing, 165–6, 173, 188
 neo-Nazi, 165–74, 177–88, 225–6, 233
 paramilitary field exercises, 170–1
 protest behaviour, 188–92
 war games, 178–81, 183
Voigt, Ekkehard, 198, 202, 205
Volksgemeinschaft, 21, 42, 216
Vorderbrügge, Sibylle, 177

Waffen SS., 8, 11, 54, 136n, 137–8, 139
war criminals
 glossing over, 53–5, 204–5
 prosecution, 218–19
 public opinion, 79, 218–19
 rehabilitation and protection, 72–6
 sentencing, 56–9, 61, 69
 sentencing chambers, 64–5, 67–8, 71–2, 139
 see also trials
war games, 178–81, 183
'war guilt lie', 29, 140, 178
Warsaw pact, 156
Wehler, Hans-Ulrich, 35
Weimar Republic, 19, 27, 85
Weinheim, 8
Weise, Gottfried, 2
Weizmann, Chaim, 31
Weizsäcker, Richard von, 35, 193–4
welfare state, 96, 197
Wilhelm II, 21
Wir selbst, 164
Wissel, Monika, 2
Wittig, Rudi, 171
Wolfgram, Kurt, 174
Worch, Christian, 181, 183, 186, 188
Working Association of Austrian Nationalist Youth Leagues, 141–2
Working Association of (formerly politically) Persecuted Social Democrats, 223
working class, 59, 145

xenophobia, 9, 46–50, 51, 157, 230

Yalta Conference, 59
Young Comradeship, 141
Young Front, 173
Young German Community, 141
Young Germany League, 142
Young National Democrats (JN), 157, 163–4, 169, 181
Youth League Eagles, 141–2, 194
youth right-wing extremism, 102–4, 235–6
 decline of organisations, 141–2

271

NPD membership, 157
protest behaviour, 188–92
violence and terrorism, 165–71, 185

Ziel, Das, 105
Zimmermann, 5
'Zyklon B' football supporters, 191